The Exemplary Husband

A Biblical Perspective

Revised Edition

Stuart Scott

THE EXEMPLARY HUSBAND
A Biblical Perspective
Revised Edition
©2002 by Stuart Scott

Published by FOCUS PUBLISHING, Inc.
All Rights Reserved

Focus Publishing, Inc.
Post Office Box 665
Bemidji, MN   56619

Unless otherwise noted, all Scripture is taken from
The New American Standard Bible
©1960, 1962, 1963, 1971, 1973, 1975, 1977, 1995
by The Lockman Foundation
Used by permission

Cover design by Richard Schaefer

ISBN 1 885904-31-2

Printed in the United States of America

This book is dedicated
to one of God's greatest blessings to me in this life:
my wife and my faithful companion,
Zondra

Foreword

I have long wished there were a convenient manual for men that would clearly outline and explain what Scripture requires of husbands and fathers. Over nearly four decades of ministry, I have counseled numerous couples with severe marital and family problems. And it has always seemed to me that in the vast majority of cases, the husband's success or failure as a spiritual leader is the key factor in determining the outcome of such conflicts. If the husband will be the kind of leader he should be, most problems within the family can ultimately be resolved. But if the husband defaults on his biblical and spiritual responsibilities, the problems invariably grow worse–and sometimes even destroy the family.

The husband's role is not simple, and it requires expertise that, frankly, doesn't come naturally to most men. The husband's various duties involve priestly elements, organizational and administrative tasks, and numerous responsibilities related to spiritual and practical leadership of all kinds. Being a godly husband requires the skill of a gifted manager, the heart of a loving counselor, and the ability to lead while gaining a follower's respect–chiefly by being a consistent example. The godly husband is a loving soul-mate, a mentor, a friend, a protector, an encourager, and a devoted listener. This is by no means a part-time calling.

The basic character requirements are a heart for God, courage, conviction, patience, devotion, love, humility, and a determined, unshakable commitment to one's wife and family. The godly husband's role calls for well-ordered priorities, a willingness to sacrifice, and above all, consistent, godly faithfulness.

So our responsibility as husbands and fathers is a weighty and often daunting burden. It is especially difficult for today's men to maintain all these priorities, because we live in an era when the very fabric of our society is being torn apart by anti-family forces. Life seems busier and more fast-paced than it has ever been. And on every front, there are distractions and temptations that pull at us. No wonder so many husbands are clamoring for help.

Finally, here is a thoroughly biblical, intensely practical, and truly spiritual look at the standard of godliness established for Christian husbands. Dr. Stuart Scott writes with the passion and insight of a godly man who is himself a committed husband and father. He handles the relevant Scripture thoughtfully. He interprets it expertly. And he applies it graciously. I highly recommend this book to all who wish to rise above the trivialized versions found in most modern manuals on manhood and see what God really requires and what He blesses.

John MacArthur

Acknowledgments

When I was approached about writing this book for husbands, I thought, "What a project that would be. I'd love nothing more than to contribute a work that would address many of the heart issues that God has confronted me with and that I counsel men about regularly." And then, reality hit me! "What am I thinking?" I asked myself. "How in the world could I pastor effectively, teach efficiently at the college and seminary, be the right kind of husband and father, and still find time to write!" Yet, the need seemed so great to me that I decided I should at least begin working on it as I could three years ago.

I tell you this because from the start I have been very much aware that this project would have to be a team effort. I have also been struck by the fact that on my own I would have *nothing* to say. I fully embrace the Apostle Paul's admonishment when he said, "What do you have that you have not received?" (1 Corinthians 4:7). There can be no boasting whatsoever. Whatever I know to be true, God has taught me either directly from His Word or indirectly through my teachers such as my parents, my past pastors, my professors, the ministry of my present pastor, Dr. John MacArthur, and the rest of the leadership at Grace Community Church (Sun Valley, CA).

I am also indebted to those the Lord graciously provided to help make this book happen. This book was truly the group effort I anticipated it would be. God has blessed me with a wonderful wife who has diligently assisted me in this project by doing the initial editing, assisting me in research, organizing the office help, and being the contact person for everyone while I was teaching at school or pastoring. I couldn't have done it without you, Honey! I am also thankful for my children who have supported me in this project and have been very patient with me throughout the process.

I want to thank the faithful men who assisted me in this task. Pastor John Crotts read over the manuscript chapter by chapter as a diligent student of the Word, offering helpful feedback. My good friend and encourager, Bryan Murphy, who serves me as my intern at the church, helped to lighten my administrative load, worked many hours on helping with layout and corrections on the book, and worked to provide a rough draft of the study guide along with Andy Snider. John Douglass and Gary Knussman were a tremendous help as our technical proof-readers. Pastor Lance Quinn and David Deuel helped me to clarify Chapter 15. Nate Prince, our favorite computer expert, selflessly served us whenever we had computer problems. Jim Rickard Sr., the director of Stewardship Services Foundation, Santa Clarita, CA, graciously provided some needed materials for the financial area. Bill Vaughan, a faithful intern helped us with some key diagrams.

I want to thank all of the ladies who worked on this project as well. Martha Peace, author of *The Excellent Wife* and a dear friend to our family, offered valuable input and encouraged me often to persevere to the end. Her daughter, Anna Maupin, who is an editor par excellance, laboriously kept me from rabbit trails, ambiguity and split infinitives, while brightening her edits with encouragement and humor. Our good friend, Bette Lou O'Brien, who has the gift of helps has served our family tirelessly and joyfully throughout the whole process of the book. Chris Green was the typist who hung in there the longest and actually enjoyed the tedious work of synthesizing the edits of five different people! Erin Sokoff and Shonna Silva sacrificially took time out from their busy schedules as students to help us on a weekly basis. MaryAnn Vaughan was a servant to us by taking over Zondra's prayer group for awhile so Zondra could assist me, helping us to create some charts we needed, typing and even feeding a delicious meal!. Our dear friend Marcia Griffiths, sacrificially gave us the best of her vacation time. Jamie Schmidt, Lioni Kuypers, Teresa Smith, Trudy Feyereisen, Gabriela Contreras, and Joan Douglass also selflessly gave several days to making needed corrections.

I want to give a special thank you to Jan Haley, Barb Smith and everyone at Focus Publishing, who have been extremely patient and encouraging throughout this three-year project. I would also be remiss if I did not express my sincere gratitude to all who prayed for us along the way. There were times it just didn't seem that this book would ever be a reality. I thank the Lord and the super team He gave me to accomplish this book for Him!

Stuart Scott

Introduction

The burden for a book such as *The Exemplary Husband* began over twenty years ago when I wished there had been a book I could read before and throughout my marriage that would guide me in the basics of being a godly man and a godly husband. I was looking for a very practical book that would deal *heavily* with my relationship with God and how that relates to my being a husband. I was interested in such topics as really knowing God, my responsibilities, proper attitudes, loving my wife, communication, conflict resolution, physical intimacy and various struggles with sin that kept me from being what God wanted me to be. Through the years as a pastor, I have longed for a book that I could use to review God's principles myself and give to other men who are looking for help in both their personal walk with God and their marriage. If you are looking for one such book, it is my prayer that you are holding it in your hands.

As one of the Christian male population, I have had to face the fact that we have a problem. Judging from my own life and the lives of many Christian men with whom I have both served and counseled, we need some sound guidance to keep us on the right track by honoring God as husbands. The problem comes when we begin to look for material that is practical, yet based on the fact that God's Word is sufficient for all of life and godliness (2 Peter 1: 2-4). We need God's wisdom and there is very little of it to be found in today's more popular books for the husband. What we don't need is humanistic and psychological mumbo-jumbo. Though there have been some very helpful and sound works on the husband's role written in more recent years, it has been my dream to have a work that would provide *a great deal* of help on the husband's relationship with God, while addressing the husband's role at the same time. How can we separate our relationship with our wife from our walk with God?

God has given us a model to follow, in order to be what He wants us to be, and that model is the person of Jesus Christ. We must first want to glorify God with our lives and then we must realize that it is Christlikeness that will help us to do just that. Christ is our example in every way and we must fix our gaze on Him whole-heartedly. This is what will enable us to be like Him in our role as a husband and in all our other roles for that matter. *The overall purpose of this book is to assist husbands toward purposeful and lasting Christlikeness for the glory of God.* Surely, a husband will not realize this goal by the mere reading of this book, but he will by the exercising of the biblical principles it contains.

I am thrilled to be a part of an effort to provide dual works for both husbands and wives so they may study together. It was even better that the "other work" was *The Excellent Wife* by Martha Peace. *The Excellent Wife* and *The Exemplary Husband* both address heart issues and the path to change which I believe can serve couples well in their walk with God and their growth together.

It is my prayer that this book will be just what you need to help you be the husband God wants you to be. In no way do I claim to have arrived. I'm still working (with God's help) to bring my life more in line with the master blueprint—Jesus Christ Himself. Won't you join me in the demolition and reconstruction necessary to be a husband who exemplifies and glorifies Christ? I promise you that every effort you make to that end will be very worth your while.

Stuart Scott

THE EXEMPLARY HUSBAND

Part One-A Husband's Recognitions
Foundational Truths for the Exemplary Husband

Part Two-A Husband's Responsibilities
Faithful Commitments of the Exemplary Husband

Part Three-A Husband's Resolves
Fundamental Commitments of the Exemplary Husband

Part Four-A Husband's Regrets
Fatal Sins to the Exemplary Husband

PART ONE

A HUSBAND'S RECOGNITIONS

Foundational Truths for the Exemplary Husband

Chapter One

A HUSBAND'S UNDERSTANDING
OF HIS PRESENT CONDITION

A Personal Testimony

I remember a time early in our marriage that was a turning point for my wife Zondra and me. It all started with one little statement that she made to me one evening after an especially hard week as a mother of two young children.

"You are being very selfish," she said. I'd *never* heard Zondra speak so pointedly to me before. At first I was speechless. "She should *not* be saying this to me," I thought. I tried desperately to figure out what I had done that was so terrible. "Where did *that* come from?" I asked after the momentary shock wore off. "How can you say that?"

I was a young pastor at the time. I had been through both Bible college and seminary. In fact, I was studying through the husband's role in marriage when this occurred. "She must be having a bad day," I rationalized. Before I could think of something else to say, she continued, only now she was in tears.

"You seem to care almost exclusively about your own desires, circumstances and interests. Now that we have children, I can't focus

3

totally on you anymore. The truth is, you act as if you couldn't care less about *my* circumstances. Do you realize that we never seem to talk about what concerns *me*? For the most part, you aren't willing to sacrifice even in the smallest ways for others, unless it costs you nothing or it serves your interests. And on top of that, do you realize that if I have to ask for your help with anything lately, your reaction shows your impatience. I really think that the concern and interest should go both ways."

So that's what this was about. "You're just upset because I was tired and didn't really want to wash the baby bottles, aren't you? You know how difficult things have been for me this week at the church. Besides, even though I didn't want to, I did wash the bottles, didn't I?" Thinking further about Zondra's statements, I became defensive. I thought, "Surely you have the wrong person. Are you talking to me? Your provider and protector? How can you so misjudge me when I am such a good husband to you?"

Blinded by my own pride, I set out to inform Zondra of the ways that I loved her sacrificially, the way Christ loves the Church. As my mind sought examples, however, I was thoroughly stumped. I mentioned a few things I had done for her. But the truth was, I did just enough to get by and there was often a kickback for me. The more I evaluated my "love" for her, the more I realized that convenience or putting on a show for others to see was almost always involved. As much as I hated to admit it, she was right. I *was* consumed with myself and my own interests.

I remember the moment of those realizations as if it were yesterday. I was like King David when he was rebuked by Nathan the prophet (2 Samuel 12:1-13). My mouth had been silenced by Zondra's words. I had never really loved my wife the way I thought I had. I came to realize that although I believed that "two shall become one," I, of course, was the one.

There followed a week of unforgettable grief and remorse. It was as if my pious world had come crashing in on me. The realities about my lack of biblical love were earth-shaking ones that I continued to recognize in all areas of my daily living. I began to see what others must have long since observed in my life. Thanks to my dear wife, who loved me enough to tell me the truth, God began a much needed work in my heart.

Since then, I have been much more aware of my pride and selfishness. Repentance began through that incident and is a continuing process. I would like to be able to tell you that I have fully arrived and become Zondra's knight in shining armor. Instead, I could be likened to a simple frog slowly being transformed into the form of her prince, not yet rid of all his warts.

The intent of this account is to illustrate my need for understanding concerning my love for Zondra. Like a builder preparing to build a home, I had to do some personal surveying before I could establish where I needed to begin building. I was lacking in true concern for her interests. My selfishness was a lack of mature Christian character.

I have entitled this book, *The Exemplary Husband*, because of its emphasis on a man's walk and character. The word *exemplary* sums up the husband's responsibility in marriage to live what God instructs. Only one other word could describe it better. That word is *Christlikeness*.

More as a goal than a full reality, Christian husbands must answer the call of God *to lead the way* in pursuing Christ's likeness. In doing this a husband will participate in the building of God's kind of marriage, and more specifically, God's kind of husband.

God's Will for Christian Husbands

God's will for every Christian husband is to shepherd and love his wife the way Christ shepherds and loves the Church (Ephesians 5:23-33). In fact, Christian men are called to follow Christ in all their ways.

**The one who says he abides in Him ought himself to
walk in the same manner as He walked.
1 John 2:6**

Christ is our perfect example in all things. We have been given many other examples in the Scriptures as well. Some are good examples and some are bad ones. We are given good examples that we might clearly see God's pattern. Bad examples show us wrong patterns. By these poor examples God is seeking to reveal what is often difficult for us to recognize in the middle of our *own* circumstances. God uses both good and bad examples to move us toward His own likeness.

God not only wants us to look to the right examples, but He also wants each one of us to *be* the right kind of example for others. We need to remember that we already *are* some sort of example to others. The question is, what kind? The following are charts of Scriptures about Christ, (our perfect example), and our need to *be* exemplary. As you read them you will see that God has spoken clearly and powerfully to us about exemplifying Christ.

The Ultimate Pattern: Jesus Christ

Servanthood
"For I gave you an example that you should always do as I did to you."— John 13:15

Suffering
For you have been called for this purpose, since Christ also suffered for you, leaving you an example for you to follow in His steps... while suffering. He... kept entrusting Himself to Him who judges righteously...— 1 Peter 2:21-23

Mindset
Have this attitude in yourselves which was also in Christ Jesus, who... emptied Himself, taking the form of a bond-servant...— Philippians 2:5-7

Self-Denial
"If anyone wishes to come after Me, let him deny himself, and take up his cross daily, and follow Me."
— Luke 9:23

Obedience to the Word
The one who says he abides in Him ought himself to walk in the same manner as He walked...
— I John 2:6

Hated by the World
"If the world hates you, you know that it has hated Me before it hated you; if they persecuted Me, they will also persecute you; if they kept My word, they will keep yours also."— John 15:18-20

Other Good Examples

God-honoring Spiritual Care
I do not write these things to shame you, but to admonish you as my beloved children... I exhort you therefore, be imitators of me.
— 1 Corinthians 4:14,16

God-honoring Evangelism
Just as I... not seeking my own profit, but the profit of the many, that they may be saved. Be imitators of me, just as I also am of Christ.
— 1 Corinthians 10:33-11:1

God-honoring Pursuits
Brethren, join in following my example, and observe those who walk according to the pattern you have in us.
— Philippians 3:17

God-honoring Life Patterns
The things you have learned and received and heard and seen in me, practice these things...
— Philippians 4:9

God-honoring Faith in Difficult Times
You also became imitators of us and of the Lord, having received the word in much tribulation... so that you became an example to all the believers...
—I Thessalonians 1:6-7

We desire that each one of you show the same diligence... imitators of those who through faith and patience inherit the promises.— Hebrews 6:11-12

God-honoring Reception of His Word
When you received from us the word of God's message, you accepted it... for what it really is... For you, brethren, became imitators of the churches of God in Jesus Christ...
— 1 Thessalonians 2:13-14

God-honoring Motives and Walk
You... know how you ought to follow our example, because we did not act in an undisciplined manner... in order to offer ourselves as a model for you, that you might follow our example.— 2 Thessalonians 3:7-9

God-honoring Leaders
Remember those who led you, who spoke the word of God to you; and considering the result of their conduct, imitate their faith.— Hebrews 13:7

God-honoring Suffering
As an example... of suffering and patience, take the prophets who spoke in the name of the Lord.
— James 5:10

7

Commands To Be An Example

All Believers
Therefore be imitators of God, as beloved children; and walk in love, just as Christ also loved you, and gave Himself up for us...— Ephesians 5:1-2

Young Men
Let no one look down on your youthfulness, but rather in speech, conduct, love, faith and purity, show yourself an example of those who believe... — 1 Timothy 4:12

Elders
Therefore, I exhort the elders among you... shepherd the flock of God among you... proving to be examples to the flock...— 1 Peter 5:1-3

Poor Examples

Israel —
Example of Sinful Lusts
Now these things happened as examples for us, that we should not crave evil things, as they also craved... Now these things happened to them as an example, and they were written for our instruction, upon whom the ends of the ages have come.
— 1 Corinthians 10:6,11

Israel —
Example of Disobedience
Let us therefore be diligent to enter that rest, lest anyone fall through following the same example of disobedience...
— Hebrews 4:11

Sodom & Gomorrah —
Examples of Immorality
Just as Sodom & Gomorrah... are exhibited as an example, in undergoing the punishment of eternal fire.
— Jude 7

Evil Doers —
Examples of Ungodliness
Beloved, do not imitate what is evil, but what is good. The one who does good is of God; the one who does evil has not seen God.— 3 John 11

Following the Perfect Pattern

You may be amazed to learn how much the Scriptures have to say about examples. You may also feel that a biblical example is a shoe you could never fill. In the Scriptures, the Greek terms for example (*typos*), pattern or model (*hypodeigma*), and imitator (*mimetes*) are key words. *Typos* in particular, can shed much light on our endeavor to be exemplary. This word carries with it the assumption of an accompanying guide. It was used to refer to the tracing or practicing of one's letters. A clear example of this definition is seen in elementary schools across our country. Our children learn to write the alphabet by first seeing the letters (which serves as their guide), then by tracing the letters, and finally by attempting to form the letters freehand.

The emphasis of this word is not necessarily on the perfection of the resulting copy, but rather on the careful attention given to the *perfect example and on the determined purpose* of following it. Likewise, we as husbands must be focused on our perfect example, the Lord Jesus Christ. We must carefully and purposefully strive to copy Him, no matter how inadequate our attempt may be at first. As we continue to grow in this endeavor we *will* be **exemplary**. There *will* be more and more of a resemblance to Christ that others can follow. As the Apostle Paul said,

> **Be imitators of me, just as I also am of Christ.**
> **1 Corinthians 11:1**

So what does it really mean to be exemplary? From our study so far, we can put together a working definition. To be "exemplary" is:

> **To serve as an improving copy of our perfect pattern, Jesus Christ, by deliberately focusing on and practicing His likeness.**

The Fruit (Traits) of the Exemplary Husband

It is God who produces real fruit within the heart (Matthew 7:17-18; Galatians 5:22,23). Only the heart that truly knows and walks with

God can even begin to look like the heart of God. *A husband will bear good fruit in his character and work only when the thoughts and intentions of his heart seek God, love God, and desire to glorify God.* Such a man will leave behind a legacy that will continue to be an example long after he is gone.

Who Can Be the Exemplary Husband?

Not that I have already obtained it, or have already become perfect, but I press on so that I may lay hold of that for which also I was laid hold of by Christ Jesus. Brethren, I do not regard myself as having laid hold of it yet; but one thing I do: forgetting what lies behind and reaching forward to what lies ahead, I press on toward the goal for the prize of the upward call of God in Christ Jesus.
Philippians 3:12-14

Whatever condition you believe your heart and life fruit to be, you need not and must not remain in this condition. To be an exemplary husband you must first be in a right relationship with God; then, you must recognize that growth is needed and purpose to begin following your perfect example. Next you must realize that sin is the only thing that can stand in your way. You should take great hope in this truth because sin *can* be confessed and turned away from with God's help. No Christian husband is destined to be a slave of his flesh, helplessly bound by his past or "personality type," nor helplessly affected by poor examples lived before him. Once one accepts responsibility for his own sin, he *can* change through God's provisions (Romans 12:2). (See the "God's Provision of Sanctification" section of chapter 3). So who can be the exemplary husband? *Any* Christian man can.

Are You Ready?

Becoming the exemplary husband will be a growing process. In the end we want to look like Christ. Each husband must do his own honest survey of his heart's condition before he can begin to build an exemplary life. Next, he must acknowledge God's perfect standard and determine his commitment to pursue it. You must count the cost of following Christ. It will most certainly cost you your own will and always getting your own way, because we cannot have both God's way and our way. This fact must be recognized at the outset of the commitment to build an exemplary life and marriage.

There is only one thing that will truly motivate men to follow Christ's example. That one thing is knowing Christ Himself. In other words, it is a right relationship with God that produces the desire for Christlikeness. You must truly be one of His disciples, or you will not be able to be an exemplary husband. Of course, a right relationship with God is based on an accurate knowledge of Him as He is revealed in the Bible.

Chapter Two

A HUSBAND'S UNDERSTANDING
OF GOD

In chapters 2-6 I will lay the foundation for becoming an exemplary husband. If a husband does not have a biblical understanding of God, man, relationships, marriage and his role, it will not benefit him much to work at his marriage.

Because of this fact, you will find that we purposely address these foundational topics more fully than does *The Excellent Wife*. It is the husband's responsibility to lead his wife (and family) spiritually. In order to do this, he must have a knowledge of the awesome God of the Bible that will enable him to call his family continually to faith.

> **Therefore everyone who hears these words of Mine and acts upon them, may be compared to a wise man who built his house upon the rock. And the rain descended, and the floods came, and the winds blew and burst against that house; and yet it did not fall, for it had been founded upon the rock. And everyone**

who hears these words of Mine, and does not act upon them, will be like a foolish man who built his house upon the sand. And the rain descended, and the floods came, and the winds blew, and burst against that house; and it fell, and great was its fall.
Matthew 7:24-27

The Main Foundation

We said in chapter one that Christ is our example. Naturally we need at least a basic understanding of who He is before we can be more like Him. We know from the Bible that Christ is fully God (John 1:1-3, 14; Colossians 1:15-18). The Bible also teaches us that God is triune. This means that God is three Persons in one God: Father, Son and Holy Spirit. Christ is the second Person of our triune God, God, the Son (Matthew 28:19). Each Person of this Trinity possesses all of the divine attributes. They are identical to each other in character. In this way, God is one God (Deuteronomy 6:4). Knowing Christ means knowing the basic character of this one (and triune) true God of the Bible.

There are foundational truths an exemplary husband needs to know. Of these, an accurate perception of God is the most important understanding a husband can gain. Having a right view of God is basic to a right relationship with Him. Certainly a husband must first be in a right relationship with God before he can love his wife as he should. Holding to a faulty view of God will make it impossible to know Christ and build a life that resembles His.

Popular Views About God

Before exploring what the Bible teaches about God, let us briefly look at some popular yet unbiblical ideas about Him. These fall far short of the One who has revealed Himself in Scripture.

1.   A Domesticated Genie

Some people believe God is obligated to deliver based on their behavior, the same way a genie is obligated to grant wishes to the one who rubs the lamp. Man, in his own pride, thinks that if he is "good" or uses the name of God, he will be granted what he desires in life—maybe even be assured of heaven. In this case, God is merely a means to one's *own* end. To look at God in this way is to live as though we are the source, means, and end of all things, and as though God owes us what we want. Truly when this person looks in a mirror he is seeing his god. He, himself, is his own god.

2.   A Distant Ogre

Others see God as a heavenly Distant Ogre. I can remember hearing some missionary speakers say things like, "Don't tell God that you don't want to go to Africa, because guess where you'll end up? Africa!" Such a person is conveying to others (perhaps unintentionally) that God is someone who enjoys inflicting hardship on His children. For those who see God in this light, He is a reluctant and distant provider who is ready to punish those who step out of line. When He is called upon, He is bothered, slow to respond, or perhaps even angered. But Jesus described the Father this way:

> **"Or what man is there among you, who when his son shall ask him for a loaf, will give him a stone? Or if he shall ask for a fish, he will not give him a snake, will he? If you then, being evil, know how to give good gifts to your children, how much more shall your Father who is in heaven give what is good to those who ask Him!"**
> **Matthew 7:9-11**

God is neither quick nor glad to punish. In fact, the parables found in Luke 15 portray God as one who goes after and cares for the lost ones, rejoices over the repentant, and has compassion on the wayward child. God is not an Ogre.

> **The Lord is gracious and merciful; slow to anger and great in lovingkindness.**
> **Psalm 145:8**

3. Spiritual Psychotherapist

Still others see God as a Spiritual Psychotherapist. Those who see Him in this way live as though He exists merely to help them feel better, function better and get more out of life. This god is also seen as one who is non-directive (one who simply listens and gives unconditional and positive regard to the person). This god would never discipline for that would hurt one's "esteem." He is only an "encourager." This is a very low view of God and a very high view of man.

4. A Kindly Old Grandpa or a Cosmic Santa Claus

God is also sometimes viewed as a Kindly Old Grandpa or a Cosmic Santa Claus. In this case, God is seen as one who cannot bring Himself to really hold us responsible for our actions. Instead, this god tends to overlook or ignore our sin. Like some grandpas, he may be hard of hearing or seem to have failing eyesight when it comes to our wrong-doing. If he is more like a Santa Claus, he is going to come through for us and give us what we want or what we think we need. He accepts our excuses for bad behavior and is easily convinced to grant us our wishes.

The God of the Bible is not here to spoil us, nor is He overlooking or ignoring our ways. He is working *His* plan for *His* glory and will one day require an accounting from each one of us.

These are some of the popular views of God. There are also many other wrong ideas about who God is. A good book to read on this subject is *Your God is Too Small* by J. B. Phillips.[1] This book addresses other distortions of God's person more fully than we are able to do here. The truth is that unless a man's heart is changed by God, he is bent on having a distorted view of God (Romans 3:11). Men have labored diligently since the Fall to create a god of their own design, rather than submit themselves to their sovereign Creator.

In spite of our bent, God who is rich in mercy has revealed Himself to us in His Word. We must examine whether or not our God is the God of the Bible.

Regardless of your past beliefs, God can be known as He is. It takes knowledge of Scripture, faith in the fact that God is who He reveals Himself to be, and the daily practice of taking specific wrong thoughts captive. As you begin the next section, ask God to reveal Himself to you as He really is in the pages of God's Word. Ask Him to reveal to you any ways you have viewed Him wrongly. Ask Him to reveal to you any way you have not specifically lived according to what the Bible says about Him.

The God of the Bible

Though we are very good at fashioning "another god" (Psalm 115: 4-8), the truth is there is only one true God (Deuteronomy 6:4-5). There is no one who compares to Him. He stands alone in His character and attributes.

> **For this reason You are great, O Lord God; for there is none like You, and there is no God besides You, according to all that we have heard with our ears.**
> **2 Samuel 7:22**

We must bring our view of God in line with His Word. The following is not a complete study of the nature and character of God, but it should serve as a clear and brief biblical overview of who God is.

1.   God is the sovereign, all-powerful Lord of all creation.

> **"Remember the former things long past, for I am God, and there is no other; I am God, and there is no one like Me, declaring the end from the beginning, and from ancient times things which have not been done, saying, 'My purpose will be established, and I will accomplish all My good pleasure'".**
> **Isaiah 46:9-10**

Every exemplary husband must come to the place where he is humble before the Almighty, Sovereign God. He must truly believe that he is small while God is great and completely in control. God is sovereign over the earth, the heavens, people, events, and even Satan and evil (Isaiah 40:12-31). By faith this attribute must be seen along with God's other attributes. By faith we must believe that an all-wise

17

and loving God knows why a particular event was allowed as part of the perfect plan for an individual and for His glory. Remembering that God's character is perfect, with no darkness at all, can help us view His sovereignty rightly. Not only is He perfectly sovereign, but He is also perfectly good, perfectly loving, and perfectly wise. Seeing God's sovereignty in light of His whole character can actually lend comfort concerning past, present and future events.

In His sovereignty, God has perfect purposes for the world and a perfect plan for *each husband*. This means that no one could improve on them. They are much higher, much better and much more suited to His whole plan than our self-centered and shortsighted plans could ever be (Isaiah 55:9). Every man who hopes to honor God and know true contentment in this life must be thoroughly convinced that God's ways are *perfect*.

Understanding God's sovereignty can also put husbands in the place they need to be. It can help them to be humble and grateful. Yes, as husbands we have been given a place of authority, but we are still mere creatures and under the authority of Almighty God. This fact should make us careful with our loved ones, submissive to God's will, and grateful that He, the Almighty and Sovereign God, desires to be intimately acquainted with us (Psalm 8:4; Romans 9:19-21).

2. God is Holy.

> **Who is like you among the gods, O Lord? Who is like you, majestic in holiness, awesome in praises, working wonders?**
> **Exodus 15:11**

God in His holiness is absolutely pure, perfect, and right in *all* His ways. The word *holy* generally means "set apart." Wayne Grudem, in his *Systematic Theology*, says that "God's holiness means that He is separated from sin and devoted to seeking His own honor." [2] There is absolutely no sin or evil in Him.

> **And this is the message we have heard from Him and**

> **announce to you, that God is light and in Him there is no darkness** *at all.*
> **1 John 1:5**

Only God is holy. When we look at God we must not be proud, because imperfection is looking at perfection; impurity is looking at purity. When we see the holiness of God we should respond as Isaiah did when he understood the holiness of God.

> **Then I said, "Woe is me, for I am ruined! Because I am a man of unclean lips, and I live among a people of unclean lips; for my eyes have seen the King, the Lord of hosts."**
> **Isaiah 6:5**

3. God is a just judge.

> **Let the rivers clap their hands, let the mountains sing together for joy before the Lord, for He is coming to judge the earth; He will judge the world with right-eousness and the peoples with equity.**
> **Psalm 98:8-9**

God righteously hates sin because it is an affront to who He is and His Kingdom, and because of what it does. He must judge sin and He must judge every person. All of God's judgments are right and just. He is the perfect judge.

As a just judge, God has rightly judged all of mankind to be sinners and deserving of hell. He is full of righteous anger toward the wicked (those outside of saving faith in Christ) for their sin (Psalm 7:11). Only those who have had their penalty paid and have placed their faith in God's substitute (Christ) will escape the judgment that is deserved. Even those who have been forgiven for their sins through Christ will face a judgment of their lives in which they will gain or lose rewards (Romans 14:10-13; 1 Corinthians 3:11-15).

Only God can perfectly examine a person and then execute the right judgment. Because God is perfect, He has the *right* to judge sin.

Because He is just, He <u>must</u> judge sin. King Solomon gave this warning to God's people in Ecclesiastes 12:13-14:

> **The conclusion, when all has been heard, is: fear God and keep His commandments, because this applies to every person. For God will bring every act to judgment, everything which is hidden, whether it is good or evil.**

4.   God is merciful and gracious.

> **Through the Lord's mercies we are not consumed, because His compassions fail not.**
> **Lamentations 3:22 (NKJV)**

God is not only a just judge but He is also full of mercy and grace. We can define *mercy* as "not giving what is *deserved*." *Grace* can be defined as "giving what *is not deserved*." It is God's mercy and grace that provided a way for Him to remain just and yet save us from the judgment we deserve. That way was to judge His own Son for the sins of the world. If God were not merciful, we would all be hopelessly doomed and receive our just condemnation. In His mercy, God has decided to save some from the destruction they deserve and father them as His very own, just as if they had never sinned. When we think about what man deserves, God has been gracious to *every* person. He provides the air we breathe and many undeserved blessings (Psalm 103).

5.   God is full of compassion.

> **He has made His wonders to be remembered; the Lord is gracious and compassionate.**
> **Psalm 111:4**

God is a compassionate God. In fact, He is exceedingly more compassionate than any one of us.

> **The Lord's lovingkindnesses indeed never cease, for His compassions never fail.**
> **Lamentations 3:22**

The fact that God is perfect in His compassion means that He is affected by our suffering. He sees, identifies with and is moved to action by our suffering. He is not a far-removed God who simply is doing what needs to be done. Jesus Christ can empathize fully with us in our humanness. He understands and cares about our circumstances.

> **Therefore, since then we have a great high priest who has passed through the heavens, Jesus the Son of God, let us hold fast our confession. For we do not have a high priest who cannot sympathize with our weaknesses, but One who has been tempted in all things as we are, yet without sin. Let us therefore draw near with confidence to the throne of grace, that we may receive mercy and may find grace to help in time of need.**
> **Hebrews 4:14-16**

6. God cares for His own as the Good Shepherd and the perfect Father.

> **The Lord is my shepherd, I shall not want.**
> **Psalm 23:1**

Regardless of how things may appear at times, God is perfect in His care. He is the Good Shepherd and the perfect Father. Out of true love, both the right kind of shepherd and the right kind of father take full responsibility for the ones they oversee. Both are committed to the good of those who are in their care. Likewise, God has the same heart of concern and commitment toward us.

> **Just as a father has compassion on his children, so the Lord has compassion on those who fear Him.**
> **Psalm 103:13**

7. God is love.

> **The one who does not love does not know God, for God is love.**
> **1 John 4:8**

God is so characterized by perfect love that love is equated with Him. Furthermore, His love is so perfect, complete, and selfless that it is described as incomprehensible apart from His revelation of it (Ephesians 3:14-19).

Once we understand that God is love, we need to know that God has set His love on His own people *fully*. The kind of love He has for us who believe is made clear in Christ's death for us. *Everything* that He does and allows in our lives is consistent with that kind of love and commitment, even though we may not understand how.

God in His love seeks to do us good all the days of our lives, even through the hard things. Nothing can separate us from the love that God has for us.

> **For I am convinced that neither death, nor life, nor angels, nor principalities, nor things present, nor things to come, nor powers, nor height, nor depth, nor any other created thing, shall be able to separate us from the love of God, which is in Christ Jesus Our Lord.**
>
> **Romans 8:38,39**

God's Judicial and Parental Aspects Reconciled

Now that we have seen a glimpse of the character of God, we need to take a moment and explore some basics of how God relates to man. While still being true to all of His attributes, God does indeed relate differently to two groups of people described in the Bible. If this distinction is not made between the saved and unsaved, confusion about one's relationship with God can result. Every husband needs to determine the group to which he belongs before He can have a right relationship with God.

1. God is angry at the wicked.

Due to the sin nature we possess through Adam, we all begin life under the wrath and condemnation of God. God is justly and righteously angry with those who have not had their sins forgiven through

Christ. God is angry with them in the sense that He rejects them, condemns them, and hates their wicked ways.

> **God is a righteous judge, and a God who has indignation every day.**
> **Psalm 7:11**

All who have not come to true faith in Christ are in the realm of the wicked and are separated from God and under His wrath. God, however, is even merciful and gracious to the wicked. Even though they are His enemies, He allows them to live, to enjoy many things, and to escape much of the suffering that is possible in this life. God does not treat even the wicked as they truly deserve (Matthew 5:45).

God will remain angry at the wicked unless they repent and will punish them in hell. Even their good deeds are described as filthy rags by God, because they are not done for the right reasons (Isaiah 64:6). However, the Bible tells us that God so loved us that He gave His Son to die that they might be reconciled to Him.

> **Much more then, having now been justified by His blood, we shall be saved from the wrath of God through Him. For if while we were enemies, we were reconciled to God through the death of His Son, much more, having been reconciled, we shall be saved by His life.**
> **Romans 5:9-10**

2.   God is faithful to His own.

When we are reconciled to God through Christ, we are undeservedly moved from the realm of the wicked to the realm of sonship. Now God does not relate to us as the condemned wicked, but He *relates to us as He does His own Son* (John 1:12; Ephesians 2:4-10).

> **There is therefore now no condemnation for those who are in Christ Jesus.**
> **Romans 8:1**

From the point of salvation and forevermore there is:

- No condemnation.
- No wrath.
- Perfect fatherly love.
- Loving discipline as needed.
- Everlasting commitment and faithfulness.

No longer must God punish (repay) our sin. Our punishment was fully taken by Christ (Colossians 2:13-14). Now the Father seeks only to do us good. Now when we go astray, He seeks to teach and discipline us in love so that we grow in maturity. Because of Christ's payment for our sin, we can know that the disciplining afflictions of the redeemed are designed only to do His child good and to glorify Him. God is a loving and faithful parent who allows hardship only when He must help His child turn from the way of darkness and/or be conformed to His likeness.

The fact that our punishment has been paid does *not* mean that God condones sin. It is clear that His true sons will not rebelliously continue in sinful patterns (1 John 2:3-6). We are commanded to walk in obedience. If our faith is genuine we will sincerely desire to please Him. Even though a true son is forgiven through Christ, God still abhors any sin in his life and is very grieved by it. This fact is especially true since Christ suffered and gave His life that we might turn from sin and glorify Him instead (2 Corinthians 5:15). When a person is saved, God does not change His view of sin. The difference is that He now deals with the believer's sin as the sin of a beloved son, rather than the sin of an enemy.

**For those whom the Lord loves He disciplines, and He
scourges every son whom He receives.
Hebrews 12:6**

At salvation, the new position of *sonship is permanently* given. Just as it is not gained by our merit, likewise, it cannot be lost on the basis of our performance. Those who truly understand God's grace will no longer be driven by fear, duty, or the need to appease God. Obedience and service flow out of *gratitude* and *an understanding of the submission of sonship*. Those who are truly His will want to obey and serve Him because they have already been forgiven so much, and because they have received an undeserved but *permanent* commitment from God.

> **Know therefore that the Lord your God, He is God, the faithful God, who keeps His covenant and His lovingkindness to a thousandth generation with those who love Him and keep His commandments.**
> **Deuteronomy 7:9**

What Christian Husbands Need to Believe About God and Their Lives

In light of what we have learned, there are at least six things that every *Christian* husband needs to believe about God's involvement in his life.

1. God is powerfully, purposefully and perfectly working in your life:

> **And we know that God causes all things to work together for good to those who love God, to those who are called according to His purpose. For those whom He foreknew, He also predestined to become conformed to the image of His Son, so that He would be the first-born among many brethren;**
> **Romans 8:28-29**

2. God perfectly understands your life (past, present, and future). He understands every detail, all you are going through and every-thing you truly need (Matthew 6:25-7:12).

> **But He knows the way I take...**
> **Job 23:10**

3. God will compassionately and graciously walk with you through life.

> **"I will never desert you, nor will I ever forsake you," so that we confidently say, "The Lord is my helper, I will not be afraid. What shall man do to me?"**
> **Hebrews 13:5b-6**

4.   God has a ministry planned for you.

In His wise sovereignty, God saved us and left us here on this earth for a reason. That reason is two-fold. First, that we might be conformed into His image. Second, that we might fulfill our ministry for Him. God intends for us to fulfill our ministry to the wife (and family) He has given us (Ephesians 5:25-28), to the local church in which He has placed us (Ephesians 4:7-12), and to the lost world around us (Matthew 28:19-20; 2 Corinthians 5:18).

God has specifically outlined our role and responsibility as husbands. We should be sure that we are doing what He has already told us to do. Outside of being a witness for Christ *wherever* we are, our in-home ministry must be our primary ministry. God has made it clear that our faithfulness in the home qualifies us for outside ministry in the Church (1 Timothy 3:4-5). The Lord has a ministry planned for you, which begins with your responsibility as a husband.

> **For we are His workmanship, created in Christ Jesus**
> **for good works, which God prepared beforehand so**
> **that we would walk in them.**
> **Ephesians 2:10**

5.   God must be preeminently sought, reverenced and worshiped in your life.

We need to know why we exist. It certainly is not for our own personal fulfillment or happiness. We are here to seek first His kingdom and His righteousness. Life is for and about God, not about us. We must realize that God created us and saved us to be God-centered. J.C. Ryle says in his book, *Walking With God*, "True Christianity is not simply believing a set of abstract truths. It involves living in daily personal communion with a Person." [3]

> **So that He Himself will come to have first place in**
> **everything.**
> **Colossians 1:18b**

6.   God is your authority.

Man is not his own authority. I cannot tell you how many husbands I have counseled who quickly want to point out how their wives ought to submit to them. In such a case, I say, "That's right and I'm glad you brought up the subject of submission. Let's talk about submission—*your* submission to Jesus Christ." Husbands *are* the head of their wives, but they are also in submission to *their head*, Jesus Christ.

Every husband must continually see himself in submission to God and His authoritative Word. In doing so he will desire to conform his life to the Word of God and seek to walk as Christ walked. The exemplary husband will also seek to do nothing of his own initiative (John 8:28-29), but rather place God's will over and above his own (Luke 22:41-42).

> **But I want you to understand that Christ is the head**
> **of every man, and the man is the head of a woman,**
> **and God is the head of Christ.**
> **1 Corinthians 11:3**

Your View of God

We must have a correct view of God before we can exemplify Him. A. W. Tozer wrote:

> What comes into our minds when we think about God is the most important thing about us. The greatest question before the Church is always God Himself, and the most [important] fact about any man is not what he at any given time may say or do, but what he in his deep heart conceives God to be like. [4]

By faith every man must line up his thinking with each aspect of God's person. If one does not see God rightly, he cannot see himself rightly either. Hopefully, this chapter has helped you to evaluate and/or to refresh your view of God. If you have become aware that your view of God is off the mark at some point, pray and ask God to give you biblical insight and faith in His person before you move on.

Thus says the Lord, "Let not a wise man boast of his wisdom, and let not the mighty man boast of his might, let not a rich man boast of his riches; but let him who boasts boast of this, that he understands and knows Me, that I am the Lord who exercises lovingkindness, justice, and righteousness on earth; for I delight in these things," declares the Lord.
Jeremiah 9:23-24

Chapter Three

A HUSBAND'S UNDERSTANDING
OF MAN and SIN

In counseling I find it common for both husbands and wives to have a wrong view of man. When the husband has a wrong view of man, he may be like Bob or like Ralph. Bob is a middle-aged man who works hard, supports his family, and considers himself to be somewhat above average. After all, he comes home after work and brings his paycheck every week. He prides himself on being a good man. Bob does not have a clue as to why his wife is so frustrated with him. In Bob's opinion, she should be grateful for all he does for her instead of complaining that he is selfish. What more could she possibly want? Bob goes to church almost every Sunday and he gives money on a fairly regular basis. When he thinks about God and heaven he confidently says to himself, "I'm as good as the next man. I would never do what some of those men at work do."

Whereas Bob prides himself on being good, poor Ralph feels he is a victim and a failure. He cannot believe he is trapped in a marriage with a wife who is quick-tempered and disrespectful. She sounds just like his mother when she yells at him, "Ralph, that was a really dumb thing you did!" Ralph says with a sigh, "I sure don't need this. I just wish that someone would accept me and support me as I am. But that's never happened for me. Just like everyone else, my wife gets angry with me and tells me how terrible I am. I can't change what life has made me, so I avoid her as much as I can. What I want is a wife who makes me feel like somebody worthwhile."

Neither Bob nor Ralph has a biblical view of himself and it affects each man's relationship with God and with his wife. Now that we have a clearer picture of who God is from the last chapter, let's take a good look at who we are.

Who Are We?

Not only is there misunderstanding about who God is but there is also great confusion about who man is. This confusion comes from man's own desire to elevate and justify himself, which is certainly fanned by the twisted humanistic influences that have taken over our society. We must establish from the outset that the source of truth concerning man is not sociology (the study of our society), psychology (the humanistic study of the soul), or secular anthropology (the evolutionary study of man), but the very Word of God. Remember, we must build upon the solid ground of God's Word rather than the shifting sand of man's opinion.

> **See to it that no one takes you captive through philosophy and empty deception, according to the tradition of men, according to the elementary principles of the world, rather than according to Christ.**
> **Colossians 2:8**

False Views of Man

In this chapter we will address some of the most popular wrong views of man and compare these views with the Scriptures. Our goal is to find out exactly what God says about who man is and how he can live as God intended. Then we will begin our practical look at the kind of life the exemplary husband can model with God's help.

1.   Man is basically good.

> **The heart is more deceitful than all else and is desperately sick; who can understand it?**
> **Jeremiah 17:9**

God says that apart from His grace and work, man's heart is bent on wickedness (Romans 3:9-20). We may not be as bad as we could be but that is *only* because of God's restraining grace in our lives. Even the good that natural (unsaved) man does is often done for the wrong reason.

> **All have turned aside, together they have become useless; there is none who does good, there is not even one.**
> **Romans 3:12**

2.   Man is getting better.

> **But realize this, that in the last days difficult times will come. For men will be lovers of self, lovers of money, boastful, arrogant, revilers, disobedient to parents, ungrateful, unholy, unloving, irreconcilable, malicious gossips, without self-control, brutal, haters of good, treacherous, reckless, conceited, lovers of pleasure rather than lovers of God, holding to a form of godliness, although they have denied its power; avoid such men as these... and that from childhood you have known the sacred writings which are able to give you the wisdom that leads to salvation through faith which is in Christ Jesus**
> **2 Timothy 3:1-5, 15**

The truth is, men are not getting better and better, but worse and worse. While it is true that science, medicine, technology, and many arts are more sophisticated and more highly developed than at any time in history, we have to admit that with these greater skills we have become, not greater men of God, but greater sinners. Our societies in the United States and across the world are not models of godliness, peace, and love. Instead, our societies have consistently improved in the ability to sin.

3.   Man can be good enough.

> **For whoever keeps the whole law and yet stumbles in**
> **one point, he has become guilty of all.**
> **James 2:10**

The Bible is very clear that man cannot be good enough to impress God (Isaiah 64:6). God's holy standard is perfection (Habakkuk 1:13a; Matthew 5:48). Man is condemned by his sin nature, which is revealed by the committing of only one sin against a holy God.

4.   Man is a non-responsible victim of tragic and senseless circumstances.

> **So then each one of us will give an account of himself**
> **to God.**
> **Romans 14:12**

The Bible teaches that each person is a great sinner and will be held accountable for his own actions, regardless of his circumstances. It also says, anyone who truly knows God and abides in His truth can lead the kind of life God wants him to lead, even if he has been greatly wronged (2 Peter 1:2-4). That person simply must learn to *adequately* apply the Word of God to his circumstances.

We are also taught from Scripture that while some events in our lives may indeed be tragic, God is in absolute control (Romans 8:28). While this fact may be hard to reconcile in our own minds, God is the one who knows the end from the beginning. Therefore, only *He* knows how a circumstance can serve to:

*   Humble a person (Job 42:1-6)
*   Draw a person to Himself (John 6:44)
*   Show Himself to be a greater-than-anything God
    (Jeremiah 32:17; Genesis 50:20)
*   Reveal Himself to a believing sufferer as Refuge, Strength and
    Helper (Psalm 46:1; Isaiah 57:15; John 9:1-3).

God's View of Man

Every man desiring to know God and be the husband he should be must reject false views about man and adopt God's view. In the first chapter of Genesis, God has revealed the truth about our beginning.

1. Man was created by God.

The first thing that we must believe is that God is the Creator and man is His creation.

> **And God created man in His own image, in the image**
> **of God He created him; male and female He created**
> **them.**
> **Genesis 1:27**

There are at least three things we can learn from God's creation of us. The most basic thing we need to grasp is that we are not our own. We are neither in control nor independent.

> **The earth is the Lord's and all it contains, the world,**
> **and those who dwell in it.**
> **Psalm 24:1**

Secondly, we need to understand that there is a great distinction between God who is our Creator, and us, who are His creatures (Psalm 8:4-8). Even though we are an amazing work of God that is unique from the rest of creation (personal, as God is), we are still *merely* a creation made by One who is *far greater*.

> **The Lord is high above all nations; His glory is above**
> **the heavens. Who is like the Lord our God, who is**
> **enthroned on high, who humbles himself to behold**
> **the things that are in heaven and in the earth?**
> **Psalm 113:4-6**

Thirdly, we need to be aware that life does *not* revolve around *us*. As our creator, God is the cause and center of all things. *He* is the rightful focus. *He* is the only one worthy of all glory (Revelation 4:11).

2. Man was created *for God*.

The fact that God created man in His own image gives us a hint as to why we were created. We were created *for Him*.

...all things have been created by Him and for Him.
Colossians 1:16b

This truth may be quite a shock to the one who believes his purpose here is to "get all I can out of life." It may even be a surprise to professing Christians who live as though God is there for them, rather than the other way around. But, the one who views God and himself rightly counts it a privilege to exist *for Him*.

To Worship Him

We were created for God that He might receive the worship He deserves. God is entirely holy, powerful, and true. He, therefore, fully deserves our focus, adoration, praise, and honor. He is worthy of our worship and He rightfully expects it.

Yours, O Lord, is the greatness and the power and the
victory and the majesty, indeed everything that is in
the heavens and the earth. Yours is the dominion, O
Lord, and You exalt Yourself as head over all.
1 Chronicles 29:11

Every human being is born with a *debt of worship* to God (Psalm 96:7-9). Not one of us has paid that debt fully. Some people are oblivious to their need to acknowledge the Creator. Others willfully refuse to worship Him. It is amazing that God patiently waits for the right time to judge mankind for its lack of worship (Psalm 96:13).

We must ask ourselves if we have embraced this *first* purpose for which we were created: to worship God. Is the central activity of your life the worship of God? The Father is seeking worshippers.

"But an hour is coming, and now is, when the true
worshippers will worship the Father in spirit and
truth; for such people the Father seeks to be His wor-
shippers."
John 4:23

To Be a People of His Very Own

We were also created *for God* so that He might have a people. The primary meaning of the word *holy* in the Bible often involves the idea of *separation*, or of being *cut off* from something. It is frequently used in the Old Testament of people or things being "set apart as holy to the Lord" (Exodus 13:12,14,15; Numbers 3:11-13). Something that is "set apart" for the Lord is specially marked as His possession and is reserved for His righteous purposes and use. In the beginning, man was set apart *for Him* with a specific purpose in view. God was going to have a people of *His very own.*

> **Know that the Lord Himself is God; It is He who has made us... we are his people and the sheep of His pasture.**
> **Psalm 100:3**

God has stooped very low to even concern Himself with us. Even so, He has revealed His desire to walk with man throughout history. As early as the Garden of Eden, God walked with man (Genesis 3:8-10). He continually called the nation of Israel to abide in a relationship with Himself (Deuteronomy 7:6,9,11). Through Christ, God is still calling people to walk with Him today.

> **[Jesus Christ]...Who gave Himself for us, that he might redeem us from every lawless deed, and purify**
> *for Himself a people that are His very own...*
> **Titus 2:14 [emphasis mine]**

To Put His Character on Display (Glorify Him)

Through our creation, God not only could receive the worship He deserves and have a people of His very own, but He could also be glorified in an awesome way. By creating us, loving us, working among us, and showering us with grace, God's character has been on display. He has been on display before the angels in heaven, man and even Satan and the demons (1 Timothy 3:16; Job 36:24-25; Mark 1:23-24).

> **Come and see the works of God who is awesome in His deeds toward the sons of men.**
> **Psalm 66:5**

Those who have been forgiven of their sins can join God in the awesome display of His character by acknowledging Him, by proclaiming His great deeds, and by making disciples (Psalm 96:1-6; 1 Peter 2:9-10). Even those who rebel against God will have a part in putting God's character on display. His justice will be seen by all (Psalm 9:8).

Throughout history, man has turned away from God's purpose and has chosen a selfish and sinful way. Many seek the pleasures of this life. Others seek God for their own ends. The truth is, our greatest purpose in life is *God's* pleasure.

3.   Man is God's enemy by nature.

As much as God desires to receive our worship and have an abiding relationship with us, He cannot and will not unjustly ignore the great barrier that our sin has created between Himself and us.

> **But your iniquities have made a separation between you and your God, and your sins have hidden His face from you so that He does not hear you.**
> **Isaiah 59:2**

We may not ever feel like God's enemy, but by the simple fact that we inherit the sinful nature of Adam, we are His enemies from birth. Our sinful condition is seen in both our failure to worship God as He deserves and in our bent toward sin and selfishness (Romans 1:18-25; 5:10). But God did not leave us in this hopeless situation. We need not remain the enemies of God!

> **And although you were formerly** *alienated and hostile in mind*, **engaged in evil deeds, yet He has now reconciled you in His fleshly body through death, in order to present you before Him, holy and blameless and beyond reproach.**
> **Colossians 1:21-22 [emphasis mine]**

So far we have learned that man is sinful to the core, dead in his trespasses and sins, an enemy of God, fully responsible, and unable to meet God's standard or to help himself (Ephesians 2:1-7). Man was born with a debt of worship to his Creator, but instead has worshiped and served himself, even in his "good deeds." He is bound to the lustful, selfish and sinful desires of his flesh and is deceived by his sin-stained mind and foolish heart. Even though man is restrained from full expression of his sinfulness, he is doomed (apart from God's direct intervention on his behalf) to suffer the consequences of his own sin and rebellion by spending an eternity in hell, paying for his sins against a holy God (2 Thessalonians 1:9; Revelation 20:11-15). What an ugly picture of ourselves! But God in His mercy is willing to make you into a *different* picture—a different man.

Defining Man's Needs

So, what then is every husband's need? Surely, some good news! Understanding what our specific needs are will lead us right to that good news. Until a man has a right relationship with God through salvation, he will not see his needs rightly (2 Corinthians 4:4). This failure can greatly affect the marriage relationship. What God says your needs are may be quite different from what you have been taught.

Psychology's List

Psychology (the secular study of man) offers us a myriad of personal needs. We are told that these needs must be met before we can be what we should be. God says no such thing. Contrary to popular thought, we do not *need* to be well respected and honored or to have our sexual appetites satisfied. We do not *need* to be comfortable, rewarded for our efforts, or recognized for our accomplishments. We do not *need* to have a good marriage, good kids or a great job. We do not *need* for others to "understand" us or where we are coming from. God also does not say that we *need* the love of others or security. Certainly, we may *desire* all these things, but we do not *need* them (2 Peter 1:2-4).

It is very important that we guard against calling something a need that God does not. Usually when we look at desires, blessings, or things that are normative as needs, we are saying (whether we realize it or not) that we cannot live as God intended for us to live without them. The reasoning that often follows is that God must supply them *if* He is good. However, many of God's people have gone without these so called "needs." The Scriptures are full of such individuals (Joseph, David, Jeremiah, Paul, and many more). And yet, look what God says in Psalm 34:10:

> **...The young lions do lack and suffer hunger;** *but they*
> *who seek the Lord shall not be in want of any good thing.*
> **[emphasis mine]**

God has promised to give us exactly what we need or is good for us. He is the only one wise enough to know what our needs are in the whole scheme of things.

God's List

The Bible, however, portrays these issues and the needs of man very differently than man does. Who is right? God is, of course. He is clear about two basic needs of man:

1.   Man needs to walk with God in His truth.

The truth is, our most basic need is God Himself (Ecclesiastes 12:13; Luke 10:42)! We need to be forgiven for our sins so we can be reconciled with Him (2 Corinthians 5:17, 20-21). This is the need of man only God can meet. When we really know God and are humbly walking with Him, we have everything we need. He alone is enough.

> **For he has satisfied the thirsty soul, and the hungry**
> **soul He has filled with what is good.**
> **Psalm 107:9**

What we also *need* is to glorify God by walking according to His principles (Deuteronomy 10:12-22). Therefore, we *need* the Word of God (2 Peter 1:3-4), we *need* to love God and others (Matthew 22:37-40), and we *need* to serve God and others (1 Peter 4:10-11). In fact, *every command of God* is a need. Beyond these needs, God *alone* determines what is necessary in our lives (Philippians 4:19). This *certainly* is *not* the way our society looks at man's need, is it?

2.   Man needs God to act.

Since Christ is our only hope to walk with God, the great gospel message is the *chief* need of man (John 14:6). The Bible says, "the wages of sin is death, but the free *gift* of God is eternal life" (Romans 6:23 [emphasis mine]). God the Father sent God the Son to provide a way for us to be forgiven and reconciled (brought back together) with Himself. God acted on our behalf to make a way of salvation.

In this is love, not that we loved God, but that He loved us and sent His Son to be the propitiation for our sins.
1 John 4:10

Each person also needs the Spirit of God to act in his heart. Until God works we are spiritually dead and would never seek God on our own.

Jesus answered and said to them, "Do not grumble among yourselves. *No one can come to me unless the Father who sent me draws him;* **and I will raise him up on the last day."**
John 6:43-44 [emphasis mine]

So God the Son, in His great display of graciousness, was willing to initiate a way of salvation for mankind and draw many to Himself (Acts 13:48). He loved us first in order to meet our greatest need of all.

God's Provisions for Man's Needs

God specifically provided for our needs. He has made a way for our salvation, our sanctification, and our glorification. If you partake of these three provisions you can become the man you were created to be.

1.   God's provision of salvation

God has provided a Savior in the person of Jesus Christ. Amazingly, He was willing to pay the penalty for the sin that *we* owe. This means that even though Jesus lived a sinless life, He, Almighty God, left heaven and the adoration He deserves in order to endure the conditions of this world, suffer shame, be rejected by men, die a criminal's gruesome death, bear the guilt of all our sins, be bitterly rejected by the Father (with whom He knew only love and harmony), and suffer the hell we so richly deserved (Philippians 2:6-8). Only Christ could do what was necessary to bring us to God.

> **For Christ also died for sins once for all, the just for the unjust, so that He might** *bring us to God,* **having been put to death in the flesh, but made alive in the spirit.**
> **1 Peter 3:18 [emphasis mine]**

It was through Christ's suffering and rejection on the cross that God's righteous wrath against sin was satisfied and a way to obtain forgiveness was made (Romans 5:9). This forgiveness is possible because God is willing to exchange Christ's righteousness for our sinfulness (2 Corinthians 5:21). For this exchange to take place a husband must have saving faith. Saving faith involves:

- Acknowledging the true reason for our existence and God's full right to our lives and how we live them (Matthew 16:24-26; Romans 11:36; 1 Corinthians 6:20).
- Coming to God in humbleness, recognizing you have nothing to offer God in your defense (James 4:6).
- Asking Him for His mercy and forgiveness, instead of what is deserved (Luke 18:9-14).
- Believing in who Christ is and His payment for your sin (1 Corinthians 15:3).
- Believing that Christ rose from the dead as Lord over all and sits at the right hand of the Father pleading the case of all those who believe (1 Corinthians 15:4; Philippians 2:9-11; Hebrews 7:25).

Christ also taught that in order to enter the kingdom of God we must be like a little child. This may smack at our manly pride but Christ was talking about important attitudes of the heart. A little child knows his place and has humble faith. A little child is dependent and needy. We must come to God with this kind of faith in order to receive His gift of salvation.

> **"Truly I say to you, whoever does not receive the kingdom of God like a child will by no means enter it at all."**
> **Mark 10:15**

If we really contemplate saving faith, we can understand why Christ said what He did to those who came to hear Him speak.

> **"Enter through the narrow gate; for the gate is wide
> and the way is broad that leads to destruction, and
> there are many who enter through it. For the gate is
> small and the way is narrow that leads to life, and**
> *there are few who find it."*
> **Matthew 7:13-14 [emphasis mine]**

Don't be deceived. A prayer said or a profession made in the past should not assure you of your salvation. Are you *having* saving faith *now*? Are you believing *now*? It is an ongoing (obedient and persevering) belief that demonstrates that you are a child of God. Christ offered this warning to all who would listen,

> **"Not everyone who says to Me, 'Lord, Lord,' will
> enter the kingdom of heaven."**
> **Matthew 7:21a**

If you have never yielded to God's plan (to be forgiven and walk with Him) I beseech you, take time right now to talk to Him about these things. Ask Him to be merciful to you, not because you deserve it, but because you know that He is the Lord God who created the universe. Confess your sins (of motive, thought, word and deed) to God and seek His forgiveness on the basis of Christ's payment for your sin. If you come to God in humility and with saving faith, He will grant you salvation.

> **[Jesus said] "All that the Father gives Me will come to
> Me, and the one who comes to Me I will certainly not
> cast out."**
> **John 6:37**

2.   God's provision of sanctification

Salvation does not automatically cause us to be all that we should be. Not by a long shot! It does, however, mean that we will wholeheartedly enter into a dependent effort with God toward *change* into Christlikeness (Philippians 3:12-14; 2 Peter 3:18).

Remember Ralph who was without hope? He would be inclined to believe that little could be done to change his life, but obviously he is wrong. Once we are saved, God initiates the sanctification or *growth process*. God Himself provides His Word, His Spirit, and His Church for our growth (2 Peter 1:2-11). Without these provisions we could not change in the least. On the other hand, God commands that we "exercise ourselves unto godliness" (1Timothy 4:7-9). What does this mean? The Greek word for "exercise" (*gumnazo*) is where our words gymnasium and gymnastics come from. This means that we are to put a strenuous effort into becoming more like Christ. When we do our part, we trust in God's work and God's promise.

> **For I am confident of this very thing, that He who began a good work in you will perfect it until the day of Christ Jesus.**
> **Philippians 1:6**

When we do our part as a Christian, we are cooperating with God in the growth process. We do our part, first of all, by *devoting our lives to loving and living for Him, rather than self*. When a person truly comes to faith in Christ he will have a new passion—Christ.

> **And He died for all, so that they who live should no longer live for themselves, but for Him who died and rose again on their behalf.**
> **2 Corinthians 5:15**

We are to be so devoted to our Creator, that we labor to please Him with every fiber of our being. Our love for the God who created and saved us should be so great that walking with Him is more important to us than anything else in the world.

Dependently working with God in the change process also means that *we will deal with any known sin God's way*. Some people believe that God's way of dealing with sin is to simply confess it and ask forgiveness. The Bible teaches that we are to deal with our sin in a fuller and much more practical way.

When we sin, God wants us to do three things:

- Confess our sin as sin (Proverbs 28:13; 1 John 1:9) and ask forgiveness with the resolve to repent (Matthew 6:12).
- Ask God for His transforming grace to change, with the same

resolve to repent (Psalm 25:4; John 15:5).

- Repent according to God's process for change by:
  a. *Working to renew the mind with Scripture* . (Romans 12:1-2). This involves knowing Scripture about whatever sin issue is at hand well enough to *specifically* change wrong or incomplete thinking into thinking that is in agreement with God's principles and promises. We must purposefully guard and renew our minds. (See Appendix One for a form to assist you in mind renewal).

Example Thoughts to Renew	
Sinful Thoughts, Void of God	**Thankful, Trusting, Hopeful Thoughts**
I've had it! I can't take this job anymore. (discouragement / giving up)	Lord, You know all about this difficult situation. Thank you that I have a job and that you can help me to endure. I pray that you might supply a different job if that is best. (Philippians 2:14; 4:13)
I just want to be left alone. (selfishness)	Lord, You know I don't feel like giving right now but I thank you that I have a family and that you can give me your strength. Help me to serve you and others now. (Philippians 2:3-4)
What if I lose my job? (worry)	Lord, I pray that I don't lose my job but if I do, I know that you will somehow provide. I thank you that you are faithful and in control. I trust you. (Matthew 6:25-34)

b. *Working to put off sinful actions and to put on righteous ones* (Ephesians 4:20-24). This involves putting enough thought into one's life to: (1) specifically plan how and when a particular sin will be avoided, and (2) determine specific ways to apply its righteous alternatives. True repentance does not take place without these things (See Appendix Two for a fuller explanation of God's process of change).

Sinful Thoughts to Replace				
Put Off I need to stop...	**Put On** I need to start...	**When** I need to practice when...	**Thoughts** I need to renew...	**Where Temptation Begins** I need to avoid...
<u>Being angry:</u>	<u>Being gentle and self-controlled:</u>	I am very tired	"This is my time to rest and relax!"	A lack of sleep
Speaking: - Mean words	Speak with: - Only words that edify	The children are disobedient	"I can't handle this!"	Being slack in training my children
- Raised voice - Harsh tone	- Gentle tone of voice	I need to do something and I'm being hindered	"Leave me alone! I can't do anything anymore!"	Over-committing myself
- Angry face Verses: Ps. 37:8 Eph. 4:31 Pr. 29:11a	- Kind face Verses: I Thess. 2:7 Eph. 4:29 Pr. 29:11b	Someone sins against me	"How dare they!"	Expecting good treatment and respect

3.   God's provision of glorification

God promises to bring us to heaven where He is and to free us from our sinful bent (1 Corinthians 15:50-58). What a great hope we have! This life is not all there is! Our short time on Earth is not what life is even about. Everything is working toward the great end of God's people being with Him for eternity (Revelation 21:3, 7).

Every Christian husband needs to be heavenly-minded (Colossians 3:1-3; Matthew 6:33). We will look forward to heaven more if we fully accept the fact that this life is *not* heaven, and never will be. If we live with heaven in our sights we will please God and be less likely to grow weary in the hardships of life (Hebrews 11:8-10; 12:1-3). Remembering that we will see Jesus face to face one day can also have a very purifying affect on our lives (1 John 3:2-3). We should strive to keep an eternal perspective and place *all* our hope in our future with Christ.

> **Therefore, prepare your minds for action, keep sober in spirit, fix your hope completely on the grace to be brought to you at the revelation of Jesus Christ.**
> **1 Peter 1:13**

We must renew our minds because our actions flow out of our motives, thoughts and beliefs. This fact can be pictured something like this.

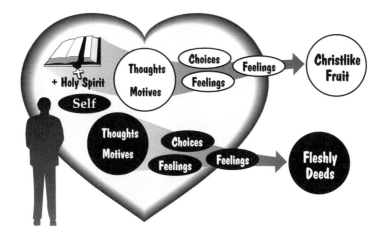

Be Assured

We have looked at false views of man that we need to reject, who man is according to God, and what man's true needs are. We have also looked at what man was created to be and God's provisions to attain that. Unless Bob and Ralph change their thinking about themselves, there is no hope for them to be the husband God wants them to be. You, on the other hand, have great hope if you grasp these foundational truths about who you are. Most important, they will allow you to relate to God properly.

I cannot guarantee that if you devote yourself to God and His will that your wife will respond in kind. In fact, for some, things may get worse if you become more like the man you were meant to be. But, based on God's Word, if you have saving faith in Christ, I *can* guarantee that the same God who died for your sins and rose again will never leave or forsake you, no matter what the circumstances (Hebrews 13:5-6). I can assure you that you *can* (by grace) walk with God and be His kind of man (Colossians 1:9-12). And, I *can* tell you with certainty that if you are a believer, one day you will see Christ face to face (Revelation 22:4). It is in focusing on these three sureties that you will find joy in your pilgrimage to heaven.

Chapter Four

A HUSBAND'S UNDERSTANDING
OF RELATIONSHIPS

Fear not, O man of God! God's Word does not (nor do I) intend to send you off on some questionable pursuit to get in touch with your so-called *feminine side*! On the other hand, I cannot go so far as to say, "You're okay—I'm okay" either. I do believe that our society and the church are in big trouble when it comes to our relationships. Given the heart of man, the state of our society, and the often-lacking influences of one's upbringing, this situation is no surprise. In many cases, there is simply a lack of foundational understanding about relationships.

Webster defines a relationship as, "the state or character of being related or interrelated." This is a rather basic understanding of the word. In a broad sense we have some type of relationship to anyone or anything. Our purpose is to define God's perspective of a *personal* relationship. We are talking about an interconnection with the persons to whom we have commitment or responsibility, such as God, family, spouse, friend, spiritual leader, brother or sister in Christ, boss, co-worker, etc. Obviously, all of these relationships will not be equal in degree, but they should have the key elements of a biblical relationship.

The question I would like to answer in this chapter is, "What does God think about our relationships?" Remember, it is our aim to be the exemplary husband God has called us to be, by patterning our lives after that of Christ. To fulfill this goal we have to look at Him through His Word. But first, let's take a closer look at many relationships today.

The Current Relationship Scene

Many Americans seem mainly interested in three things; getting things done, achieving personal goals, and protecting their personal space. Often we are so busy with things that do not involve other people, there is no time for and eventually no interest in relationships. Some people have pulled out of the relationship idea altogether because they have been wronged or "burned." Other people are reluctant to pursue relationships simply because relating well requires effort. Our flesh (sinful nature) is an enemy to the effort that is needed to maintain relationships. If the "Church" continues to follow our society in becoming more and more lovers and servers of self, the pursuit of biblical relationships will fall more and more by the wayside.

Often a wife's primary complaint about her marriage is, "We have no relationship." In turn, a common response of the husband is, "What's the problem? I think we have a great— or at least a good— relationship." This response is often (at least in part) because of the husband's relational deficiency. Put this deficiency together with the idealistic expectations of some wives, (the wrong idea that men should be just like women in how they relate), and the presence of unresolved issues in the relationship, and you have a blueprint for marital disaster.

> **But realize this, that in the last days difficult times will come. For men will be lovers of self, lovers of money, boastful, arrogant, revilers, disobedient to parents, ungrateful, unholy, unloving, irreconcilable, malicious gossips, without self control, brutal, despisers of good, treacherous, reckless, conceited, lovers of pleasure rather than lovers of God, holding to a form of godliness, although they have denied its power; avoid such men as these.**
> **2 Timothy 3:1-5**

The qualities in these verses do not make for good relationships! Both genders are involved in these sins, but we cannot ignore that there seems to be a growing number of men who have little interest or know-how when it comes to relationships.

Any pastor who is involved with his people can attest that more and more individuals are coming forward in the church with problems in husband/wife, parent/child, employer/employee, and friend/friend relationships. Furthermore, some husbands have excused themselves from their God-given responsibilities with deceptions such as, "It shouldn't take so much effort to be together." Or, "My wife should be thrilled that I am her faithful provider and protector. Why can't that satisfy her?" Or, "I don't really need relationships because I'm just not a needy person." Are relationships just for needy people? Nothing could be further from the truth.

A Book of Relationships

Thankfully, rather than leaving us to fend for ourselves, God has in His Word given us a blueprint for relationships. We must look to Him for guidance about our relationships. No other book can so quickly tell us what God wants for our relationships.

The first step to relating in a God-honoring way is to fully accept the truth that our relationships are extremely important to God. Once a husband has come to saving faith, he will hopefully become aware that the Bible is a book of relationships. It continually addresses first our most important vertical relationship with God and then our horizontal relationships with others. Christ Himself summed up the whole law into two relational categories in Matthew 22:37-40:

> **And He said to him, "You shall love the Lord your God with all your heart and with all your soul, and with all your mind." This is the great and foremost commandment. The second is like it, "You shall love your neighbor as yourself." On these two commandments depend the whole Law and the Prophets.**

Our Relationship To God

Everyone is related to God as creator and sustainer, but as we saw in chapter 3, those of us who know Him as Savior have the privilege of a much deeper relationship (Titus 2:14). God gives to us and we give to God. He gives grace, love, guidance, care, compassion, protection, strength, comfort, teaching, commands and many desires. We give praise, thanksgiving, honor, love, obedience, trust and service. The relationship between God and the believer is not a one-sided relationship. Both God and man are actively involved.

Our Relationship To Others

Christ gave us an even closer look at how relational our three-in-one God is when He was here on earth. He not only taught about the two greatest commandments but He lived them as well. His life was all about God the Father and people. Everywhere He went He was interested in people. Since our God is a relational God, then *we* must be also. Remember, Christlikeness is our goal. We cannot be exemplary husbands and balk at the need to take our relationships with others seriously. (See Appendix Three for a list of relationships that God has addressed in the Scriptures.)

Created Dependent and Interdependent (Not Independent)

From the very beginning, man was dependent on God. Man was not created in such a way that he could provide for himself (out of nothing) nor sustain himself. God provides the air we breathe, the place we live, the food we eat, the water we drink, and the instruction and strength we need for living. We need God!

Man was also created to be interdependent (involved) with others. After being placed in the Garden, God said that it was not good for man to be alone and provided for him a helper (Genesis 2:18). Here is our first clue that we are meant to depend in some way on one another. Consistent with this fact, God has included many "one another commands" in the New Testament (See Appendix Four for a sample list of one-anothers).

Now, if we are created from the beginning to relate with one another and to be interdependent with one another, how is it, men, that we seem inclined to think that it is neither macho nor necessary to be involved with others? Some of us need a serious change of mind in this respect. We must rid ourselves of the pride that says, "I can do this by myself," or *excuses responsibility to love others* with, "Just me and the Lord is all I need." To be like Christ, we must pursue involvement with others.

Even though our efforts to be involved in a two-way biblical relationship (for God's glory and the other's good) are sometimes resisted or rejected by the other person, we must remain committed to trying, until the other person dissolves the relationship with finality. Even when there has been rejection, there may still be an occasional opportunity to do that person good (Romans 12:17-21). Though it is difficult, we can love others with God's kind of love, even if they are not loving toward us. God requires that we love, serve, and even suffer for those who are indifferent or hostile toward us, because that is exactly what He has done for us. (This does not mean one cannot appeal to the governing authorities for protection when someone is breaking the law by physical abuse—Romans 13:1-7).

God's Blueprint for Relationships

We have already learned some things about relationships by looking at how God has pursued us and created us. Before creating a clear description and definition of a biblical relationship, we must look at the most crucial part of our relational blueprint—**how God relates to Himself**. This is the best pattern for our relationships. It is unfortunate that in most theology books the three members of the Trinity are presented as only relating to one another functionally. In reality, they relate to one another personally as well. Within the relationships of the Godhead (Father, Son and Holy Spirit) there is:

- A willingness to deny self (Mark 14:32-36; Philippians 2:5-9).
- Honor and respect—though equality exists (John 8:49; 2 Peter 1:17).
- Submission to an order of authority—though equality exists (John 8:28-29; 14:31; 16:13; 1 Corinthians 11:3).
- Humility (John 16:14; Philippians 2:1-11; 1 Corinthians 11:3).

51

- Unity (Deuteronomy 6:4; John 10:30, 38; 14:10-11, 23; 17:11).
- Uniqueness of Personhood—three distinct Persons
  (Luke 3:21-22; John 1:31-34; 14:23-26; Acts 5:3-4).
- Perfect communication (John 8:28; 15:15; 16:13; 2 Peter 1:17).
- Involvement and cooperation (Genesis 1:26; Luke 4:1; John 14:23;
  Colossians 1:12-20).
- Knowledge of the other Persons (Matthew 11:27; John 8:55; 15:15; 1
  Corinthians 2:10).
- Expressions of thankfulness (Matthew 11:25; 15:36; 26:27;
  Luke 10:21; John 11:41).
- Verbal expressions of love
  (John 10:17; 14:31; 15:9; 17:23; Romans 5:5).
- Visible expressions of love, goodness, blessing and service (John
  15:9-10; 17:4,23; Romans 15:3; Galatians 5:22; Colossians 1:19).
- Truthfulness/Trustworthiness
  (John 3:33; 14:17; Titus 1:1-2; Hebrews 6:18).
- Utmost concern for God's truth and glory (John 16:14; 17:1,5,24).

What an excellent pattern we have to follow! These are the key elements of a biblical relationship. One of the major elements God has expanded for us is the *visible expressions of love* element. The effects of our expressions of love for one another also include: encouraging one another when discouraged, forgiving one another, stirring up one another to love and good deeds, gently admonishing one another, firmly and lovingly rebuking one another; and bearing each other's burdens.

The most important thing for us to remember in our relationships is that the way the Trinity relates to one another gives us our model for relationships. The basic elements seen among the Godhead should be present in a biblical relationship. If you seek to implement these things in your marriage, you will be well on your way to becoming an exemplary husband.

Don't Even Go There!

In our relationships with others, we must address any tendency **to give or require an *inordinate* amount of attention**. People who have this wrong focus are actually in the relationship for themselves since they are not in it for God's glory or the good of the other person. They may be under the mistaken assumption that giving this worshipful attention is the way it is supposed to be. The theater has encouraged this thinking, depicting that life is about an all-consuming and near-perfect human love. To pursue such a fanciful relationship is neither right nor living within reality. God is the one with whom we should be consumed.

> **Their sorrows shall be multiplied who hasten after another God; O Lord, You are the portion of my inheritance and my cup; you maintain my lot. I have set the Lord always before me. In your presence is fullness of joy; at your right hand are pleasures forever more.**
> **Psalm 16:4-5, 8, 11 [NKJV]**

Two Surrounding Necessities

There are two more things always present in the way God relates to us. First of all, God's perfect love overshadows all of His dealings with us. His love for us is never inactive. We know this because of the biblical word *hesed*. This Hebrew word refers to God's relationship with us and means "steadfast loving-kindness" or "covenant loyalty" (Psalm 36:7; Isaiah 63:7). The word carries with it the ideas of both *love* and *faithfulness*. Therefore, a biblical relationship has **enduring love.** Everything that is done in a biblical relationship should be in keeping with this kind of love.

> **Therefore as the elect of God, holy and beloved, put on tender mercies, kindness, humility, meekness,** *longsuffering; bearing with one another,* **and forgiving one another, if anyone has a complaint against another; even as Christ forgave you, so you also must do.**
> **Colossians 3:12-13 [emphasis mine] NKJV**

Secondly, each of God's relational qualities rests on the foundation of truth. He loves in a way that is in keeping with His character and word (James 1:17). Everything we do should also be in keeping with all of God's principles and commands.

> **My little children, let us not love in word or in tongue, but in deed and *in truth*. And by this we know that we are of the truth, and shall assure our hearts before Him.**
> **1 John 3:18-19 [emphasis mine] NKJV**

This is how we relate biblically. A biblical relationship, then, must possess both the quality of *enduring love* and *obedience to the Scriptures*.

GOD'S TRUTH
A
Biblical
Relationship
ENDURING LOVE

Putting It All Together

Having taken a close look at God and His dealings with us, we can create a definition of a biblical relationship. Our relationships must be:

A joint participation between two distinct Christian persons in which there is involvement, Christ-like love (sacrificial, enduring, and in keeping with God's Word), good communication, appreciation, edification, and service—all in an attitude of respect and humility—and all for God's glory and the benefit of the other.

In non-mutual relationships, our responsibility remains the same. We cannot force others to relate the way God wants them to but we can honor God *ourselves*. We are all related in some way to unbelievers. Some of you have unbelieving wives. Unbelieving wives do not have the capacity to relate as God relates, but by carrying out your responsibility, you can be a witness of *God's* love and bring great glory to Him. In this case, you must engage in:

A pursuit of involvement and faithfulness toward another distinct person by *your own* Christ-like love (sacrificial, enduring, and in keeping with God's Word), good communication, appreciation, edification, and service —all in an attitude of respect and humility—and all for God's glory and the benefit of the other.

Major Pitfalls in Relationships

Before we leave the subject of relationships, I want to address some of the pitfalls that we must avoid if we are going to achieve what we just described. Sin has always been the problem in relationships. As a result of the Fall of man, not only was man separated from his God, but he also immediately began to have difficulty in his horizontal relationships. This is demonstrated clearly in the book of Genesis (Adam and Eve, Genesis 3:12-13; Cain and Abel, Genesis 4:8; etc.). Relationship problems have continued through the ages because sin has continued. Even after salvation, our sinful bent is still present (Romans 7:21-25).

As exemplary husbands, we need to avoid these sins and seek with all diligence to replace the following unrighteous characteristics with God their Christ-like counterparts:

1. Not pursuing Christ first and foremost (see also chapter 7).

    Our relationship with Christ will always affect our horizontal relationships with one another. If we are not loving God with all our heart, soul and mind, we are putting something or someone else in His rightful place. We will inevitably find ourselves having difficulty in our other relationships.

    Instead: Make Christ your life and treasure. Pursue Him as your "first love."

2. Pride (the mindset of self—see also chapter 13).

    a. Self-exalting pride

    Pride will cause us to look down on others and lord it over others rather than lovingly lead. A person who is self-exalting will also get defensive, blame-shift, rename, or ignore sin

55

rather than admit sin and ask forgiveness. He will also be reluctant to be accountable to anyone, and will rarely see anyone as capable of giving advice or beneficial input.

Instead: Put on the humility that treats others as more important than self (Philippians 2:1-4), admits sin (Psalm 32:5; James 5:16), seeks counsel (Proverbs 1:5, 15:22), welcomes accountability (Hebrews 10:24-25), only makes requests that consider the glory of God and the good of others (Philippians 2:1-4).

    b. Self-centered pride

The focus of the sinful flesh is **Self**! It finds great difficulty in being others-minded and considerate. Its thoughts, words and efforts are consumed with "*my*" agenda, "*my*" problems, "*my*" lacks, "*my*" desires, "*my*" needs.

Instead: Seek to focus on God's desires and serving the good of others.

Be devoted to one another in brotherly love; *give preference to one another in hono*r.
Romans 12:10 [emphasis mine]

3.   Sinful communication (see also chapter 16).

It is important to be sensitive to both self-initiated and reactionary sins of communication. Deceitful, unwholesome, or hurtful words, as well as the tone of voice and body language with which they are said can also be sinful. The flesh wants to excuse these sins based on the circumstances, but God's Word does not give us any exceptions about our communication.

Instead: Communicate with truthfulness and love at all times.

Let no unwholesome word proceed from your mouth, but only such a word as is *good for edification* **according to the need of the moment, that it may give grace to those who hear.**
Ephesians 4:29 [emphasis mine]

4. A lack of appreciation and thankfulness.

    When we are focused on the negative aspects of a person or of a relationship, rather than on the positive, we are reluctant to relate as we should. Letting someone's strong points and demonstrations of love (no matter how small or how few they may be) fade into the background of whatever negative qualities there may be breaks the command of God to be thankful at all times (1Thessalonians 5:18). Even when Christ had to reprove the seven churches in the book of Revelation, He started with appreciation and commendation. This is a good pattern for us when there are negative things that we have to address with others (Revelation 2-3).

Instead: Regularly think and share thoughts of appreciation and thankfulness.

> **Therefore encourage one another and build up one another, just as you also are doing.**
> **1 Thessalonians 5:11**

5. Self-focused expectations.

    Looking and waiting for another's growth, time, care, or attention is always a bad idea. We must not live in expectation or put conditions on our love and care for others. *Our* focus is to be on loving God and others for God's glory, not on having personal desires met. We must also seek to keep any decisions in balance with real life and the many responsibilities the other person may have. It is a danger to have unrealistic expectations as far as Christian growth is concerned. We *cannot* expect immediate perfection from a repentant spouse. But, we can biblically expect *improvement* (for their good and God's glory), bearing in mind that it takes time to create new habits.

Instead: Focus most on *God's* desires and *your own* responsibility *to* others, rather than on *your* desires and the performance or responsibility *of* others. See your own sin as large and others' sin as small.

And why do you look at the speck in your brother's eye, but do not notice the log that is in your own eye? Or how can you say to your brother "Let me take the speck out of your eye," and behold, the log is in your own eye? You hypocrite, first take the log out of your own eye, and then you will see clearly to take the speck out of your brother's eye.

Matthew 7:3-5

Take Time to Evaluate

We are all involved in relationships of one kind or another. They are either poor and worsening, or good and growing. Men, we cannot escape the fact that God is very concerned about our relationships. He has pointedly addressed them throughout His Word. He has given us a pattern or blueprint to follow. By giving careful attention to God's way of relating, and by seeking to live in the same way, we can exemplify Christ.

Do you view your relationship with your wife as importantly as God does? Are you committed to involvement with your wife? Does your relationship with your wife have the key elements of a biblical relationship? Are you ready to guard against common pitfalls to a good relationship with your wife? The marriage relationship is a great gift from God, intended to bring Him glory and intended to bring blessing to those who enter into it. The more you and your wife seek to relate as God relates, the more you will experience what God intended.

Chapter Five

A HUSBAND'S UNDERSTANDING
OF MARRIAGE

"Marriage is a fine institution, if you're ready for an institution!" How often has that tired old joke been repeated? Sadly, people are frequently in agreement with the many derogatory jokes made about the state of marriage. According to the contemporary statistician, George Barna, nine out of ten adults believe that marriage is an outdated institution.[5] Many men of the world (and some in the Church) think it is a virtue to hold out in singleness as long as possible. To them, only the weak or insane would allow themselves to be "conquered" by the opposite sex and be destined for a life of cowardly conformity or hopeless conflict.

While we as Christian men may not take such extreme viewpoints, our own ideas and frustrations about marriage can leave us with similar apprehensions. A negative viewpoint certainly is not God's perspective, nor what He had in mind when He instituted marriage. The husband who is seeking to imitate Christ will want to know and fulfill God's intentions. In doing so, he will also take part in the blessings that come from honoring God in this marvelous arrangement called "marriage."

Whether a marriage is disastrous or marvelous depends greatly on the couple's views of marriage. How a man thinks about marriage will certainly affect his perspective of his role, his wife's role, and the relationship itself.

God's Purposes for Marriage

Since it was God Himself who instituted or began marriage, we know that marriage is good and has perfect purposes. God's overall purpose for marriage is to bring Himself glory. This is clearly accomplished through the more specific areas of *companionship, assistance, characterization, sexual satisfaction*, and *procreation*.

1. Companionship

After creating Adam, God made this statement:

> **Then the Lord God said, "It is not good for the man to be alone; I will make him a helper** *suitable* **for him."**
> **Genesis 2:18 [emphasis mine]**

This verse makes it clear that God planned to make someone "suitable" for Adam. The Hebrew word used here (*kenegdo*) means "comparable or corresponding to him." Then, immediately following the revealed plan, God brought the animals to Adam for naming. This is an interesting order of events. The Bible states that among all the animals "there was not found a helper suitable for Him" (Genesis 2:20).

Certainly, *God* knew that none of these animals would be right for Adam. So who was doing the searching? It must have been Adam. It is as if God purposefully called attention to the paired animals for Adam's awareness. Now both God and man were anticipating someone more than just a presence (any animal) and someone more than just a helper (like an ox). God was going to provide a *companion*. Only someone like him (or "comparable" to him) could be a companion.

From the creation account, it is clear that one reason God provided marriage is for companionship. In the Bible, the actual word for companion (chaber) is used in speaking of one's wife (Malachi 2:14). It means "an associate knit together." Even though this aspect of marriage can grow somewhat by time alone, the exemplary husband will *purpose to treat his wife as his special companion.* He will also do all he can to become a better companion to her. He will do this because it is the will of God.

Ways a Husband Can Treat His Wife As His Companion

By being with her and involving her.

> • Plan time to spend with her alone. • Develop common interests with her. • Let her know how she can help you/work along side you. • Call her from work . • Tell her about what you do.

By seeking to understand her and help her.

> • Ask what she did today and then listen. • Inquire as to her well-being and then pay attention. • Plan a regular time to talk about her concerns and then pray/study/and help her find solutions. • Ask her how you can pray for her. • Pray with her. • Assist her when she needs it.

By appreciating her.

> • Thank God for her. • Think and verbalize specific qualities or deeds that you are thankful for. • Speak well of her to others. • Leave her a note of appreciation.

By treating her special compared to others.

> • Open doors for her. • Plan dates. • Put her "needs" and desires above others. • Show her non-sexual affection. • Be sexually intimate with her, focusing most on her enjoyment.

By revealing yourself to her.

- Communicate your thoughts, perspectives, and goals to her.
- Let her know how she can pray for you.

2. Assistance

God has spoken clearly that the wife is to assist her husband in this life. The root meaning of the Hebrew word for helper (*'ezer*) means "to aid." A wife, then, is supposed to, in a very real sense, *aid* her husband. Since this is God's design, it is good and the way of blessing for both husband and wife.

> **Then the Lord God said, "It is not good for the man to be alone; I will make him a *helper* suitable for him."**
> **Genesis 2:18 [emphasis mine]**

Like that of companion, assistance is obviously another *major* purpose for marriage. In fact, in this verse about the creation of woman, the word "helper" *precedes* the word "suitable"!

God had just put Adam in the garden to "tend and keep it" (Genesis 2:15). He had been given a task to do. God decided it was not good for man to be alone and declared that He would make him a *helper*. The most straightforward way to interpret this passage is that God intended for Eve to assist her husband in the work that he had been given to do. Naturally, since this was before the Fall, Adam had only one kind of work, tending and keeping the garden. Apparently God intended for Adam to have a part in the provision of food and the maintenance of God's creation. Adam was supposed to be busy at work and so was Eve. He was to work for God and she was to work for God by assisting her husband.

God has always intended for the wife to assist her husband in *his* work for God. This is a principle that our society and many in the Church do not grasp. Many wives are doing their own thing for their own "fulfillment." This is not a biblical attitude. The world sees pursuing one's own fulfillment as necessary to well-being and "happiness". Sadly, even husbands are encouraging their wives in this pursuit. Certainly a wife is *very capable* of doing her own thing, but this is *not* God's design. In the end doing one's *own thing* is a very empty and fruitless pursuit. Neither the Christian husband nor his wife should be seeking self-fulfillment, but should be using their gifts, talents and skills to serve God's purposes (Matthew 28:19-20).

Assisting her husband does not necessarily prohibit "other" work for the wife, so long as it is helpful to the man and the wife is still seeking to fulfill her function of assistant (i.e., a job to help with the finances that does not hinder her from fulfilling her God-given responsibilities to her husband and children). Husbands and wives can find joy and fulfillment in doing what they were created to do. Even the wife of an unbelieving husband (who is not doing his work for God) can fulfill God's purpose by assisting her husband in whatever work he does.

Ways a Wife Can Assist Her Husband

As Christian men today, we have *more* work than Adam had. Since the Fall of man, our work of providing has been expanded to include clothing and shelter from the elements. Also, husbands have been given the work of ministry (the furtherance of God's Kingdom) and the work of leading our families spiritually. Since God did not specify how the wife is to assist her husband, I believe that this principle should be applied as much as possible to all of the husband's work.

A husband should look for ways for his wife to be of assistance to him *generally, personally, and specifically*. God has commanded the wife to be the primary worker in the home (Titus 2:4-5). This certainly helps a husband to have the time he needs to do his work. Your wife can also help you *personally* by prayer, encouragement, support, understanding, and respectful and loving admonishment when you need it.

In helping you *specifically*, it would be good for her to ask daily how she can assist you. She can assist you in the shepherding and training of the children since she is with them a great deal of the time.

She can assist you in the work of ministry as well. Wherever you are ministering, your wife should be doing whatever she can to help you to carry out your ministry as unto the Lord. In fact, this should always be her *outside* (the home) ministry priority.

For God's Glory, Not Your Own Advantage

There are two obvious cautions when it comes to understanding God's intent here. First of all, the man must be careful not to see the woman *only* as a worker to help him. We have already discussed how she is to be his *companion* as well. She also has responsibilities to her relationship with God, her children, and the Church (Colossians 2:6-7; Proverbs 31:10-31; Titus 2:3-5; 1 Peter 4:10). A husband needs to take into consideration his wife's other duties and not expect her to be at his side helping him twenty-four hours a day. Secondly, it might be tempting to use his wife's role as assistant to give himself a break or to abandon his own responsibilities. A husband should not selfishly encourage her role as assistant, but rather encourage it because it is God's will and it is for her good.

Understanding this purpose for marriage should affect your efforts to involve your wife in your life. It should also affect the decisions the two of you make concerning *financial lifestyle, the wife working outside the home* (if, when, and how much), *use of time* and *ministry choices*. Our goal is to carry out the work that God has given us to do, and we need to enlist the assistance of our wives in the making and carrying out of those plans.

> **For man does not originate from woman, but woman from man; for indeed man was not created for the woman's sake, but woman for the man's sake.**
> **1 Corinthians 11:8-9**

3. **Characterization**

Characterization is the picturesque representation of something for the purpose of illustration. The marriage relationship is to be a characterization of Christ's relationship to His people. Included in this picture is a snapshot of the Gospel, in that the husband's love is to imitate Christ's sacrificial love on the cross.

Husbands, love your wives, just as Christ also loved the church and gave Himself up for her; **that He might sanctify her, having cleansed her by the washing of water with the word, that He might present to Himself the church in all her glory, having no spot or wrinkle or any such thing; but that she should be holy and blameless. So husbands ought also to love their own wives as their own bodies. He who loves his own wife loves himself; for no one ever hated his own flesh,** *but nourishes and cherishes it, just as Christ also does the church,* **because we are members of His body.**
Ephesians 5:25-30 [emphasis mine]

There are many principles concerning marriage that we can draw from the analogy God has purposely used in this passage. For now, we will summarize that the husband is to portray Christ and the wife is to portray the Church.

What Are You Portraying?

Both husband and wife should seriously consider the picture they are painting to a watching world. Husband, are you portraying Christ's demonstration of love and leadership to the Church? Or do you perhaps see yourself in one or more of the following roles?

- A king lording it over his vassals—dictating and waiting to be served.
- A hireling over sheep—leaving when the going gets tough and not willing to sacrifice.
- A tolerant roommate—making no commitment, ignoring sin and doing his own thing—just basically sharing expenses and a roof.
- A business partner—splitting and doing everything 50/50, with equal benefits and equal say.
- An irresponsible steward or drifter—leaving responsibilities undone, letting others take care of your responsibilities, or just going with the flow with no purpose or direction.
- A preoccupied worker—staying too busy and distracted to fulfill marital responsibilities (lack of involvement).
- A patrolling supplier—provides sustenance, room, clothes, etc., and offers a level of protection over his interests, but is not personally involved.

4. **Sexual Union**.

"...and they shall become one flesh."
Genesis 2:24c

As we have already seen, becoming one is more than becoming one physically, but from the beginning God intended for physical union to take place in marriage. There are two reasons why.

a. God intended to provide for procreation.

One intention behind God's command to become "one flesh" was to provide children. This is more clearly seen in Genesis 1:27-28. Obviously at the time this verse was given there was a need to fill the earth. He also wanted to bless Adam and Eve with children. Generally speaking, God gives a husband and a wife the ability to have children, unless He has an even better plan for them.

God created man in His own image, in the image of
God He created him; male and female He created
them. God blessed them, and God said to them, "Be
fruitful and multiply; and fill the earth and subdue it."
Genesis 1:27-28a

There is a great deal of misunderstanding about this verse, since it might be understood only as a command. Actually, the introductory statement of the second sentence of this verse, "Then God blessed them," identifies the rest of the verse as a *blessing* and not only a command. Robert Jamieson, in his commentary on Genesis said, *"Be fruitful and multiply"* is a benediction of fertility, not a requirement per se.[6]

It is also important to note that in both the instances when this blessing was given, the earth was virtually empty (the second time was Genesis 9:7, after the flood). Each time the blessing and ability was given for a specific time and a specific purpose. What one can learn from careful study of these passages is that *God was doing something for them, as well as commanding them to do something.* Unfortunate results of misunderstanding this verse can be: feelings of guilt about not being able to have children, undue pressure to have children and have many children, and the condemnation of all types of birth control.

The truth is, each couple has the freedom and the responsibility to plan for the number of children that seems in keeping with good stewardship principles (common sense based upon biblical balance). Along with the ability to bear children, comes the responsibilities to care for them (1 Thessalonians 2:7) disciple them (Deuteronomy 6:6-9; Ephesians 6:4) and provide for them (1 Timothy 5:8). For some families, medical issues play a part in decision-making as well. You and your wife should plan, knowing that God is sovereign and that He is the one who opens and closes the womb in perfect wisdom (Genesis 30:2,22). Then you have the assurance of God that there is a *better* plan. He will over-rule. There have been many blessed surprises!

When God Does not Give the Ability to Bear Children

When God does not give a couple the ability to procreate it is for a special purpose. God is always working His plan (Isaiah 46:9-11; Ephesians 1:11). When he does not give this ability, He has a *better* plan. One possibility is that He may not grant natural children in order to provide the opportunity of adoption to one of His precious un-parented children. Another possibility is that He may not allow a couple to bear children simply to do a good and perfect work in the husband's life, the wife's life, or both. He may not grant children because He has a vital and extra time-consuming ministry planned for the couple. Each barren couple must trust the *sovereignty* and *goodness* of God and ask Him for wisdom as they test various *medical* (within reason and according to biblical ethics), *adoption*, and *ministry* options.

b.   *God intends for a couple to be sexually satisfied.*

When God gave the blessing for Adam and Eve to be able to procreate, He instituted sexual intimacy (Genesis 2:24). In 1 Corinthians 7:3-5, God clearly commands the husband and the wife to fulfill the sexual desires of their partner in this way (an exception would be physical incapacity). God has also commanded that this should only take place within the marriage relationship.

> **Let marriage be held in honor among all, and let the marriage bed be undefiled; for fornicators and adulterers God will judge.**
> **Hebrews 13:4**

God also intends for husband and wife to "richly enjoy" their sexual union. The sexual relationship can be a complex one. We will fully discuss this and many other issues related to the topic of *Physical Intimacy* in chapter 11.

The Right Level of Commitment in Marriage

In the Scriptures, the marriage commitment is always associated with *covenant* language (Malachi 2:14, Proverbs 2:17). Indeed, *it is a covenant*. A covenant is a very serious commitment made before God Himself. In Bible times breaking this covenant by marital unfaithfulness meant certain death (Leviticus 20:10-21). Wouldn't death be far more common in our society today if the same punishment were still being practiced for unfaithfulness and abandonment?

When we marry, we are covenanting before God to become "one flesh." We are promising to permanently join our lives with another in the most permanent and comprehensive way possible.

> **For this cause a man shall leave his father and his mother, and shall cleave to His wife; and they shall become one flesh.**
> **Genesis 2:24**

"One flesh" definitely includes sexual relations but also much more. The Apostle Paul uses it in connection with having sex with a harlot in 1 Corinthians 6:16, but it is far more than this. The animals are never said to be "one flesh" with their mates. Furthermore, with the command to be "one flesh," God mentions *leaving* mother and father and *cleaving* to one's wife. If we put these things together with the companion purpose of marriage, it is obvious that God is also talking about *relational oneness*, being bonded together.

In context then, "one flesh" actually means something more along the lines of *woven lives*. The oneness God is speaking of seems to be a total sharing of one another. It is a sharing of ideas, beliefs, joys, difficulties, triumphs, failures, possessions, and bodies. The motivation of oneness must be to obey and glorify God (Matthew 22:37-38). There are two commands given by God to bring about oneness.

1.   The command to leave one's parents.

Though the word *'azab* or "leave" literally means "to forsake," it obviously cannot mean to abandon one's parents thoroughly (Genesis 2:24). God has clearly commanded that we are still to love, respect, and care for our parents after marriage (Exodus 20:12; 21:15; Ephesians 6:1-3; 1 Timothy 5:8). What it does mean is that there is now:

*   a new primary relationship
*   a change of authority
*   an exchange of dependence

After marriage, key changes must take place. Each spouse is to be the other's most significant person on earth. Their relationship is to take priority over that with their parents. When a son of one family and a daughter of another marry, the husband becomes the new authority (under God's authority) of *his own home*. Now the wife is under the husband's authority and neither wife nor husband is required to obey their own parents any longer, though they *are* required to treat them with respect (Ephesians 6:2-3). Unless a child has already been living on his or her own, marriage creates the first experience of not being under the authority of parents. This change may be a significant adjustment for everyone involved.

In addition to the primary *relationship change* and the *authority change*, there is one more change. There is a *dependence change*. Neither marriage partner should depend on their parents for provisions any longer. It is now the husband's responsibility to shoulder the task of providing (Ephesians 5:29: the term *nourish* actually means "to make provision for", coming from the root word, *to feed*). God gives a strong warning to irresponsible husbands.

> **But if anyone does not provide for his own, and especially for those of his household, he has denied the faith and is worse than an unbeliever.**
> **1 Timothy 5:8**

2.   The command to cleave to one's spouse.

Not only are the husband and wife to leave mother and father, they are to *cleave* to one another (Genesis 2:24). The Hebrew word for cleave (*dabaq*) means "to pursue hard (like continual pressing) a firmly joined state." This joining is a permanent and abiding union, like "super glue." Only our pursuit of God is to be a greater pursuit than this one. This kind of pursuit and abiding will create an intricate weaving of two lives, thus making them into *one* in most respects.

There are some men who indeed want to be joined together with their wife as one, but *they* want to be the one (I should know, I was such a man, remember?)! Instead there should be a *mutual* cleaving and a *mutual* weaving of two lives together.

God's Intentions for the Marriage Relationship

As we sum up what we have learned about marriage, there are three basic intentions that God has for the marriage relationship.

1. God intends for the marriage relationship to be our *primary* human relationship.

    > **The man said, "This is now bone of my bones, and flesh of my flesh; she shall be called Woman, because she was taken out of man." For this reason a man shall leave his father and his mother, and be joined to his wife; and they shall become one flesh.**
    > **Genesis 2:23-24**

    Marriage is the only relationship that is described as a "one flesh" relationship. No other relationship should compare, not even the parent-child relationship. An exemplary husband will be careful to pursue his relationship with his wife over that with any other human being.

2. God intends for the marriage relationship to be a *permanent* relationship (on earth).

    > **"Consequently they are no longer two, but one flesh. What therefore God has joined together, let no man separate."**
    > **Matthew 19:6**

This verse is clear concerning the permanency of marriage. Thousands of years after creation, we find God's original intent stated in the Scriptures. (See Appendix Five for a Biblical Position on Divorce and Remarriage). Divorce must not even be a remote option for true believers. God hates divorce (Malachi 2:16). Therefore, anyone who causes or contributes to the breaking of this covenant made before God, excluding the two exemptions below, is in rebellion against the command of God and will one day give an account (Matthew 5:33-37; 2 Corinthians 5:10).

The Cooperation Clause

The reality is that some husbands and wives choose to rebel against God's will. Every husband should be aware of the four major views on divorce and remarriage. You can read about each in the book, *Divorce and Remarriage: Four Christian Views* (H. Wayne House, Editor, InterVarsity Press, 1990). I believe the Bible teaches us that there are two situations in which God allows a believer to cooperate with a rebelling partner's decision to break the covenant agreement. One situation is when the partner is an unbeliever (by his own admission or the church's declaration by the fourth step of church discipline: (Matthew 18:17) who doggedly wants a divorce or has abandoned the spouse with no intention to return.

> **...If any brother has a wife who is an unbeliever and she consents to live with him, he must not divorce her. And a woman who has an unbelieving husband, and he consents to live with her, she must not send her husband away. For the unbelieving husband is sanctified through his wife, and the unbelieving wife is sanctified through her believing husband; for otherwise your children are unclean, but now they are holy. Yet if the unbelieving one leaves, let him leave; the brother or the sister is not under bondage in such cases, but God has called us to peace.**
> **I Corinthians 7:12-15**

The other situation is in the case of sexual unfaithfulness with another person by one's spouse. The sinning spouse may evidence sorrow without true repentance (complete change of intentions, thoughts, and actions). A person should rely on the counsel of church leadership in determining whether or not a husband or wife is truly repentant.

71

"But I say to you that everyone who divorces his wife, except for the reason of unchastity [*porneia*; sexual unfaithfulness], makes her commit adultery; and whoever marries a divorced woman commits adultery."
Matthew 5:32 [explanation mine]

In both of these situations, the believing and obedient partner is not forsaking the covenant agreement. It has already been forsaken by their spouse. For further explanations of these two exceptions, a husband can also refer to John Murray's book *Divorce*,[7] and to Jay Adam's book *Marriage, Divorce, and Remarriage in the Bible*.[8] And, by all means, a husband who is in a very unusual situation should submit to the guidance of his church leaders, assuming that he is in a biblical church that practices church discipline.

3. God intends for the marriage relationship to be a *perfecting* relationship.

God uses everything in our lives for His perfecting (growing) purposes (Romans 8:28-29; James 1:2-4). As we learned earlier, our growth as Christians toward Christ-likeness is a life-long process, often referred to as *sanctification*. Because God is so intent on sanctifying us, we know that He will certainly use our most important human relationship to do this. Since marriage is the closest of relationships, it provides the greatest potential for self-denial and obedience to the relational principles in God's Word.

We also saw that the husband is specifically commanded in Ephesians 5:25-33 to love his wife as Christ loves the Church. In this passage we are given an explanation of what that love entails, including the responsibility of the husband to lead and care for his wife spiritually. Certainly, that care involves lovingly admonishing his wife when necessary. We will discuss more fully the husband's responsibility to lead the wife spiritually and how he is to help his wife with her sin in Chapters 10 and 15, respectively.

While the wife is not to lead her husband spiritually (other male leadership is needed), and while she always is to evidence a respectful and submissive attitude, she should be allowed to address her husband's sin. Your wife is your sister in the Lord and your helper. An exemplary husband will encourage his wife to respectfully reprove his sin (Proverbs 27:5-6). Even if your wife should reprove you incorrectly, you should sincerely consider and respond to her reproof, because Christ taught us to always deal with our *own* sin first (Matthew 7:3-5).

What is Your Intention?

By now your understanding of marriage should have been broadened and/or strengthened. If there is clear knowledge and sincere adoption of God's purposes, God's level of commitment, and God's intentions for marriage, you will be well on your way to becoming an exemplary husband. Are your marriage purposes biblical? Is your marriage commitment at the right level? Are your marriage intentions the same as God's? If so, you will be better able to fulfill your role as husband.

Chapter Six

A HUSBAND'S UNDERSTANDING
OF HIS ROLE

As Creator and ruler of this world and everything in it, God is the one who has the perfect plan for marriage. We must accept His plan and depend on His infinite wisdom concerning the roles of both husband and wife. In this chapter we will seek only to gain a basic understanding of the husband's role, exploring how it correlates to the wife's role. This biblical perspective is needed for Christ-likeness in marriage. It is through his role that the husband exemplifies Christ to his wife, his family, and the world.

In this century our society has managed to confuse thoroughly the roles of husband and wife. Even many "Christians" have taken the viewpoint that it is okay for everyone to do what is right in their own eyes. This individualistic mindset has historically brought heartache to God's people and shame to God's name (Proverbs 18:1-2; Isaiah 5:21). The exemplary husband must see the importance of doing things God's way. For the husband to truly understand God's way he must first understand God's perspective of man and woman.

God's Perspective of Man and Woman

There are varied views about the nature of man and woman. Some say they are equal, while others say they are not. Both the authoritarian man and the feminist woman have muddied the waters concerning the issue of equality. As Creator, God has the right view about their nature and equality. In actuality, they are both equal and unequal, depending on what aspect of their person is being considered.

1. The two are *positionally* and *personally equal.*

Both man and woman were created in the image of God. This means that each was created with the ability and responsibility to know and glorify God. It also means that both genders were created the same in nature and intellect. Neither gender is viewed, loved, or accepted by God more or less. From God's perspective they are equal in essence and standing.

> **God created man in His own image, in the image of God He created him; male and female He created them.**
> **Genesis 1:27**

> **There is neither Jew nor Greek, there is neither slave nor free man, there is neither male nor female; for you are all one in Christ Jesus.**
> **Galatians 3:28**

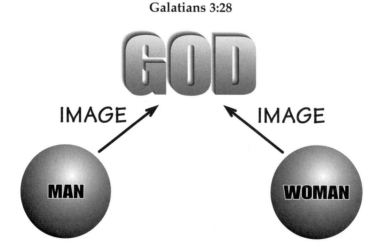

2.   The two are functionally unequal.

As with the Trinity, there is to be an order of function between the husband and wife. God has wisely assigned who gets which function. This delegation of function has nothing to do with worth or ability. It has everything, however, to do with love, humility, and the goal of effectively glorifying God. The husband is given authority over the wife and the wife is to submit to the husband's leadership because this can best glorify God. Since the goal of every sincere Christian is to glorify God, the husband and wife can each accept their role with joy.

The husband and wife are unequal only in *authority*. This is in keeping with the rest of life, is it not? Parents are in authority over children, the government is in authority over citizens, employers are in authority over employees, church leadership is in authority over church members, and so on. A good question is, "Why all the difficulty surrounding the authority of the husband?"

The Godhead has no problem with the right view of submission or the abuse of authority. They have perfect unity and contentment. So, the answer to our previous question is: "Our difficulties with authority and/or submission come from our own sinful pride." The husband must humble himself to realize that he does not have unlimited authority, (it is delegated authority), that his authority is not for his own benefit, and that his authority should be carried out lovingly. A wife must humble herself to realize that she obeys Christ by respecting her husband's position at all times.

Both leadership and submission should also flow out of a love relationship between the husband and wife. Alexander Strauch writes in his book, *Men and Women, Equal Yet Different*:

> The husband-wife relationship is not a boss-employee, a commander-soldier, or a teacher-student relationship. It is a love relationship in which two adults become united as one. Within this union, one partner lovingly takes the lead and the other willingly and actively supports that lead. [9]
>
> **But I want you to understand that Christ is the head of every man, and the man is the head of a woman,**

and God is the head of Christ.
1 Corinthians 11:3

As we learned earlier, the functional roles of the husband and wife should be patterned after that of Christ and the Church.

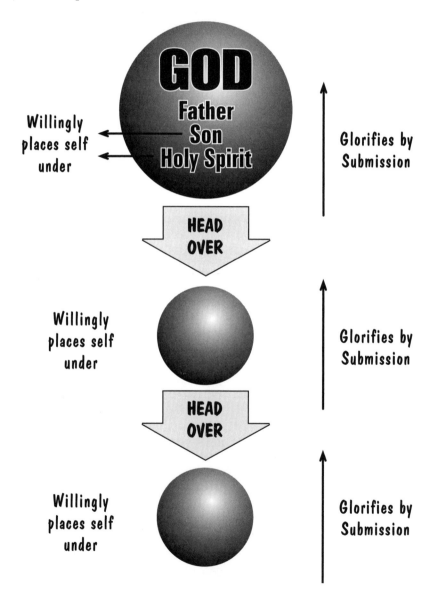

With the delegation of authority comes glory. A person in authority receives a certain amount of glory or prominence by virtue of his position and the submission of those under him. In this sense, woman is the glory of man and man is the glory of God. The husband must keep in mind that he is in this place of glory by no merit of his own and that he should "pass on" all glory to God. Men, be reminded that God caused King Herod to be eaten by worms when he kept glory for himself (Acts 12:20-23).

There are some who suggest there should be a mutual submission between husband and wife. Naturally, there is a sense in which both husband and wife are to lay down their own wills and give preference to one another. Certainly a husband is to take into account (and whenever he deems appropriate and possible, *act upon*) his wife's requests, counsel and admonitions. However, there should never be a time when the wife takes the position of authority over the husband. The favorite (and only) passage that proponents of mutual submission site is Ephesians 5:21. However, the meaning and context of "one another" in this verse does not support their view, nor does it negate the several times that God commands the wife to be in subjection to her husband (Ephesians 5:22; Colossians 3:18; 1 Peter 3:1; Titus 2:4-5). Based upon the context, a better rendering of "one another," is "some to others." Then the Apostle Paul proceeds to develop the "some to others" in the remaining verses.

The Husband's Role Specifically Involves Leadership

We have already established that the husband is head over the wife and his family. We have also established that he is to lead as Christ leads the Church (Ephesians 5:23; 1 Corinthians 11:3). What do these things actually mean in a practical sense in the marriage? We can see some of the specifics from our Ephesians 5:22-33 passage.

The Pattern of Ephesians Five			
Christ/Husband		**Church/Wife**	
:22-24,30	Presides as Head	:22,24	Follows as a respectful submissive body
:25,28,33	Pursues to actively love (sacrificially giving his own life for her) includes 'protecting' and 'cherishing'	:24,33	Honors and serves Christ's/husband's righteous goals
:29	Provides physically and spiritually—includes 'nourishes'	:29,30	Depends on, looks to, wisely uses resources to give back and serve

The Husbands Role Specifically Involves Loving

The command for husbands to love their wives is repeated several times in Scripture. Obviously this is to be a major aspect of the husband's role. His wife bears the responsibility to love him as a person (friend or foe—Matthew 5:44; 22:39), as a believer (1 John 4:7), and as a spouse (Titus 2:4). But we as husbands have been told specifically four times to love our wives! We must seek to love her as a person, as a believer (if she is one), and as our spouse. Then, on top of this three-fold responsibility to love, we are given the command to love our wives as Christ loved the Church.

> **Husbands, love your wives, just as Christ also loved the church and gave Himself up for her.**
> **Ephesians 5:25**

> **So husbands ought also to love their own wives as their own bodies. He who loves his own wife loves himself; for no one ever hated his own flesh, but nourishes and cherishes it, just as Christ also does the church.**
> **Ephesians 5:28-29**

An exemplary husband is to love his wife:

• *Actively*

He must show his love in tangible ways. He will not simply *say*, "I love you," but he will assure her of his love by his deeds. It is also important that he refrain from pointing backwards to isolated demonstrations of love as if they are *frozen in time* and sufficient for *today*. He must continue to display his love daily.
(1 Corinthians 13:4-8; Ephesians 5:25-33).

- *According to knowledge*

He will take the time and make the effort to know the best way to love her. *Understanding* her and her circumstances well will help him love her better. Another way he can love her according to knowledge is to *study* and *apply* God's kind of love and God's principles of marriage to his relationship with his wife. It is a lack of love for God and one's wife that causes a husband to say, "I don't like to read," "It's just not me to study," or "I can't take the time to read or become knowledgeable." I venture to say that if a man were offered a million dollars to study God's principles of marriage or to attend a marriage conference, he would make a great effort to make it happen (1 Peter 3:7).

- *Sacrificially*

He must put his wife before himself and serve her, even when it means a personal sacrifice on his part. Christ sacrificially loved us to the point of death. Our goal is to model our love after that of Christ. We must be willing to lay our lives down for our wife daily. A wife who is sacrificially loved will usually have no doubt of her husband's love (Ephesians 5:25).

Much more will be said about the husband's love in Chapters 8 and 14. You can look forward to exploring in greater detail what these three things mean, and also to discovering many specific ways to apply them.

There is a great deal of confusion surrounding the roles involved in marriage. It can be difficult to understand how the multiple authorities (the Lord, church leaders and husbands), relationships (with the Lord, with each other as spouses, fellow believers), and responsibilities (companionship, leadership, submission, etc.) all fit together. When we are trying to sort it all out we have to keep all of the relationships involved in mind. We could picture the marriage roles in this way:

Ephesians

Husband
Role: Child of God
Relationship: Fellow Disciple
Responsibilities: Walk with God

Role: Brother
Relationship: Members of
                One Another
Responsibilities: Mutual
                Sanctification
                Loving Attitude

Role: Husband
Relationship: One Flesh
Responsibilities: Lead, Love,
                Pursue Oneness

Wife
Role: Child of God
Relationship: Fellow Disciple
Responsibilities: Walk with God

Role: Sister
Relationship: Members of
                One Another
Responsibilities: Mutual
                Sanctification
                Submissive
                Attitude

Role: Wife
Relationship: One Flesh
Responsibilities: Submit, Assist,
                Pursue Oneness

What About You?

Now that we have taken a good look at the Bible concerning our role as husbands, it is time to compare yourself to it. Are you whole-heartedly ready and willing to take up the role that God has laid out for you? If so, you are desirous to be a better leader and a better lover. If you're not quite sure how to grow in these areas, there will be some practical helps to come in later chapters. The first step is for you to adopt God's viewpoint of your role as a husband.

Most likely you have become aware of some area of your role that needs restructuring. If this is true, confess it to the Lord and to your spouse. Strive to live in light of your new understanding. Remember, an exemplary husband knows that he is not perfect but keeps Christ ever before him as his example.

PART TWO

A HUSBAND'S RESPONSIBILITIES

Faithful Commitments of the Exemplary Husband

Chapter Seven

A HUSBAND'S RESPONSIBILITY
WORSHIPING CHRIST ONLY

In the previous section, we laid the all-important foundational truths of God's Word. As we move into the more practical areas of our role as an exemplary husband, we must choose to *walk daily* in God's truth.

> **How blessed are those whose way is blameless, who walk in the law of the Lord. How blessed are those who observe His testimonies, who seek Him with all their heart.**
> **Psalm 119:1-2**

In the next six chapters we will see five areas of the husband's responsibility take shape. The exemplary husband will be committed to his responsibilities in the areas of worshiping Christ alone, love, leadership, physical intimacy and stewardship. The most important commitment for the Christian husband is to have a heart of worship toward God alone.

Every Heart Is a Worshiping Heart

We saw in Chapter 3 that man was created *by God* and *for* God (Colossians 1:16). We were created to worship Him (Romans 1:25; Colossians 1:13-18). We are all by nature, worshipers. The question is, who or what are we worshiping? Once God has drawn a man to seek Himself, opened that man's eyes to the truth of the Gospel, and reconciled that man with Himself (on the basis of his faith in and commitment to Jesus Christ), that man is able to worship the God of the Bible in "spirit and truth" (John 4:23).

What God is Looking For

Once the condition of a man's heart is initially remedied (salvation), the vocation (or preoccupation) of his heart should then, and forever, be the worship of his God "in spirit and in truth" (John 4:23).

The Bible tells us that God is greatly concerned with just exactly what is going on in the heart (Proverbs 4:23). While man tends to focus on outward appearance and actions, God looks at and tests the heart (I Samuel 16:7). We can see from the following verses that He tests our heart to reveal whether or not we worship Him alone.

> **You shall not listen to the words of that prophet or that dreamer of dreams; for the Lord your God is testing you to find out if you love the Lord your God with all your heart and with all your soul.**
> **Deuteronomy 13:3**

> **But the Lord said to Samuel, "Do not look at his appearance or at the height of his stature, because I have rejected him; for God sees not as man sees, for man looks at the outward appearance, but the Lord looks at the heart."**
> **1 Samuel 16:7**

What Is the Heart?

In order to have a heart of worship for God alone, we need to know two things. First, we need to know what *the heart of man* actually is. It can basically be described as man's control center for living. It involves his thoughts, intentions, beliefs, desires and attitudes. Because all these things really take place in the mind, we can say that the heart could be thought of as the mind. What a man truly wants, thinks and believes about something is his heart on the matter (no matter if his lips speak differently).

> **For as he** *thinks in his heart* **so is he.**
> **Proverbs 23:7a [emphasis mine] NKJV**

> **"for the heart of this people has become dull, with their ears they scarcely hear, and they have closed their eyes, otherwise they would see with their eyes, hear with their ears, and** *understand with their heart* **and return, and I would heal them."**
> **Matthew 13:15 [emphasis mine]**

What Is Worship?

Secondly, if we are going to maintain a heart of worship for God alone, we must have a clear understanding of what *worship* is. Some people believe that worship equals praise or adoration. In actuality, worship involves this and much more. Worship is to be an all-consuming and all-encompassing preoccupation (Deuteronomy 6:5; Luke 4:8; 14:25-33).

<u>What we worship we will:</u>

- Adore
- Sacrifice for
- Focus on
- Submit to
- Seek after
- Hope in
- Serve/give to
- Speak about
- Look to for peace, meaning and happiness
- Spend a great amount of thoughts, time, energy, and resources on

What God Hates: Idol Worship

I am indebted to Dave Powlison from the Christian Counseling and Educational Foundation, Glenside, PA, for his teaching on this subject. Worship in the broad sense encompasses all of these aspects. God is the only one worthy of this worship (Revelation 4:9-11; 5:11-14). If we revere something other than God in the above ways, we will not live our lives unto God alone. God does not want His people to worship anything or anyone else because He wants their hearts to belong to Him (Joshua 24:23). Since we know that God deserves to have us live our lives unto Him, we can understand why God forbids us to worship anyone or anything else (Exodus 20:2-6). In the Bible, God warns us often about misplaced worship because He knows that every man's heart is prone to worship other things. He refers to this misplaced worship as *idolatry*. This is an abomination to God, because it robs Him of the glory that is due Him. Idolatry is the worst thing we can do before

God (Leviticus 19:4).

> **Little children, guard yourselves from idols.**
> **1 John 5:21**

Even those who know Christ as Savior and Lord can find themselves involved in idol worship when they wane in their worship of God. We can understand this better if we more clearly define an idol.

What Is an Idol?

Perhaps when you think of idolatry you think only of graven images or the gods of false religion. But we can be engaged in idolatry, even though we are not physically bowing down to someone or something (Colossians 3:5).

How We Can Recognize Idols of the Heart

When we make something other than God our *primary* focus and goal we are clearly engaged in idol worship. We worship what we believe we desperately need or must have in order to be happy (James 4:1-3). When we place this kind of emphasis on something, it is actually a sinful lust. Even a good desire can turn into a lust. If we *habitually sin in order to get something* or we *habitually sin because we cannot have something*, chances are, we are worshiping that thing. Some of these sins might include: lying, manipulating, being selfishly moody, withdrawing, complaining, compromising, getting sinfully angry, having a pity party, having a bitter attitude, worrying, despairing, judging God, and so on. The truth is, when we worship idols we are living for self.

Thus, **an idol is anything that we <u>consistently</u> make equal to or more important than God in our attention, desire, devotion, and choices.**

<u>What people may worship other than or in addition to the God of the Bible:</u>

- Security
- Material things

- Knowledge
- Control
- Wealth
- Themselves
- Good health
- Other gods of the cults
- Another person
- A god of their own making
- Pleasure/comfort
- Pain-free/trouble-free life
- An accomplishment
- Fair or good treatment
- The good opinion of others
- Significance/success/impact
- Physical appearance
- A desired circumstance of life (a good marriage, children, financial stability, etc.)
- Ambition

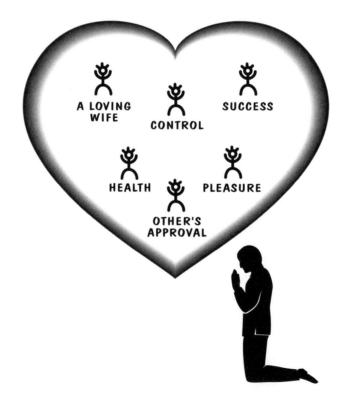

When we worship an idol we give our heart to it rather than God (Ezekiel 14:5). A Christian, of course, will not give his heart over entirely, but he can certainly have *divided* allegiance (James 1:6-8). Setting our heart steadfastly ("I *must* have") on something other than on God (even though we still seek to worship God also), is being unfaithful (or *adulterous*) toward God.

We must not revere any person or thing in a way that is only meant for God. Nothing is to take His place or even come close to it (Matthew 10:37; Luke 14:25-35). A divided heart leads to the self-deception of divided worship. We can not truly worship God with our lives and someone or something else at the same time. God does not accept divided worship (1 Kings 18:21). We will not even be able to continue in our deception of divided worship very long. When one is attempting to serve two masters, he will naturally forget God more and more and begin to serve only the wrong master (Matthew 6:24; Psalm 135:15-18). We need to ask God to help us unite our heart to seek only Him.

Teach me Your way, O Lord: I will walk in Your truth;
Unite my heart to fear Your name.
Psalm 86: 11

Thankfully, God's children will not continue to forget Him because God is faithful to act. He does not forget (Isaiah 49:15-16; Romans 8:31-39). He is determined and faithful to reveal our idols or "vanities" (1 Kings 16:13 KJV) and to reclaim our heart. God must do this for us because idols are self-deceiving, self-serving, and self-destroying (Psalm 106:35-36; 115:4-8). He is faithful to do this in at least four ways.

Four ways God reveals idols to us:

1. God has given His Word and His Spirit to consistently speak to this issue (Hebrews 4:12; 1 Corinthians 6:19).
2. God may frustrate our idols by withholding them, or He may allow us to experience the futility of our idols and refuges by granting them (Psalm 106:13-15).
3. God may give us a living example (a person) of true worship to convict us (e.g., Elijah; 1 Kings 18:26, 36).
4. God may administer loving discipline. Because God cares for His own, a person who is not being convicted, frustrated, or chastened

in his idol worship may not be one of God's children at all (Hebrews 12:5-11).

False refuges In Marriage

When we worship other idols, we naturally distance ourselves from fellowship with God who is the one true refuge (Ezekiel 14:5b, 1 Kings 11:4, Deuteronomy 29:18). God does not move, but we do (Revelation 2:4). This allows us to continue our idol worship. Consequently, in our disappointments and/or in the difficulties of life, we turn from trusting in God to trusting in other things for help, comfort, peace, strength and even safety.

> **"This is your lot, the portion measured to you from Me," declares the Lord, "because you have forgotten Me and trusted in falsehood."**
> **Jeremiah 13:25**

What many turn to as false refuges in our marriages:

- Food
- Sleep
- Drugs
- Travel
- Sports
- Music
- Reading
- Television
- Another person (man or woman)
- Strong drink
- Sex/pornography
- Fantasies/ imaginations
- Shopping/ spending money
- Fleeing (leaving, driving)
- Busyness at work, church or hobbies

We can picture our turning to false refuges in this way:

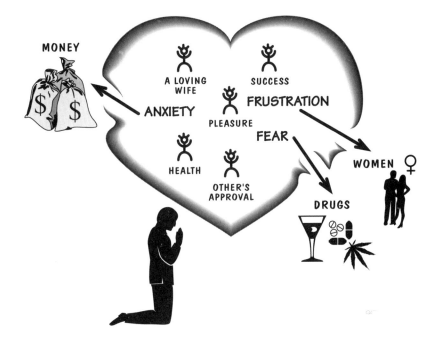

You may be asking, "What's wrong with some of these things you have listed as idols?" The fact is, there is absolutely nothing inherently wrong with some of these things. The problem lies in the place of importance that we give them. Our desire and focus can become inordinate and our trust can be misplaced (Luke 14:25-33). When we think of worship and refuges in these terms, we can make *anything* an idol or refuge, even something good. Our desires must remain *unessential* and our trust must be in God *alone*. When He is all we really must have and He alone satisfies, then we know that we are worshiping and trusting God alone.

> **My soul, wait in silence for God only, for my hope is from Him. He only is my rock and my salvation, my stronghold; I shall not be shaken. On God my salvation and my glory rests; the rock of my strength, my**

> **refuge is in God. Trust in Him at all times, O people;
> pour out your heart before Him; God is a refuge for
> us.**
>
> **Psalm 62:5-8**

What God Wants from *You:*

Forsake Any Idols in Your Marriage

We have seen that God in His amazing mercy and love goes to great lengths (including loving discipline) to capture the heart completely. To you, God is saying the same thing He said to Israel, "Repent and turn away from your idols" (Ezekiel 14:6). You must actively seek to forsake any tendencies toward idol worship that you may have.

> **Little children, guard yourselves from idols.**
> **1 John 5:21**

You can forsake idols by:

1. Asking God to search your heart and reveal any idols you may be worshiping as you evaluate your life and worship of God (Psalm 139:23-24).

2. Confessing your abominable sin to God (Psalm 51:3,4,17).

3. Repenting. Turn away from the pursuit of your idol and turn to the worship of God alone by: (a) determining how to rightly view your idol and (b) pursuing a passion for God (Ezekiel 14:6).

4. Removing the possibility of idol worship. For some this may mean taking radical steps to remove temptation. In Christ's discussion about adultery in Matthew 5:29-30, His point is not that we should literally do ourselves bodily harm but that we should take extreme action (if necessary) to guard our hearts from sin. This means we may not be able to participate in things that other people may participate in nor go everywhere other people can go.

5. Being on guard. Be watchful and prayerful concerning habitual or new idol worship (1 Peter 1:13-16; 1 Thessalonians 5:6; 1 John 5:21).

Have the Right Passion

What we worship is our passion. When we are passionate about something other than Christ, we will have the wrong desires and expectations. When we are passionate about Christ alone, we will have the right desires and expectations. In turn these desires will have a profound effect on our decisions, our actions, and our joy.

Some wrong desires and expectations in our marriages:

*   That my wife will please me with her physical looks and dress, her talents, abilities and accomplishments outside the home.

*   That I could do what I really like to do with my time.

*   That my wife won't be late or keep me waiting.

*   That my wife will be the sexual initiator, or be ready sexually when I desire her. That she would be the perfect sexual partner, no matter what is asked of her.

*   That she would treat me with respect.

*   That I would have plenty of money to be able to live as I please, or live the "good" life.

*   That I would know/find total love on a human level.

*   That there would be peace and harmony around me always.

Some right desires and expectations:

*   That I may know Christ and delight to walk with Him (Philippians 3:10-14).

- That I may know God's Word and obey it
  (Psalms 119:18; 101; 112; 131).

- That I may seek Christ with my whole heart and become more like
  Him (Psalm 119:2).

- That I may be used of God to witness for Him
  (Matthew 28:19-20).

- That I may be pleasing to Christ regardless of my circumstances
  (2 Corinthians 5:9).

- That I may cultivate an attitude of joy and gratitude in what God
  is doing in my life (1 Thessalonians 5:16-18).

- That I may have confidence and joy in how God has decided (place
  and circumstances) He can use me best for His glory (Romans
  8:28-29; James 1:2-4).

- That I may serve others rather than be served (Galatians 5:13).

- That I may look forward to heaven as the place of bliss with Jesus
  (John 14:1-3).

The Right Heart Before the Right Life

You've heard the expression "putting the cart before the horse."
This is not a very effective way of getting anywhere. Likewise, we cannot expect real change if our heart is not "after God" (Acts 13:22). I am
not suggesting that we wait for the desire (feelings) before we do what
is pleasing to God in a particular situation. Often in the Christian life,
we are called to go against our feelings in order to obey God (Mark
14:36). However, a husband's attempts to reform his ways will in the
end be futile if he has not determined in his heart that he wants to worship Christ alone. We can picture the devotion we should have for
Christ alone in this way:

Husband, what is really important to you? I mean really? What is your passion as far as your marriage is concerned? Is it for your wife to be the perfect, ever-satisfying wife, or is it for you to know and glorify Christ in your marriage? What is your passion in *life*? Is there any other thing that you think you must have in life besides Christ and His will? Is there anything or anyone other than God that you are worshiping? Be careful not to move too quickly past this chapter. Only when a husband's heart is right, is he ready to work on the problems in his marriage.

Chapter Eight

A HUSBAND'S RESPONSIBILITY
LOVE

"Pastor, we don't love each other anymore. How can we stay in a marriage if we don't really love each other?" Couples bring this concern to my office thinking, "Love is gone forever."

This kind of thinking is especially difficult for those who remember how it used to be, or notice how "love" is portrayed on the movie screen. Others are aware that a lack of love has always been a problem in their marriage. A husband might say, "She has *never* loved me." If you see yourself in one of these situations, let me assure you, there is still hope.

You may not be in as desperate a state as these couples. Perhaps you think that the love level in your marriage is fine just the way it is. In reality, no Christian marriage is "fine just the way it is." We have already seen that every exemplary husband needs to become more and more like Christ in his marriage. We are to love our wives as Christ loves the Church. Since Christ's love is perfect, we know that we will not fully reach that goal this side of heaven, but our love for our wives ought to be always growing. We must never be satisfied with our love, "just the way it is."

> **And may the Lord cause you to increase and abound in love for one another, and for all people, just as we also do for you; so that He may establish your hearts without blame in holiness before our God and Father at the coming of our Lord Jesus with all His saints.**
> **1 Thessalonians 3:12-13**

> **Be on the alert, stand firm in the faith, act like men, be strong. Let all that you do be done in love.**
> **1 Corinthians 16:13-14**

Whether you are someone who fears that love is gone forever, someone who is aware that complacency has set in, or just someone who wants to excel still more in his love, what you need to do is look closely at biblical love. Biblical love is derived from God's love. The starting point for us is to gain an understanding of God's love for us. A man who does not know the *magnitude* of God's forgiveness will not love God properly either. It is only through this understanding and appreciation of God's great love toward us that we can begin to love others with the right motives and to have enduring love.

What Biblical Love is *Not*

The word *love* is a loosely used term in our day. We love this food or that movie. We love sports or the way a woman looks. Then, among these frivolous declarations, we say to our wives, "I love *you*." It is no wonder that this phrase has come to have less and less meaning in our marriages.

Love needs to have great meaning to the exemplary husband. In turn, he must seek to understand and copy God's kind of love. Unfortunately, we are probably more familiar with worldly love. Without exposure to God's truth about love, we too can have a warped or limited understanding.

1. Romantic feelings = love

    Romantic feelings come and go, but real love is a continuous commitment. Romantic feelings are often based on superficial matters and/or unrealistic infatuation. True love can produce intermittent romantic feelings but romantic feelings are not necessarily an indicator of God's kind of love (1 Corinthians 13:7).

2. Physical attraction = love

    Appreciation, desire or passion that is initiated by and/or based upon outward appearance is not true love. Liking the way someone looks or being physically attracted to someone's body does *not* mean that you love them. These things can be a result of pure selfishness. A husband whose "love" is merely or largely based on physical attraction will have great difficulty in his relationship with his wife if her appearance becomes significantly altered by age, event, or weight gain (1 Samuel 16:7).

3. Sex = love

    In our society, to be a "good lover" means only one thing—to be good at sex. Many believe that love is synonymous with the sex act. Like physical attraction, the sex act can be nothing more than selfish lust. Fulfilling the sexual desires of one's spouse should be an expression of the love commitment that is already present. Even though sex may be related to love in marriage, it can never be equated with love (Ephesians 5:2-3; Hebrews 13:4 NKJV).

4. Needing = love

    For some, a sense of great *need* is the prevailing attraction toward another person. The needy person may feel as if he or she cannot live without the relationship, and they may become desperate at the thought of losing it. In this case, they are gaining something from the other person that they feel they desperately need. Actually this neediness is more selfish than it is loving. Needing is *not* the same as loving (1Corinthians 13:5b).

5. Benefitting = love

    Other individuals may not sense such great need, but they believe themselves to be "in love" because they receive great benefit from a person. When they say, "I love you," what they really mean is, "I like what you do for me." If biblical love has never been understood or experienced, the person benefitting may not be aware of their selfishness. The clearest indication of this false kind of "love" is the response that follows a lapse or the removal of the benefit that is being received (1 Corinthians 13:5b again).

6. Loving words alone = love

Some find it very easy to "talk the love talk" but do not "walk the love walk." They are under the impression that loving words are all that matter. They are quick to say, "I love you" but then consistently make selfish or inconsiderate choices. Their words rarely find active expression. This is not God's kind of love (Romans 5:8).

7. Loving actions alone = love

This distortion can be the closest thing to the real thing, but it is not necessarily love. The situation may be that there is a true commitment and proper awareness that love is thinking of the other person, but verbal expression of it is lacking. If selfish motives are behind one's actions, the actions really have nothing to do with real love at all. If the problem is that a person is embarrassed to express their love verbally, they need to practice doing it until it is not embarrassing any more (1 Corinthians 13:3).

Some men and women are under the mistaken impression that it is unloving to do anything that might cause sadness or disappointment. This viewpoint can cause a person to leave off very important aspects of love such as protection, truthfulness, admonishment, and accountability. Those who believe this lie fail to do what is best for the other person in order to keep them "happy." This may be because they actually care more about themselves and what they may lose in the process of doing what is right, than because they care about the other person (Proverbs 27:5-6; Ephesians 4:15).

8. Being "in love" = love

This is not a biblical term. God always refers to love as a commitment; a choice; an action, *not* a state. Usually the phrase "in love" is associated with the idea that one can fall in and out of love.

While there may be *something* that individuals fall in and out of, it is not true love.

What Biblical Love Is

Let's compare these erroneous definitions of love to God's kind of love. The controlling command for us to love our wives as *Christ loved the Church* can give us our most comprehensive understanding (Ephesians 5:20-33). Christ's love for us is both perfect and undeserved. This is the kind of love we should show our wives.

Christ's love:

- is initiated first by Himself (1 John 4:9-11)
- is enduring (Psalm 17:12)
- is verbalized (Jeremiah 31:3)
- is compassionate (Psalm 112:4)
- is demonstrated by action (Romans 5:8)
- does what is best for us (Romans 8:28)
- is self-sacrificial (John 10:11)
- involves treasuring us, even though we are not worthy (Luke 15:11-32)
- is not based on performance (Psalm 103:10)

In some marriage situations the wife becomes so embittered that she begins to relate to her husband in the same way that an enemy would. God still holds a husband, in this situation, responsible to love his wife. He commands us to *love our enemies*.

> **"But I say to you, love your enemies and pray for those who persecute you, so that you may be sons of your Father who is in heaven; for He causes His sun to rise on the evil and the good, and sends rain on the righteous and the unrighteous."**
> **Matthew 5:44-45**

<u>A husband can love his wife who is treating him like an enemy</u>
<u>in these ways:</u>

- by confessing, repenting (changing mind and actions) and asking forgiveness of any personal sin (Matthew 5:23-24)
- by doing good to her (Matthew 5:44)
- by returning a blessing instead of evil for evil (Romans 12:14,17)
- by lovingly confronting her sin, *after* you have dealt with your own (Matthew 18:15; Ephesians 4:15)
- by praying for her (Matthew 5:44c)

A Working Definition of Love

In a world where everyone has his own definition of love, it is important to remember that only God defines love perfectly. God's kind of love is:

A selfless and enduring commitment of the will to care about and benefit another person by righteous, truthful, and compassionate thoughts, words and actions.

True love has no ulterior motive to only benefit self. True love is always thinking of the other person. True love is like God's love.

The Determination to Love

The determination or decision to love cannot be made according to our feelings. A Christian *must* love. By determination I mean our decision or our intention to love. It is God who has already determined the *basic* how, when, where, and why of real love. God's Word tells us that those who do not love do not know God.

> **The one who does not love does not know God, for God is love.**
> **1 John 4:8**

We are only truly able to love *by the Spirit of God* (the basic how). God's Word also tells us that we must strive to love *continually* (the basic when) and *in every situation* (the basic where), *because we love God and want to be like Him* (the basic why).

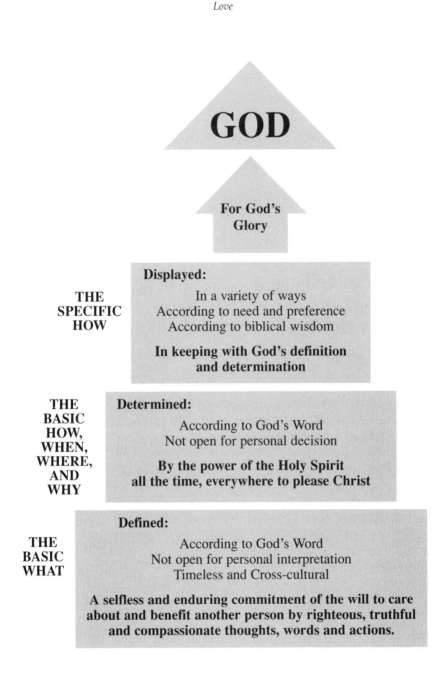

GOD

For God's
Glory

**THE
SPECIFIC
HOW**

Displayed:
In a variety of ways
According to need and preference
According to biblical wisdom

**In keeping with God's definition
and determination**

**THE
BASIC
HOW,
WHEN,
WHERE,
AND
WHY**

Determined:
According to God's Word
Not open for personal decision

**By the power of the Holy Spirit
all the time, everywhere to please Christ**

**THE
BASIC
WHAT**

Defined:
According to God's Word
Not open for personal interpretation
Timeless and Cross-cultural

**A selfless and enduring commitment of the will to care
about and benefit another person by righteous, truthful
and compassionate thoughts, words and actions.**

LOVE ACCORDING TO GOD

The Display of Love

There is a measure of personal freedom in how love is communicated. *As long as God's Word is taken into account*, it is okay for couples to share what actions communicate "I love you" best to one another. Men, be sure to recognize as love *any* selfless act of consideration your wife shows, and demonstrate your appreciation.

Each husband must evaluate his own love for his wife. Does it fit the above descriptions? Is it true love according to God's standards? The opposite of love is selfishness. Perhaps you know that your love is not what it should be. Perhaps you never have loved your wife with biblical love—what then?

Renewing Love and It's Feelings

If we are honest, we must admit that our love often falls short of God's kind of love. Thankfully, you can *renew* love that seems gone forever. If positive feelings toward your wife have decreased or disappeared, it is most likely because you are not actively loving her as you should. Your lack of love may be a result of not really understanding God's love. It may be simple laziness. In some cases, the lack of love is a sinful response to unresolved issues in the marriage. Before we can renew love, we must deal with past sin issues God's way (Ephesians 4:32; see also Chapter 15: "Helping His Wife Deal With Her Sin").

To renew love, you must confess your lack of love to God and your wife, begin putting off any selfish or unkind ways and put on real love. Usually positive feelings will eventually follow *consistent actions* of true love. You *demonstrate love* in order to *build* love.

Hindrances to Love

Wrong Motives

A husband's motives are wrong when they are aimed at benefitting himself. Ask yourself why you do what you do for your wife, or why you don't do what is loving toward her. Ask God to search your heart and reveal any wrong motives.

And see if there be any hurtful way in me, and lead me in the everlasting way.
Psalms 139:24

Wrong	Right
To serve self To feel good about self To get love or favors	To show God's kind of love with no goal of personal benefit To glorify and bless God

Pride

A husband is proud when he focuses on himself, does not consider others, sees himself above or better than others, refuses to admit or consider that he might be wrong and/or believes he has nothing to learn.

Proud thoughts to put off:	Loving thoughts to put on:
Self-focused: Why doesn't she think of me more? Why isn't she doing _____ for me?	*Others-focused:* How can I think of her now? What can I do for her?
My life is so hard. She should _____	God will help me—how can I bless her?
I'll never be what I should be, why even try? Woe is me.	Lord, help me to please you by being the husband I should be. Thank You that You promise to help me grow.
Selfish: I will do this if she will _____.	*Selfless:* I'm going to do this just to bless her and for You, Lord.
I want to do what I want to do.	What would she like to do?
I don't want to_____.	I don't feel like _____, but I will because I want to love You, Lord, and her.

What's in it for me?	I want nothing in return.
This is an inconvenience to me.	Christ was inconvenienced for me. I'll be inconvenienced.
She should do it my way.	What would she like? I can prefer her and still do Your will, so I will.
I'm tired. I'm not going to _____.	I'm tired. Lord, give the strength to continue loving and giving.
Arrogant: She gets on my nerves. She is so _____ (negative trait).	*Humble:* She is, (positive trait). Everyone (especially me) has their weaknesses.
She doesn't know anything. I don't need her or anyone's input.	She has a lot to offer. I need to listen to her. I don't know everything.
I'm a real catch, a gift. What's her problem? She should appreciate me more.	If she has a problem with me maybe I need to learn and change. She probably has a point.
I know I'm right. Anyone who doesn't agree with me is wrong. I don't need this.	I will listen, consider and study God's Word and think about it. I could very well be wrong.
I'm fine. I've been faithful in everything.	I have not been completely faithful. God sets the standard. I must grow in faithfulness.

Proud actions to put off:	Loving actions to put on:
Bragging about my goodness, good qualities, or accomplishments	Thanking God for any good in me or that is accomplished through me
Waiting or looking for her to love me or do for me first	Initiating affection and other acts of love
Just pointing out her wrong-doing and not mine	Focusing on my wrong-doing
Not asking what my wife would like but choosing what brings me pleasure or allows me to avoid discomfort or effort	Asking what she would like; suffering discomfort for the sake of love and pleasing God
Planning my day off around me	Considering my wife and her desires when planning my only day off
Rejecting or tuning out my wife's input or admonishments	Listening to what she has to say, asking questions and committing to think about it, pray about it, and/or study it out—whatever applies; then getting back to her about it

Fear

A husband is sinfully fearful when he is consumed with an outcome that will affect him negatively or jeopardize his "happiness". He is concerned about self most of all.

Fearful thoughts to put off:	Loving thoughts to put on:
If I do or say that, she will get mad.	If she gets mad, I will deal with it God's way.

She's going to find someone else. I'm going to isolate her.	I will believe the best of her, and let her carry on life in a normal fashion
If I give an inch, she'll take a mile.	I will love her and do what I can for her
I have to be in control and keep her dependent or I might lose her.	God is in control. I don't need to control her. I need to love her.

Fearful actions to put off:	Loving actions to put on:
Staying quiet when I should speak	Speaking up and facing any consequences for God's glory
Being jealous and controlling to protect my interests	Letting her have other interests and other people in her life
Doing something to keep her happy and/or happy with me	Doing loving things to please God and show His kind of love to her

Bitterness

A husband is bitter when he continually finds fault with his wife, and finds it difficult to think good thoughts about her or do good things for her. He might punish his wife by withdrawing from her, by verbally attacking her, or by making life difficult for her.

Bitter thoughts to put off:	Loving thoughts to put on:
I've had it! If she does _____ one more time, that's it. Phooey on her. I'm going to leave her!	I will keep loving her. Christ loved me when I didn't deserve it. My love is forever; no matter what.
I'll show her. I'll get even with her.	I will return good for evil. My

	love does not depend on her love. I have promised before God to love her.
I'll never forgive her for that. She doesn't deserve it.	God forgave me and says I must, therefore, forgive others. I have sinned against her too. She is just acting sinfully because she is not in a right place with God. I will choose to show love to her even if she may not deserve it and I will be willing to say, "I forgive you," when she repents and asks.
She did that deliberately to hurt me or embarrass me.	I need to believe the best and ask her about that.
I'm not going to do anything for her or love her. Look at what she is doing or at what she has done to me.	I will love her with Christ's kind of love no matter what she has done. And, I will seek to help her turn away from sin.

Bitter actions to put off:	Loving actions to put on:
Cutting my wife down to others or to her face	Saying good things about her
Not believing the best of my wife Holding her past sin against her	Thinking the best of her and remembering that I forgave her for the past
Planning or doing wicked or vengeful things so that my wife suffers	Planning what I will not do when she sins against me.
Continuing to think negative thoughts about my wife	Planning thankful thoughts to think about my wife

Refusing to do loving things for my wife	Planning loving things to do for my wife and then doing them

Preoccupation

A husband is sinfully preoccupied when he is consistently focused on other things of a lower priority than his wife, or when he is ignoring problems in the marriage. He is distracted by things that are of lesser importance to God. It is sin to be task-oriented, money-oriented, success-oriented, or leisure-oriented.

Preoccupied thoughts to put off:	Loving thoughts to put on:
I'm too busy to talk, pray, or spend time with her.	She is more important. God's priority will be my priority. I will show her love.
I have too many things on my mind to handle another thing.	I can do all things through Christ who strengthens me. I will put forth the effort (even though I don't feel like it) because I love her and God.
This is more important (when it is not) or I have to do this (when I don't).	I will let go of what I want to do and do the more important thing. I will have God's viewpoint.
God has called me to my ministry, not to be caught up with relational things with my wife.	My ministry to my wife qualifies me for other ministry. God is relational. I am committed to her and our relationship.

Preoccupied actions to put off:	Loving actions to put on:
Ignoring problems	Talking to my wife about issues and seeking biblical solutions

Neglecting my wife	Planning time with her and putting that time before other things
Not praying with and for my wife	Planning time to pray for and with her
Over-extending myself	Cutting back on whatever I can to make the time that is needed to love her as I should and thereby strengthen our marriage

Everyone is tempted to sin in these ways at least on occasion. Hopefully these lists will help you to love your wife better. It is also a good idea to ask your wife if she has any opinion about how well you are loving her.

Ways You Can Show Love to Your Wife

We must put off any ideas that love is unnecessary, a sign of weakness, or a feminine characteristic. Clearly, increasing in love for our wives must be a major pursuit. The exemplary husband's wife will never accuse him of not loving her because the message will be loud and clear.

Every husband should think about and investigate specific ways he can show love to his wife. I have already mentioned some ways in the put off-put on lists. Below is a list of basic ways we can show love to our wives. It is up to each of us to make application to our own marriages.

To Love Your Wife:

- Prefer her over yourself.
- Show interest in her interests.
- Encourage her with words of appreciation.
- Brighten her day with an unexpected card, note, flowers, or gift.
- Spend time with her having fun (what she enjoys).
- Spend time listening with interest to her concerns while showing

compassion, giving her *encouragement* from God's Word, and helping her find a *solution*; all in *that* order (trust me!).
- Help her when she looks as if she needs it (don't wait to be asked!).
- Do chivalrous things to let her know how special she is to you (open doors, wipe off benches before she sits down, pull out chairs, etc.).
- Show her non-sexual affection.
- Seek to please and satisfy her during sexual intimacy.
- Confront her sin in love, pray with her about it and encourage change.
- Pray with her and lead her spiritually (Read Scripture with her). See to it that she is serving and using her spiritual gifts within the church.

Does Your Love Pass The Test?

The man who truly loves God will seek to love his wife with the love that God has shown for him. He will define love as God does, putting off counterfeits and putting on biblical love. By changing self-focused thoughts and actions to loving ones, he can be sure to renew or increase his love.

Husband, as you seek to obey God, pray that He will work His kind of love in you. Plan and carry out ways to show biblical love to your wife and most likely she will respond with great enthusiasm. Men, I have never heard a wife say, " Pastor, please help! My husband is loving me too much!" Some wives may be more cautious and wait to see if you are sincere, but unless a wife is an unbeliever or very embittered, she should eventually respond. You *must* persevere for the glory of God. Regardless of your wife's response, you are called to be exemplary in your love. One day you will answer to God for how you have or have not loved your wife. Most important, you can show gratitude for God's love toward you by loving your wife more and more.

> **Therefore be imitators of God, as beloved children; and walk in love, just as Christ also loved you and gave Himself up for us, an offering and a sacrifice to God as a fragrant aroma.**
> **Ephesians 5:1-2**

Chapter Nine

A HUSBAND'S RESPONSIBILITY
LEADERSHIP—PART I

A common expression, "Take me to your leader!" should not create confusion, especially within a Christian family. The husband's leadership is a mandate from God, and as such is a privilege and responsibility. With the backdrop of true worship of God and Christlike love fresh in our minds, we can now turn our attention to the skill and art of leading. In this chapter, we will examine the general characteristics of Christlike leadership. Christ's way of leading is very different from the worldly leadership we often see and the fleshly leadership that comes so naturally.

The Natural Man*	The Spiritual Man*
•Self-confident •Knows men •Makes own decisions •Ambitious •Originates own methods •Enjoys commanding others •Motivated by personal considerations •Independent	•Confident in God •Also knows God •Seeks to find God's will •Self-effacing [to erase self or make self inconspicuous] •Finds and follows God's methods •Delights to obey God •Motivated by love for God and man •God-dependent

* J. Oswald Sanders, *Spiritual Leadership* (Chicago, IL: Moody Press, 1967), p. 21.

Poor leadership is the cause of many conflicts in marriage. Any time a husband's method of leadership helps him to accomplish his own *fleshly gain*, enables him to *lord it over* his wife or allows him to be *irresponsible*, his method of leading is *wrong* (1Peter 5:2-3). Christlike leadership qualities are indispensable to the exemplary husband's marriage.

The Husband Has God-Given Authority

The responsibility to lead always comes from holding a position of authority. "Headship" is bestowed by God on the husband at the time of the marriage vows. There are abuses and distortions of the privilege of leadership, however, because there are misunderstandings about the headship or authority the husband has been given by God. Following are some important aspects of the authority God has given the husband.

Your Authority Is Limited

Only God has unlimited authority. You are limited in your authority by the commands of God's Word, just as the authority of the government can go only so far. Even though all Christians are commanded to be in subjection to the government, the government's authority is limited. It only has the authority that God gives it. Its authority is not above God's. Paul makes this point well in Romans:

> **Every person is to be in subjection to the governing authorities. For there is no authority except from God, and those which exist are established by God. Therefore whoever resists authority has opposed the ordinance of God; and they who have opposed will receive condemnation upon themselves.**
> **Romans 13:1-2**

This same principle applies to the authority the husband has been given. Some husbands seem to think they have the authority to say anything, do anything, or require anything. A husband does *not* have the authority to sin or to ask his wife to sin. You are under God's authority and have been given a *measure* of authority to carry out God's revealed will. While it is true that your wife must obey you unless you ask her to sin, *your concern* must be that you are obeying God and loving your wife in whatever decisions and requests you make. God will hold you accountable for your leadership. We must honor God by using our authority in the way that He intended. Anytime a husband sees his authority over and above the ordained limits, or without God's other very important commands, he will be a poor leader. He will not be leading in the way a Christian husband should.

Your Authority Must Be Active

You need to remember that your authority requires you to lead. It is not an option. God has made this very clear:

> **For the husband is the head of the wife, as Christ also is the head of the church, He Himself being the Savior of the body. But as the church is subject to Christ, so also the wives ought to be to their husbands in everything.**
> **Ephesians 5:23-24**

God is a God of order. Chaos, confusion, and disorganization should not be present in anything that God has designed or instituted. In His wisdom, God knows that order is necessary to accomplish a purpose. He has required order in the way that creation functions (Genesis 1-2), in the way that the nation of Israel functioned (Exodus 35-Numbers 9), in the way that the family should function (1 Corinthians 11:3; Ephesians 6:1), in the way that the Church should function (1 Corinthians 14:40), and so on. We have even seen that there is order in how the Godhead (Father, Son, Holy Spirit) itself operates. I believe it is obvious that one reason God has given you your authority is to put order in the institution of marriage, so that His purposes might be accomplished (Ephesians 5:21-33; Colossians 3:18-4:1).

<u>Some purposes for the authority you have been given are:</u>

- To help others see how God leads his people
- To develop humility and obedience in all those concerned
- To guide the family in righteousness
- To give a sense of order and stability in the home
- To provide what is needed for the family
- To protect the family
- To accomplish ministry for God more effectively
- To help the family be a good witness to the world

All for God's glory

God has given you your authority *to use.* He will, one day, hold you responsible for your faithfulness in this area. Are you above reproach before God and man in this area? In Paul's instructions to Timothy, he writes that overseers and deacons must be men who are "above reproach" even in how they manage their home (1 Timothy 3:2, 10). Paul then goes on to explain *how* a man is to be" above reproach." In his list of ways he says:

> **... Not addicted to wine or pugnacious, but gentle, peaceable, free from the love of money. He must be** *one who manages his own household well*, **keeping his children under control with all dignity (but if a man** *does not know how to manage his own household*, **how will he take care of the church of God?). Deacons must be husbands of only one wife, and** *good managers of their children and their own households.*
> **1 Timothy 3:3-5, 12 [emphasis mine]**

In these verses the word "manage" (*prohistemi*) means "to lead and care for." If you want to be a man who is "above reproach" or "blameless" (NKJV), you must lead and care for your home well.

The Exemplary Husband is a Type of Shepherd-Leader

In the Scriptures, God is pictured as the Shepherd of Israel (Psalm 80:1; Isaiah 40:11). He cared for them as He led them. He always knew the direction that He wanted His people to go, but He exercised great patience along the way. He often allowed His people to serve Him with their own talents and goals, but He also had boundaries that He decisively required them to stay within (e.g., Joshua 1:7). Christ referred to Himself as "The Good Shepherd" and was the perfect human example of leadership (John 10:11). Even though our God has all power and authority, He always leads His people like a shepherd:

> **"I am the good shepherd, and I know My own and My own know Me."**
> **John 10:14**

Since our goal is to be like Christ, and if Christ is a shepherd to those He leads, then we need to be caring to those we lead also (1 John 2:6). As much as possible, our leadership needs to have similar qualities as the shepherding done by God, and more specifically, the shepherding done by Christ.

The word *shepherd* brings our leadership into perspective. We are not kings, high above our wives, but actually lowly under-shepherds, doing the bidding of the Chief Shepherd. Yes, we do have authority to make decisions, but *authority is not the goal*. Authority is a means to an end—God's end. It is the means by which we care for our wives and do God's will. Furthermore, it is only one aspect of our relationship with our wives. We are also partners and companions. Most men dwell on their authority too much. Authority is something that you exercise when you have to. I've heard it said that our perspective should not be that we love to rule, but that we rule to love. Shepherding, on the other hand, is something you should always have in the forefront of your mind because it implies complete and daily care, whatever that may entail. Let's take a closer look at the qualities of a shepherd by looking at God's shepherding and His instructions to under-shepherds of God's people.

1. A shepherd knows where he is going.

> **"For I have come down from heaven, not to do my own will, but the will of Him who sent me."**
> **John 6:38**

A shepherd must know his destination before he can lead his flock there. Christ certainly knew where He was going. He was intent on glorifying God, and He used perfect wisdom in all His decisions.

A shepherd is neither "wishy-washy" nor rash in his decisions. In order to lead, he must be decisive, but very carefully decisive. A shepherd will always be in the process of making informed and purposeful decisions in order to care for his sheep properly. He needs to be aware of the circumstances, dangers and possibilities around his sheep, as much as possible. He also needs to know his sheep well. Being decisive does not mean that the shepherd will *always* be making and expressing decisions, but that he will always be thinking, studying, and evaluating.

> **He who gives an answer before he hears, it is folly and shame to him....The mind of the prudent acquires knowledge, and the ear of the wise seeks knowledge.**
> **Proverbs 18:13, 15**

Obviously we cannot be lazy as husbands. We must not sit back and let our wives do the evaluating and the decision-making. We should certainly enlist their input, but the evaluating and the decision-making are *our own* responsibility.

Wisdom comes from the Word of God. Husband, there is no way for you to lead your wife in the ways of God and in a wise way in this world unless you, yourself, are fixed on God's truth. You must pursue knowing God's Person, goals, and ways (through His Word) with fervor. You must devote yourself to this. This is one reason that the first section of this book, "A Husband's Recognitions," was so lengthy. A man who wants to prosper in the will of God will do what God told Joshua to do:

> **"This book of the law shall not depart from your mouth, but you shall meditate on it day and night, so that you may be careful to do according to all that is written in it; for then you will make your way prosperous, and then you will have success."**
> **Joshua 1:8**

2. A shepherd knows how to lead lovingly.

**"The Lord is my shepherd... Surely goodness and lov-
ingkindness shall follow me all the days of my life...."
Psalm 23:1,6**

We have just spent a whole chapter on the need to love our wives. As Psalm 23 indicates, God (our Shepherd) is always bringing about good for His sheep and showing lovingkindness. A true shepherd loves and cares for his sheep at all times. In John 10:1-16, Jesus contrasts a true shepherd with a hireling. The true shepherd is willing to give his life for the sheep. The hireling is not. The true shepherd knows his sheep well. The hireling does not. A hireling looks after the sheep because he is paid to look after them. A true shepherd looks after the sheep because they belong to him and he cares for them.

3. A shepherd leads by example.

**"When he [the shepherd of the sheep] puts forth his
own, he goes before them..."
John 10:4a**

A shepherd leads by example, first and foremost. He may have times when he has to use a different method, but most of the time he goes before the sheep and the sheep follow him. Christ led by example while He was here on earth. He led the disciples to pray by example (Matthew 6: 5-15). He led them to serve one another by example (John 13:3-15). He taught them how to do ministry by example before He sent them out to minister on their own (Luke 8:1-9:6).

Likewise we need to be leading our wives by example. The motto, "Do as I say, not as I do" will not satisfy God or your wife. No one wants to follow a hypocrite. How we live speaks more loudly than our words. I am convinced that some of us need to do much less talking and a great deal more living!

God clearly outlined what a man who leads by example looks like in his instruction to the church on choosing godly men for service. The virtues listed in 1 Timothy 3:1-3 and Titus 1:5-9 are prerequisites for church leadership because they are exemplary characteristics. Except for two that are specific to a church leadership role, (able to teach and not a new convert), these qualities are ones that all men should possess.

Characteristics of the godly man:

- *Above reproach*: blameless because he does not practice evil. If and when he is accused, there is no evidence.
- *Husband of one wife*: a one-woman man. He is faithful and true to his wife.
- *Temperate*: in control of himself and well-composed.
- *Prudent*: in touch with reality and alert. He has sound judgement.
- *Respectable*: proper, orderly, and modest, as opposed to scatter-brained and immature.
- *Hospitable*: A friend to strangers and willing to have others in his home.
- *Not addicted to much wine*: moderate and self-controlled. He is not a drunkard.
- *Not pugnatious/Uncontentious*: not quarrelsome or easily angered.
- *Free from the love of money*: not covetous or focused on earthly wealth.
- *Manages his household well*: maintains and cares for his house well. He leads his family, rather than driving them or letting them rule him.
- *Keeps his children under control with all dignity*: has children who obey him. Because he is dignified in how he manages them, they act with dignity.

4. A shepherd knows how to oversee.

> **The Word of the Lord came to me saying, "Son of man, prophesy against the shepherds of Israel. Prophesy and say to those shepherds, 'Thus says the Lord God, "Woe, shepherds of Israel ...** *with force and with severity you have dominated them* **[God's sheep].""'**
> **Ezekiel 34:1-4 [emphasis and explanation mine]**

Shepherding is not a harsh, driving or controlling kind of leader-ship. Some men treat their wives like little children, doing everything for them or trying to control their every activity and decision. A shep-herding husband, however, does not "lord it over" his wife. There is most of the time a significant measure of freedom in the way a good shepherd leads. He takes those under him in a certain direction; he does not seek to scrutinize and control their every step. Be careful that your leadership is largely oversight and not a matter of control.

A husband who lords it over his wife does not really care for her as he should, but instead cares most about his own agenda. This kind of husband might also look down on others and have difficulty believing that they are capable (by God's grace) of doing what they need to do and becoming what they need to become. He may be tempted to see himself as the only one who must make everything happen, instead of giving others a chance and trusting God to work. He also is usually lacking in personal and relational skills and the ability to recognize his own sin and shortcomings. As an exemplary husband, we must put off any "lording it over" tendencies, and put on patience, self-control, and humility.

> **Shepherd the flock of God among you, exercising oversight not under compulsion,...nor yet as lording it over those allotted to your charge, but proving to be examples to the flock.**
> **1 Peter 5:2-3**

5.   A shepherd is involved.

> **"I am the Good Shepherd ... I know my own and my own know Me."**
> **John 10:14**

A number of husbands are too cowardly, fearful, or busy about the wrong things to be involved. Some fear the reaction of their wife and the consequences of doing the right thing. Instead, they must have courage, faith in God, and trust that His Word will guide them in whatever results from taking the responsibility to lead. Overly busy husbands do not yet grasp that they will be held accountable for their contribution (or the lack thereof) to the state of the home. In the same way that church leaders will be held responsible for the care of their flock, you will be held responsible for the care of your home flock.

6.   A shepherd is diligent in his responsibility.

Shepherd the flock ... with eagerness.
1 Peter 5:2

It is very easy to rationalize away our responsibility as husbands. I've heard (and used myself) the best of excuses: "I'm too tired." "I'm too busy." "I'm not wired that way." "That's not my style." "That's just too much to expect of me right now."   The common denominators in all of these excuses is selfishness (Philippians 2:3-4). Christ, however, is never self-focused or lazy in His care for us. A good shepherd is diligent and eager to care for his sheep. We must, therefore, be diligent and eager in our leadership as well.

If you have been letting your wife lead, you need to sit down with her and express your intention to love her and God by leading as you should. Tell her of your desire to lovingly lead without lording it over her. Discuss specific ways that she can better follow you. Once you both have the same goal of obeying God in this area, you both need to be gracious and patient as you learn new habits.

7.   A shepherd protects.

I am the good shepherd; the good shepherd lays down
His life for the sheep.   He who is the hired hand and
not a shepherd ... flees because he is a hired hand and
is not concerned about the sheep.
John 10:11-13

A shepherd is always on the lookout for danger and is ready to intervene. Certainly, he would never intentionally or knowingly put his sheep in harm's way. As husbands we need to do what we can to keep our wives safe from danger. If at all possible, we need to be with them, or see that someone is, when there is potential danger. We should do what we can to give them a safe place to live and a reliable car to drive. We also need to be on the lookout for any spiritual dangers such as heresies, known temptations, and excessive worldly input (i.e. the wrong kind of television shows, novels, friendships, etc.). It is never right for a husband to knowingly allow his wife to be in any kind of preventable danger.

8.   A shepherd provides.

> **The Lord is my shepherd, I shall not want [be in true**
> **need].**
> **Psalm 23:1 [explanation mine]**

Christ, as the Good Shepherd, provides for His Church. He cares for her every need, and makes the well-being of His flock His concern. Providing for our wives is an important part of loving our wives the way Christ loves us. The Bible is clear that we must care for the physical and spiritual needs of our wives (1 Timothy 5:8). To fulfill our responsibility we must provide food, clothing, shelter, rest, healthcare, and sexual satisfaction, as well as a good church and spiritual oversight.

9.   A shepherd instructs.

> **The Lord is my shepherd . . . . He guides me in the**
> **paths of righteousness for His name's sake.**
> **Psalm 23:1-3**

With the understanding that our instruction must be balanced by the oversight principle (see number 5), we must be sure to *give instruction*, especially in the things of God. A shepherd doesn't just let the sheep wander *anywhere without any instruction*. Taking the time to study with, review sermons with, or have devotions with your wife is a good way to lead by instruction. Having a special time to discuss concerns and decisions is also very helpful.

10.   A shepherd corrects.

> **The Lord is my Shepherd.... Your rod and Your staff,**
> **they comfort me.**
> **Psalm 23:1,4**

Out of love, a shepherd will occasionally have to correct a wayward lamb. He does this for the well-being of the sheep. Even though correction may not be pleasant, it can still be the best thing for a lamb. It may even be a comforting thing for a lamb to know his shepherd will not let him stray and that his shepherd truly cares. Sometimes a wife may need to be clearly corrected with God's staff (the Word of God). This should be done only when there is clear sin involved and for the purpose of helping her and glorifying God. You need to ascertain whether she is *weak, fainthearted* or *unruly* and respond accordingly (1 Thessalonians 5:14). Most wives who are lovingly led by their husbands rarely need anything more than a loving admonition.

Sometimes a lamb does not learn from correction, but continues to stray. A shepherd of literal sheep will do whatever is necessary to help the sheep learn what is best for them. As humans, our authority stops short of physically abusing our wives! Men, we are absolutely NEVER allowed to strike or harm our wives. Any husband who hurts his wife physically is committing a serious moral offense before God (1 Timothy 3:3). He is also committing a criminal offense and should suffer the legal consequences. Doing physical harm to your wife also will have the devastating result of breaking a trust that is difficult to regain. If you and your wife are in this position, it would be wise to seek godly counsel to restore the relationship and to gain accountability.

There may be a time when our wife needs more than *our own* correction with God's Word. After we have led by example, have given instruction, have gently admonished, and, finally, have firmly rebuked in love—all to no avail, a more drastic measure may be needed before the wife will submit to the will of God. The Lord has told us what to do in this kind of situation. If she is a professing believer, we are to bring in another believer and the whole church if necessary (Luke 17:3-4; Matthew 18:15-20). We will more fully discuss how to deal with both the believing and unbelieving wife's sin in Chapter15.

11.   A shepherd seeks to restore his sheep.

> **The Lord is my shepherd .... He restores my soul.**
> **Psalm 23:1, 3**

> **Brethren, even if anyone is caught in any trespass, you who are spiritual,** *restore such a one* **in a spirit of gentleness; each one looking to yourself, so that you too will not be tempted.**
> **Galatians 6:1 [emphasis mine]**

Whether a lamb is hurt in the process of following or of rebelling, a good shepherd seeks to restore that sheep to full health. A shepherd will compassionately receive and help the lamb that is willing to receive help. In the same way, we must be willing to forgive and/or assist a hurting wife. It is important that you seek to really understand your wife as you are trying to restore her. I would strongly suggest that you run the risk of erring on the side of comfort, until it becomes evident that your wife needs more.

The Exemplary Husband is a Servant-Leader

To some a servant leader may seem like an irreconcilable paradox (opposites that cannot be put together). But actually, the two concepts must go hand in hand. Christ was the perfect leader and yet He was very much the perfect servant.

> **"It is not this way among you, but whoever wishes to become great among you shall be your servant, and whoever wishes to be first among you shall be your slave; just as the Son of Man did not come to be served, but to serve, and to give His life a ransom for many."**
> **Matthew 20:26-28**

Serving does not lessen one's authority or leadership. Instead, it enhances it—especially the leading-by-example aspect. One who leads as Christ leads is always thinking of others, not self. He is willing to sacrifice his own comfort and even his own well-being for those he leads. He is willing to put himself last, prefer others, and even serve those he leads. Christ gave us an amazing example of serving when He humbled himself and served the disciples in the upper room:

> **"You call Me Teacher and Lord; and you are right, for so I am. If I then, the Lord and the Teacher, washed your feet, you also ought to wash one another's feet. For I gave you an example that you also should do as I did to you. Truly, truly, I say to you, a slave is not greater than his master, nor is one who is sent greater than the one who sent him. If you know these things,**

you are blessed if you do them."
John 13:13-17

Jesus' message to the disciples was loud and clear. If He was willing to be a servant, we certainly should be too. Husbands, how do you serve your wife? Even though she is called to assist you, you must serve her. A servant will be more concerned about his own responsibility than that of others. First be sure that you are serving your wife, then address her need to assist you if she is not doing her part. The greatest leader of all time was a servant-leader.

With God All Things Are Possible

Christ has left you with the perfect example of leadership. Though it is not humanly possible, God is able to make you into the leader you should be. Change will take humble and prayerful dependence on Him. Confess and repent of any sin in the area of your leadership to both God and your wife. Begin to make this aspect of your marriage a serious matter of prayer. Pinpoint where your leadership goes wrong and seek to put on right thinking and actions instead. As you seek to honor God as a shepherd and servant-leader, you will be better able to exemplify Christ.

Chapter Ten

LEADERSHIP—PART II

In this chapter, we want to press on in our endeavor to exemplify Christ in our leadership. Now it is time to get down to the basics. This chapter is intended to give you some specific helps for applying what you have learned. We must know what God expects of us and also have a plan to accomplish His expectations. If we are serious about our desire to do His will, we will take specific action (James 1:25).

Know Your Own Goals

As the leader of your household, you must first determine your personal and spiritual goals. What are your goals for your marriage? What are your educational and vocational goals? What are your ministry goals? You should not aimlessly drift from day to day taking things as they come. Remember - all your goals/plans are under God's sovereign providence (James 4:13-15).

After you have set your own personal course, you are ready to think about the direction and goals having to do with your household. When you are considering direction and goals for your household, be bibically-controlled and balanced, and be *sure* to involve your wife.

Remember that you are to be *one* with her and she is to be your *helper*. Most likely, she will be of great assistance.

<u>Direction and possible goals you can establish for your household:</u>

- Establish the Word of God as the standard for your home.
- Establish how you will provide for your family spiritually (a good church and biblical instruction).
- Establish how you will work toward financial stability and providing basic needs for the family (for both immediate and extended family).
- Establish operational guidelines for your own household (devotions, family meetings, phone use [especially for teens], family nights, bedtimes, noise level, neatness standard, etc.).
- Establish ministry goals and guidelines for you and your family (the need for ministry, how often outside ministry takes place, how you can minister together, hospitality frequency, etc.).
- Be careful not to have some inflexible schedule that is never modified

Know the Areas to Oversee

I believe we can safely (scripturally) say that we should oversee any area of our wife's life that affects her well-being (spiritual and otherwise), the lives of the other family members, the management of the home, and the family's witness of God before a watching world. An observant overseer will see areas where the Lord might already be working in his wife's life and look for ways to be of assistance in that area. (See Appendix Six for Leadership Worksheets).

<u>Areas to oversee:</u>

1. Her spiritual welfare

> **Husbands, love your wives, just as Christ also loved the church and gave Himself up for her, so that He might sanctify her, having cleansed her by the washing of water with the word, that He might present to Himself the church in all her glory, having no spot or wrinkle or any such thing; but that she should be holy and blameless.**
> **Ephesians 5:25-27**

- See that you pray for her and with her.
- Provide for her to be a part of, and involved with, your local church, <u>if she is a believer</u>.
- Be sure that you are a good testimony to her by your life and that you share the gospel with her as you have opportunity,<u> if she is unsaved</u>.
- See that you do not take on the role and responsibility of the Holy Spirit by constantly admonishing her and trying to do a sanctifying work in her heart.
- See that you pray with her. How often and how long are not mandated by God, but praying with her daily is very helpful for your understanding of her concerns and for being one with her.
- See that you look into God's Word with her regularly. This can be done through devotions, review of sermon notes, a book, or a study. You can use this time to lead and instruct in spiritual matters. Recognize that she can contribute insight as well. Make sure that you focus most on your own response to God's Word. Also study with her when she has specific questions or needs. You can use your own study methods or a study done by someone else.

2.   Her decision-making

> **For this reason also, since the day we heard of it, we have not ceased to pray for you and to ask that you may be filled with the knowledge of His will in all spiritual wisdom and understanding, so that you will walk in a manner worthy of the Lord, to please Him in all respects.**
> **Colossians 1:9-10**

- Encourage her toward the goal of glorifying God.
- Teach her about the two biggest pitfalls of good decision- making: selfishness and subjectivity (following one's feelings and one's own judgment, rather than God's Word).
- Encourage her to emphasize biblical principles in her decision-making.
- Help her to consider her priorities in her decision-making: God, husband, children, home, and the local church. This is not to be done in a strict order at every given moment.

3.   Her relationships

> **Older women likewise are to be reverent in their behavior, not malicious gossips nor enslaved to much wine, teaching what is good, so that they may encourage the young women to love their husbands, to love their children, to be sensible, pure, workers at home, kind, being subject to their own husbands, so that the word of God will not be dishonored.**
> **Titus 2:3-5**

- Make sure she understands her relationship with you.
  - to be one
  - to be a companion
  - to be your helper
  - to be submissive and respectful. Make sure she knows how to give a godly appeal when she wants you to reconsider a decision, an action, or an attitude (see *The Excellent Wife*, by Martha Peace).
- See that she is protected from sinful or evil relationships. Come to her aid when she needs help in dealing with people who try to take advantage of her kindness, are unreasonable, or act inappropriately toward her.
- Help her to balance her relationship priorities: God, you, the children, and others.
- See that she has any help and resources she needs for her relationships: you, her children, her friends, her boss or co-workers, and her extended family.

4. Her ministries

> **As each one has received a special gift, employ it in serving one another as good stewards of the manifold grace of God.**
> **1 Peter 4:10**

- See that she knows what her ministries are biblically: you, the children, the home, the church body, those outside the faith, and the proportion of time to give to each.
- See that she does not overextend herself.
- Provide her with encouragement in discovering or exercising her spiritual gift(s).

5. Her physical well-being

    So husbands ought also to love their own wives as their own bodies. He who loves his own wife loves himself; for no one ever hated his own flesh, but nourishes and cherishes it, just as Christ also does the church.
    Ephesians 5:28-29

- See that you show concern for and provide care for any medical issues.
- See that you encourage her and hold her accountable toward proper care of herself: eating, resting, safety, and exercise.

Know When To Act

I think it has been well established that a good leader is not quick to correct. On the other hand, a husband will have times when he *should* speak up (Proverbs 25:11; 27:5). A situation may call for anything from a simple question to a loving rebuke. There may even be times when a husband has to pursue church discipline. If a husband has the right heart (a shepherd's heart and a servant's heart), he will do it at the right time and in the right way. The following are good things to practice *before* you give direction to your wife:

1. Make sure you have adequate information.

    He who gives an answer before he hears, it is folly and shame to him.
    Proverbs 18:13

- Observe, but be careful not to be presumptuous (thinking you know her heart and mind just by your observation).
- Get information from your wife and any others who can be helpful.
- Obtain biblical insight by studying God's Word and/or seeking godly counsel.

2. Pray for biblical wisdom.

> **But if any of you lacks wisdom, let him ask of God, who gives to all generously and without reproach, and it will be given to him.**
> **James 1:5**

- Ask yourself:
    "Is my input really necessary at this point?"
    "What is God's perspective on the matter at hand?"
    "Is this a sin issue or an issue that is causing great difficulty for my wife or family?

3. Think through the proper approach.

Remember, you want to shepherd your wife. What is the most gracious way you can provide her with the opportunity to head in the desired direction on her own initiative? The following questions will help you determine the proper approach. They are placed in a suggested order of progression.

- Have I told my wife what I appreciate about her and what she is doing right?
- Have I made sure she has been given the knowledge or biblical insight that is needed for the change she needs to make?
- Have I given her a chance to apply that knowledge on her own?
- Have I encouraged any progress in the right direction?
- Have I offered any help?
- Have I given her general direction?
- Have I given her specific direction?

When your wife needs specific leadership, you may need to give her a direct instruction or make a definite decision. This should be done in a loving and helpful way. Hopefully, your suggestions will be appreciated, but they may be resented or even resisted. At this point, unless you are asking your wife to sin, *she* is sinning if she refuses to do what you ask. We will address what to do about the sinning wife in Chapter 15.

4. Have the right goals.

> **Whether, then, you eat or drink or whatever you do, do all to the glory of God.**
> **1 Corinthians 10:31**

- Your goals in leading your wife should be:
    - To glorify God
    - To do your wife and others good
    - <u>Not</u> to simply have your way or accomplish your preferences

5.   If at all possible, remember to communicate your reasons and goals (God's glory and the other's good) when you must go against what your wife wants or believes is best (Philippians 2:3-4; Mark 10:32-40).

> **But the goal of our instruction is love from a pure heart and a good conscience and sincere faith.**
> **1 Timothy 1:5**

Leading an Unsaved Wife

Some husbands are married to unbelieving wives. They are still responsible to be faithful in leadership. If a wife professes to believe, but there is doubt as to whether she really is saved or not, a husband should attempt to lead her in the same way a husband should lead a believing wife. In time, her true spiritual condition will become evident. If a husband is married to a wife who readily admits that she is not a believer, he needs to know the answer to the question, "How does a believing husband shepherd an unbelieving wife?"

The most important thing for a husband in this position is to focus on glorifying God no matter what happens. Leading an unsaved wife may prove to be a difficult task, but God has given us some guidance.

> **But to the rest I say, not the Lord, that if any brother has a wife who is an unbeliever, and she consents to live with him, he must not divorce her. And a woman who has an unbelieving husband, and he consents to live with her, let her not send her husband away. For the unbelieving husband is sanctified through his wife, and the unbelieving wife is sanctified through**

her believing husband; for otherwise your children are unclean, but now they are holy. Yet if the unbelieving one leaves, let him leave; the brother or the sister is not under bondage in such cases, but God has called us to peace. For how do you know, O wife, whether you will save your husband? Or how do you know, O husband, whether you will save your wife?
1 Corinthians 7:12-16

If you desire to be faithful in leading your unsaved wife:

- *Do not leave her or send her away,* but be willing to live with her and love her (exceptions: unrepentant sexual unfaithfulness or if she wants out of the marriage).

- *Be a godly witness more by your life than by your words.* Seek to be an example of love and obedience toward God. A husband should be careful not to preach at his unsaved wife or force God's Word upon her. Instead, he should share with her only if she is open to hearing about who God is and how to be rightly related to Him.

- *Genuinely love and care for her and have Christ's humble mindset.* Consider her interests and preferences above your own. In my experience, very few unbelieving wives resist coming to the Lord when a husband is living with her in a loving and understanding way. A husband of an unsaved wife must first of all be sure that he is walking humbly before God and his wife. Many unsaved wives have bailed out of their marriages because their believing husbands were very proud and difficult to live with.

- *When you sin against her, acknowledge it, confess it, ask for her forgiveness, and then repent* (change).

- *If you are newly saved, allow your unsaved wife a transition time before you try to address sin problems.* First, center on your walk with the Lord and then on her salvation.

- *Do not expect your unbelieving wife to understand her need to honor God with her life or to understand biblical submission.* Since she is an unbeliever, expect her to sin a great deal. Only address major sin that is greatly affecting her or the family. When you must deal with sin, appeal to her conscience and on the basis of what is right in the sight of God and all men. She may or may not understand these things.

- *Remember it is God who saves* (Ephesians 2:1-9). Pray for the Holy Spirit to work and then be patient.

Husbands of unsaved wives often ask questions like, "How can I expect her to submit?" "How can I deal with her sin?" "What do I do if she will not follow?" or "What about matters that pertain to the children and her dealings with them?" We will attempt to answer these questions in Chapter 15: "Helping His Wife Deal With Her Sin."

The goal of an exemplary husband who is dwelling with an unbelieving wife should be faithfulness to God's will. A husband cannot *make* his wife submit to Christ, submit to him, or even stay in the relationship. If you have an unsaved wife, you must *not* have the goal of having a saved wife or the goal of a smooth marriage. If your unbelieving wife wants out of the marriage, you should let her go peacefully, because you are called to peace and not war (1 Corinthians 7:15). When a husband has done all he can to love his unbelieving wife, but she still wants to leave, God can give you all the wisdom and grace you need to please Him in this trial. If your unbelieving wife does leave you, it will be an enormous comfort to know that you have glorified God by your faithfulness.

Know How To Make God-Honoring Decisions

A leader will only be as good as his decision-making practices. Because we make hundreds of decisions a day, we must know how to make them in a way that pleases God. The most common mistakes, by far, in decision-making are subjectivity (determining truth by one's own ideas, feelings, or experience) and mysticism (believing that God communicates His will subjectively). J.I. Packer once wrote, "wrong ideas about God's guidance lead to wrong conclusions about what to do." We cannot depend on anything subjective as being from God (see the Exemplary Husband Study Guide for more explanation concerning these kinds of practices). In His book, *Decision-Making and the Will of God*, Gary Friesen warns against making important decisions based on our feelings or impressions:

> For impressions could be produced by any number of
> sources: God, Satan, an angel, a demon, human emo-
> tion (such as fear and ecstacy), hormonal imbalance,
> insomnia, medication, or an upset stomach...Impres-
> sions are real; believers experience them. But impres-
> sions are not authoritative.[10]

Though it is sometimes easier to make decisions subjectively or
mystically, God has given us a different and better way to make decisions: by the serious and constant consideration of God's Word (Psalm
1; 19:7; 2 Peter 1:19).

The more you know the Scriptures, the more direction you will
have in your life (Psalm 119). There are more than enough principles
in the Bible to lead the way. The Bible speaks about some things very
directly (i.e., direct commands). In this sense it is a specific road map.
On other issues, however, the Bible speaks *indirectly* and acts more as a
compass, giving you a general direction to follow (i.e., supported principles). John Charles Ryle, the Bishop of Liverpool in 1880, summed up
decision-making well when he wrote:

> The Bible must be our standard. Whenever we are con-
> fronted with a question about Christian practice, we
> must apply the teaching of the Bible. Sometimes the
> Bible will deal with it directly, and we must go by its
> direct teaching. Often the Bible will not deal with it
> directly, and then we must look for general *principles* to
> guide us. It does not matter what other people think.
> Their behavior is not a standard for us. But the Bible is
> a standard for us, and it is by the Bible that we must
> live (emphasis his). [11]

Once you have investigated and applied any direct commands and
indirect principles concerning a decision, you may see that the situation
falls in the realm of *purposeful freedom*. If you have followed the map
and the compass as far as it can take you, you may still have a green
light in a certain direction. To a degree, you can then choose however
you want to choose, and then trust in the sovereignty of God. While
you may have a measure of freedom in your choice, you must always
consider the good of others and the need to be a good witness for Christ

(1 Corinthians 8:9). This consideration is what I mean by *purposeful* freedom. Your freedom can still be restricted somewhat by certain issues. Here are some questions you can ask yourself when you think you are dealing with an area of freedom:

- Will this choice be an opportunity for my sinful flesh to seek fulfillment? (Romans 13:14; Galatians 5:13; 1 Peter 2:16)
- Will this choice be inconsiderate (self-serving) of someone else? (Philippians 2:3-4)
- Will this choice cause someone else to fall into temptation? (1 Corinthians 8:9-13)
- Will this lead me toward enslavement or addiction? (1 Corinthians 6:12)
- Does this glorify God in every way? (1 Corinthians 10:31)

As you face a leadership decision, be sure to consult your wife in your initial data gathering process. Occasionally, you may go through the whole biblical decision-making process as best you can and still have some reservations due to a lack of information or the desire to get more counsel. In Romans, Paul discourages us from taking any action when we cannot act in full faith. He says, "Whatever is not from faith is sin" (Romans 14:23). Just be sure that you don't use this principle as an excuse to do *nothing*.

I have included more information on biblical decision-making in the Study Guide.

Know When To Stand Strong

A good leader will not vacillate on the basis of popular opinion. Once you believe that you have come to a biblical decision, you must not waver just because others don't like it. Strongly evaluate your wife's input and concerns, but also remember, you will answer to God for how you lead. The more carefully you have made a decision the more confident you will be. A husband should not refuse to hear and consider new information (Proverbs 18:1-2), but he must always fear God rather than man. You must ask yourself what Paul asked himself:

> **For am I now seeking the favor of men, or of God? Or am I striving to please men? If I were still trying to please men, I would not be a bond-servant of Christ.**
> **Galatians 1:10**

It is hard to follow someone who doesn't seem to know what he is doing. If you are not careful and biblical about your decision-making, you will most likely change direction or change your decisions often. This instability does not give your wife confidence in your ability to lead. Granted, she still must follow and trust God's sovereignty, but in love you should make it as easy and enjoyable as possible for her to follow you.

Now It's Time To Practice

With a good understanding of the kind of leader God wants us to be and some practical ways to get the job done, the only thing left is for us to be doing it! We need to know our direction and goals. We need to know the areas in which to oversee and lead. We need to know how to make biblical decisions. Then, depending on God, we can work at becoming more and more like our faithful Shepherd-leader and Servant-leader, Jesus Christ. For the glory of God and the furtherance of His kingdom, we need to be exemplary in our leadership. Is your leadership in place and becoming more and more like Christ's?

Chapter Eleven

A HUSBAND'S RESPONSIBILITY
PHYSICAL INTIMACY

It is the responsibility of every husband to know and live out God's will in the area of physical intimacy. It has been reported (and I have no reason to doubt it) that 80% of counseling deals with marital problems. I would suggest that within this marital counseling 60-70% of the time sexual issues are a problem. Reading this chapter together with your wife can lead to some good communication about your physical relationship and will also help you keep what you are reading in the proper context of your marriage.

There are many couples who come for counseling who need help in this area of their marriage. I have tried to be biblically appropriate and straightforward in an effort to help couples glorify God and serve one another in their times of intimacy.

The Current Scene

Any husband who is exemplary in the sexual area will certainly be unique in our society. Our country has been in a moral decline over the past fifty years which has drastically affected our culture. The light of God's Word has been steadily dimmed by a society that desires to practice the deeds of darkness. Many are not even aware of just how dark the times have become until God's light breaks through. I believe that the most obvious expression of that darkness is the perversion of one of God's greatest blessings: physical intimacy.

Our culture has become so dark in the sexual realm that shame is often not even in the picture. A case in point is the whole matter of President Clinton's immoral behavior during 1998. For the most part, we live in a country that perceives Clinton's deception and gross immorality to be irrelevant to his leadership position. As recently as ten years ago, however, a senator was disqualified from the presidential race for being unfaithful to his wife. Even as I write, citizens in California are voting on whether or not homosexuals should have the right to marry legally. The other day I was sitting with my family watching a basketball game when a disturbing advertisement came on TV. The commercial began with what sounded like a woman experiencing sexual pleasure and then continued with the revelation that the woman was only washing her hair. The announcer proceeded to use sexual language such as "stimulated" and "climax" to convince the viewer of their need to buy the shampoo that the woman was using. Unfortunately, many advertisements today unashamedly have an immoral element to them.

Society has moved so far from what God intended that, for many, physical intimacy is merely a means to selfish pleasure. This selfishness often causes problems even in Christian marriages. To God, physical intimacy is a sacred and beautiful thing (Song of Solomon). The only way to unscramble the sexual confusion in which we find ourselves is to understand and live by God's principles.

As a husband who desires to be like Christ, you must have God's perspective on sex in marriage. You can bring glory to God as you fulfill His intentions in this area and show true love to your wife.

If a husband understands the proper purpose and focus of sex in marriage it can have a far-reaching effect on the marriage relationship. This is not to say that a right understanding of sex is the answer to all marital discord. In fact, the sexual relationship is often a barometer for the soundness of the marriage relationship in general. Getting God's perspective on physical intimacy will not solve other specific problems that need to be dealt with in the marriage, but it *will* go a long way in communicating love to your wife. Certainly, applying God's principles to the sexual area will only improve physical intimacy between a husband and wife.

Six Biblical Principles of Sexual Intimacy For Husbands

1. Sexual intimacy in marriage was instituted by God; therefore it can be pure and holy and should be enjoyed.

God is the one who instituted sexual relations. He did this in the garden with Adam and Eve when He commanded them to become one and blessed them saying, "Be fruitful and multiply" (Genesis 1:28). We have already established (in Chapter 5) that becoming one means *more* than just the physical union, but it *does* include it (1 Corinthians 6:16). Everything God does is holy. Everything He tells us to do is right and good. Even after the Fall, we are told that the marriage bed should not be defiled. It is adultery (sex with someone other than your spouse) and fornication (all sexual activity outside of marriage) that defiles it:

> **Marriage is to be held in honor among all, and the marriage bed is to be undefiled; for fornicators and adulterers God will judge.**
> **Hebrews 13:4**

The original Greek word for "bed" *(koite)* in this verse, clearly refers to sexual union and is where we get our word *coitus* (sexual intercourse). If the marriage bed is not defiled, then it is holy. Sex as God

145

intended is completely pure. If the heart is pure, intimacy in marriage is just as pure as anything else we do for God. It is as pure as prayer, praise, ministry, and giving. We just need to be sure our heart and actions at the time of physical intimacy are as pure as they are when we serve and worship God in other ways. Selfish sex is *not* pure sex.

Pleasure in sex is not sinful but rather assured and encouraged in Scripture. We have already learned that our Lord intends for us to enjoy everything He has given (1 Timothy 6:17). The Song of Solomon is a marvelous example of the sexual enjoyment God permits and encourages in the marriage relationship.

> **Let your fountain be blessed, and rejoice in the wife of your youth. As a loving hind and a graceful doe, let her breasts satisfy you at all times; be exhilarated always with her love.**
> **Proverbs 5:18-19**

It is sex with the wrong person, for the wrong purpose, and/or with the wrong thinking that makes it unholy. Some men's minds have been significantly affected by their past sexual involvement or the sexual corruption that is all around us. The more we take our thoughts captive and view physical intimacy the way God does, the more we will enjoy it as the pure and wholesome act it was intended to be (2 Corinthians 10:5; Philippians 4:8).

2. Sexual intimacy in marriage should be kept in perspective.

Sex should not be the basis for any marriage. It should only be an aspect of the marriage. We have already seen that there are other more important purposes for marriage. Commitment, oneness, and companionship are the foundation of a good marriage. Husbands must not make physical intimacy more important than it should be. If sex is a consuming thing, something is seriously wrong. If your relationship revolves mostly around the physical, the physical is too important.

As your wife's companion and shepherd, you need to delight in *her person* as well as in her body (Proverbs 31:28-30). A wife is usually quite aware of a wrong perspective. She can feel very much like an object

3 reasons

being used for self-gratification if a husband is consumed with his passions and not delighting in who she is. Even though the media encourages the exploitation of women, we Christian men need to have a very different perspective.

Sexual intimacy *is important* for three reasons. The first two are weightier than the third. They are to fulfill oneness (Genesis 2:24) and to fulfill the desires of one's partner (1 Corinthians 7:3-5), so as not to be vulnerable to temptation. I say these two reasons are weightier because they are related to direct commands in the Bible. The third reason is to partake of the wonderful blessing of children (Genesis 1:28). Certainly this reason is important, but it is not connected with any specific command (see Chapter 5: "A Husband's Understanding of Marriage," under the point of "Procreation").

3. Sexual intimacy in marriage should not be self-focused.

The right focus during sexual intimacy is the other person—your wife. The sexual realm is just another area that we must apply the selfless love and servanthood we discussed earlier (1 Corinthians 13:5). This is the mindset that God wants us to have at all times. The amazing thing is, when we give the way we should, we also benefit as a byproduct. It is always "more blessed to give than it is to receive" (Acts 20:35). Both husband and wife should be seeking to please the other person in their times of intimacy. God has commanded husbands and wives to serve one another in this way:

> **The husband must fulfill his duty to his wife, and likewise also the wife to her husband.**
> **1 Corinthians 7:3**

Some husbands are quick to point out that sexual satisfaction is due them, but not that it is due the wife as well. It is interesting that God even mentions the husband's duty first.

Having the main goal of pleasing and satisfying your wife first and foremost can revolutionize your times of intimacy. This unselfish focus is real love in action. What's more, you will enjoy the sex act more fully and in the right way.

Because of God's command to fulfill the desires of one another, both husband and wife can initiate sex and should seek to satisfy the other person completely and enthusiastically. The word "satisfy" in Proverbs 5:19 means to "satiate" or "to intoxicate." There are a few Christian resources that can be helpful in learning how better to please your wife. Of course your first source (which may be enough) should be your wife. Work hard to have the kind of open and honest communication that will allow her to share her desires with you. The bulk of what follows in this chapter is a summary of the common knowledge that you will find in most Christian resources. It is intended to help both you and your wife discuss key issues of your physical relationship. In addition, it should encourage you to sincerely pursue a Christlike (others) mindset in the sexual realm. To be a husband who sincerely has his wife in mind you will:

- *Investigate and discuss the sexual desires of your wife.* Ask your wife questions about her desire. Discuss and learn to sense *how frequent* and *how strong* her desire may be. Most wives have more desire at certain times of the month. There are some women who have stronger and more frequent desire than their husbands. There are some women who have very little desire. Most women can be brought to a place of strong desire by their husband's efforts, even if they initially have none. It is a good idea to set aside some uninterrupted time to talk about these things. Both husband and wife should work through any embarrassment. The more you talk about this perfectly holy and natural part of your lives, the more at ease you will become.

- *Investigate the likes and dislikes of your wife.* As many resources indicate, most women enjoy eye contact, loving words, kissing, holding and caressing very much. Naturally, your wife will enjoy the complete fulfillment of her desires. Still, ask your wife to be as specific as possible about what she really likes. Also, assure her that she can be honest about things she dislikes. Then of course, stop doing them! A husband and wife should seek to determine what is mutually enjoyable. I am not saying, however, that a spouse should only participate in what they, themselves, like very much. Both husband and wife should be willing to serve by doing things that don't necessarily excite them. But you <u>should not</u> do something nor ask your wife to do something that you know she very much dislikes. This is thinking only of yourself.

- *Be humble enough to learn.* Bringing pleasure to your spouse is a learned skill! You can learn some things from the Bible (Song of Solomon) and other Christian books, but the best source is your wife. A husband and wife should never be too proud to be told what they are doing is wrong or even to have their hand guided to the right place. Let your wife help you learn what is best for her without getting defensive.

- *Make personal hygiene a priority.* Cleanliness or the lack of it can greatly affect your wife's enjoyment of intimacy. Showering (*at least* the day of), brushing your teeth, and being clean shaven (as opposed to the prickly-pear condition of yesterday's shave) will demonstrate consideration and avoid creating a major turn-off for your wife. It is difficult for a wife to be enthusiastic about a close encounter with bad body odor! It is nothing short of rude to ignore these seemingly small matters. If a husband is thinking of his wife, he will strive to be at his best and not his worst for physical intimacy. The various smells in Song of Solomon are appealing, not appalling (chapters 4-7).

- *Only request or do what is approved by both consciences (husband and wife) and what is not physically harmful.* It is fine for couples to experiment with new ways to bring pleasure to their spouses. Still, it is good to communicate about anything that is unusual or drastic. It is never loving to request (and certainly not to insist) that a spouse participate in anything that you know violates his or her conscience. Never use the manipulative line, "Well, if you love me, you will..." Even though certain practices are not expressly prohibited by Scripture, some people may associate a particular practice with a lifestyle of sin. Others may have always assumed that they are ungodly practices. Regardless, both the husband's and wife's consciences need to be completely clear on a matter before participating. It is also a violation of biblical principles to do anything that is harmful to either body (e.g., anal sex). Love does not harm and we should take care of the body God has given us. Anything that does not repulse either partner, does not violate either conscience and does no harm to either body can be heartily enjoyed (Romans 14:23; 1 Corinthians 6:19-20).

- *Seek to fulfill the desires of your wife even if you do not have the desire to be satisfied.* In 1 Corinthians 7:4, Paul tells the wife that she "does not have authority over her own body, but the husband does." He also says that "the husband does not have authority over his own body, but the wife does." This verse instructs us that our bodies should be available to our spouse whenever possible. We must not think only of our interests (Philippians 2:2-3). This verse also makes it clear again that both husband and wife can and should initiate sex.

  If we know that our spouse is desirous, we should offer our bodies in love. This goes for the husband who has already been sexually satisfied, leaving him extremely tired and no longer interested. Whether it is the husband or the wife who has no desire, the offer to please the other should be made in all sincerity. If the other spouse wills to be pleased, the one with no desire should do his or her very best to be totally involved for the sake of the other spouse. This is real love. There are probably few things worse to a husband or a wife than to have their spouse go through the motions while they are clearly not engaging their mind (heart) in the process. Ask God for His help to be committed to pleasing your spouse at all times.

- *Not use your own body to gratify yourself.* A man who gratifies himself (masturbates) is being self-focused. This act is clearly not the right use of our intimate parts. Our bodies are not meant to serve us, but God and our wife (1 Corinthians 7:4; 1 Corinthians 13:5). Another reason masturbation is wrong is because it usually involves engaging in lustful thoughts (Philippians 4:8). A third reason is that is becomes a very enslaving activity (1 Corinthians 6:12). Finally, it removes any need of self-control in the sexual area (1 Corinthians 7:1-2; Galatians 5:22-23).

4. Sexual intimacy should be the culmination of a loving relationship.

The sex act should be a picture of the love and commitment that is already present in the marriage relationship; the icing on the cake, so to speak. This is one of the main reasons why other marriage problems often affect physical intimacy. Physical intimacy itself should be a relational experience (Song of Solomon). This aspect of the physical relationship is something that we men typically have to work at since sexual pleasure is usually attained easily by us. Women, on the other hand, are typically much more interested in the relational aspect of the sex act. The exemplary husband will seek to maintain a loving relationship with his wife and make physical intimacy the relational experience it should be.

Some suggested ways to make intimacy more relational:

*   Seek to quickly resolve conflict and work out other marriage problems in a biblical way.
*   Regularly speak words of appreciation and say, "I love you."
*   Regularly show her affection that is non-sexual.
*   Approach physical intimacy in a tender and relational way (spend enjoyable time together beforehand, if possible).
*   Purposefully think thoughts of love and appreciation during physical intimacy.
*   Express words of love and appreciation during physical intimacy.

5. Sexual excitement seems to happen differently for men and women.

You may be well aware of the fact that sexual excitement comes about very differently for men and women. God has made us different. Usually men are quickly aroused by sight and can be ready in a moment to engage in the sex act. Our passion can react much like a match to kindling wood (to some, it's like gunpowder)! Sometimes the mere mention of the possibility has one steaming! We can also be ready for sex simply because it has been a while since the last fulfillment. Unlike many women, our desires can build when sex with our wives is infrequent. For the most part, we are set on "go," and our desires are inhibited by very little.

On the other hand, women are typically aroused by touch, rather than by sight. More time is typically needed as well. To use a helpful analogy, their passion works more like an oven that must be preheated. It has been documented that many women have to think about the prospect of sex for a while, before they have any physical reaction. A woman may have difficulty being aroused if she is tired, slightly ill, troubled by something, or even just distracted by noise. It would be interesting if we could get inside the head of a man and woman and see the difference in their thoughts about their times of intimacy together. A woman would most likely be thinking in terms of romance and touch, while a man might be thinking in terms of passion and sight.

These differences between men and women should not be cause for any offense. Instead, they should be accepted as amoral (neither right nor wrong) and they should help us be understanding during physical intimacy. A husband should not automatically take his wife's slower arousal as a rejection of his love or a reflection of his abilities. Likewise, a wife should not automatically take a husband's quick readiness as a sign of shallowness, insensitivity or a lack of love. Men and women must learn to appreciate the differences that God has given them. This does not mean that we should not pursue ways to narrow differences a bit for enjoyment's sake. But we need to understand that differences are not necessarily a matter of right or wrong, and not necessarily a matter of a spouse's love. It's just how God has made us.

Having said all that, God has also made us all individuals. There are varying degrees of these differences and sometimes a reversal of the typical tendencies. Couples may be able to lessen differences through the way they approach or perform intimacy, or by consulting with their physician.

The goal of a loving spouse will be to bring the other person as much pleasure as possible. This means that one partner will seek to bring the other partner along in their desires. Sexual intimacy is certainly more enjoyable for a spouse if he or she is experiencing physical desire as well. If similarity of desire is not achievable, the spouse with the lesser desires should still seek to fulfill those of the other person as an act of love (Proverbs 5:15-19).

A husband should bring his wife along in her desires according to how <u>her</u> body responds. This is a way that he can be understanding toward his wife (1 Peter 3:7).

<u>Your wife can usually be brought along in her desires in the following ways:</u>

- *Suggest physical intimacy in a loving way well in advance of the actual time.* Give her time to think about it. Even early in the day before an intimate evening is good for women with few desires.
- *Be personal, thoughtful, loving and gentle in your approach.* Women are not to be roughly and abruptly manhandled. Husband, you need to be as little like a ravenous beast as possible! Looking into your wife's eyes, and whispering sweet "somethings" into her ear will let her know that you care for her, and will help her to respond well.
- *Use self-control to calm yourself down in the beginning.* Control your thoughts (and your eyes if necessary) in the beginning. Perhaps it is best for your wife to remain covered initially. Focus on her pleasure and not your own. Wait as long as possible in order to reach fulfillment together or bring your wife to fulfillment first. You and your wife both will experience far more enjoyment if you do not reach fulfillment before she does.
- *Do what she really enjoys.* Hopefully your wife has communicated what is pleasurable. Many written sources indicate gentle caressing that gradually approaches the intimate parts will probably be very enjoyable to her (Song of Solomon 4-7). Still, husbands should not assume that caressing is enough to satisfy. Unless your wife communicates a lack of desire, always seek to bring her to <u>complete</u> fulfillment. Another common misunderstanding among husbands is that the mere sex act will automatically bring the wife to this complete point. In actuality, this is often not the case. If simultaneous fulfillment is not achievable, a husband can bring his wife to fulfillment manually (by hand).

Your patience is the key to your wife's enjoyment. Rushing the process will only prove counter-productive. Obviously, there may be occasions when time does not permit an extended time of physical intimacy. As we said earlier, some women are more easily aroused than others. There may be times when it is appropriate for the wife to forego her own satisfaction but still be willing to please her husband if he is desirous and time is short (however, not having enough time, men, ought to be the exception and not the rule). The husband can still seek to make the time as enjoyable as possible, especially by focusing on her and being relational. Of course, the husband should seek to fulfill his wife then as soon as he can. If at all possible, both husband and wife should be fulfilled during the same physical intimacy time.

It is important to mention that your wife may not always desire sexual completion. There should be communication with her on this issue. A wife may fully enjoy a time of intimacy with her husband without it. This fact is true when her desire is minimal. She can still enjoy being close with and pleasing her husband, as well as obtaining only a certain level of excitement. The wife, however, should be the one to decide to forego her satisfaction, not the husband for her.

6. Sexual intimacy should be regular.

The Bible is clear that we need to fulfill the desires of our spouse regularly and not deprive them.

> **Stop depriving one another, except by agreement for
> a time, so that you may devote yourselves to prayer,
> and come together again so that Satan will not tempt
> you because of your lack of self-control.**
> **1 Corinthians 7:5**

There is only one reason to abstain from satisfying the desires of one's spouse. This reason is for a specific time of prayer for a specific reason. Both partners must be in agreement about abstinence for godly purposes. We should be aware that Satan will use the sexual area to tempt either a husband or a wife to sin if he can. Great caution should be used before any decision to abstain. In fact, there needs to be a very positive and selfless perspective about physical intimacy. The thinking ought to be how often can we, rather than when must we.

A couple should also be aware that unless the frequency of the husband's fulfillment meets the general frequency of his desires, it can be very difficult for the husband to wait to please his wife first. This fact is especially true when there has been less practice in waiting as with a newly married young man. Therefore "keeping up" with the husband's desires will prove to be very helpful in the enjoyment and the satisfaction of the wife. Of course, understanding should be exercised when either spouse is virtually unable to meet the other spouse's desires due to sickness, surgery, travel or an emergency.

Enjoy What God Intended

In a society that has completely confused and degraded God's pure blessing of sexual intimacy, we must be different in our beliefs and practices. As exemplary husbands, we want our supreme love for God and our commitment to love our wife unselfishly to spill over into and flood the physical intimacy aspect of our marriages. In order to do this we must take selfish thoughts captive and replace them with loving thoughts while being focused on our wife's enjoyment. This focus will result in sincere efforts to fulfill the desires of our wife with fervor and joy. The sex act will then be the culmination of a loving relationship, rather than a means to gratify self. When a husband and wife have the right perspective of physical intimacy, they will enjoy it to the fullest and bring glory to God.

Chapter Twelve

A HUSBAND'S RESPONSIBILITY
STEWARDSHIP

There it is. The title of the sermon is "Stewardship", and you know instinctively that it is again that time of year when the pastor will shear God's sheep. To many people the word stewardship is synonymous with the words *giving, money,* and *finances*. But from God's perspective it is much more. There is a definite need for greater understanding of the *Stewardship Principle*.

The stewardship principle involves one's maturity and character. The presence of it or the lack of it has far-reaching effects on every husband's life. One of the chief complaints that I hear from wives in problem marriages is that the husband is not faithful concerning reasonable goals and his God-given responsibilities in their marriage and/or in their life in general.

Unless we as men learn to become faithful stewards, we will not be able to fulfill our responsibilities as a husband, and we will have many sins and failures with which to reckon. Good stewardship is a necessary path toward usefulness to God and His kingdom.

A Working Definition

Stewardship and steward are not commonly used words today. A "steward" is defined in the Webster's dictionary as a person who manages or attends to another's property or financial affairs. In the Bible, the Greek word for steward is *oikonomos*, meaning a house distributor, an overseer, a manager, or an employee or agent in that capacity. Being a steward is actually being a servant to someone else and someone else's interests.

Herein lies our biggest problem as men and women of this age. Pride and selfishness often stand in the way of being concerned with someone else's interests, and stand in the way of recognizing that what I have is not "mine"! We tend to have a very strong, *and wrong*, sense of ownership about those things that have been *merely* entrusted to us. When we think of the gifts God has given us (including our wives) as our own and for our own benefit, we may wrongly conclude that we can decide what our responsibility is or is not concerning them. We may think that we have the right to do with these gifts as we please.

> **The earth is the Lord's, and all it contains, the world,**
> **and those who dwell in it.**
> **Psalm 24:1**

In actuality, God has made it very clear that no one has anything unless He has given it or allows it (1 Corinthians 4:7). God owns all things and has control over all things (Colossians 1:16). Because He has authority over them, He can require faithfulness. God says that every steward should be faithful in the handling of what he has been given.

> **In this case, moreover, it is required of stewards that**
> **one be found trustworthy.**
> **1 Corinthians 4:2**

Faithfulness will be rewarded. There are many natural rewards to faithfulness. For example, living with your wife in an understanding way will naturally result in a better relationship with her than if you live with her in a harsh or an inconsiderate way. Also, God says that He will personally reward faithfulness when we reach heaven. The rewards we receive will be determined by our level of faithfulness to His commands.

> Each man's work will become evident; for the day will
> show it because it is to be revealed with fire, and the
> fire itself will test the quality of each man's work. If
> any man's work which he has built on it remains, he
> will receive a reward.
>
> **1 Corinthians 3:13-14**

With all these things in mind, we can define biblical stewardship in this way:

> **Managing, maintaining, and making the most of all
> God has entrusted to us for the furtherance of His
> interests, as we look forward to future reward.**

What Has God Entrusted to You?

God has graciously given you many things. He desires that you enjoy these things and be blessed by them (1 Timothy 6:17). However, along with each thing God has given, He requires faithfulness according to *His* standards, not man's. Your faithfulness is based on your obedience to God's Word (1 Samuel 15:22). In all of the areas in which God has blessed you, He has also given you clear instructions to follow. What has God entrusted to you?

You are a steward of	But they are
• Your wife	God's, on loan
• Your children	God's, on loan
• Your brothers and sisters in Christ	God's, on loan
• Your money	God's, on loan
• Your possessions	God's, on loan
• Your time	God's, on loan
• Your talents and abilities	God's, on loan
• Your physical body	God's, on loan
• Your spiritual gift(s)	God's, on loan
• Your ministry	God's, on loan

God's Word has made it clear that you are merely a steward of these things. Yes, He has given you these things to enjoy, *but only as you use them to accomplish His purposes.* The things He has given to us are *primarily* for God's glory and the good of others, not self (1 Corinthians 10:31; Galatians 5:13). A selfish focus will always result in a lack of faithfulness. How do you view the things God has given you?

We must take our responsibility concerning all of God's gifts very seriously. Let's look at how seriously God takes our faithfulness in just one of these areas. God has given us our families. With this gift comes many responsibilities. The responsibility to provide for your family is just one of those responsibilities. What does God say about the one who is lazy and/or irresponsible and does not work hard in order to provide for his family?

> **But if anyone does not provide for his own, and espe-**
> **cially for those of his household, he has denied the**
> **faith and is worse than an unbeliever.**
> **1 Timothy 5:8**

Every command that God has given concerning the gifts that He has entrusted to us is a serious matter (1 John 2:4). Some men will be very disappointed at the end of this life when most of what they have lived for will be burned up (1 Corinthians 3:13-15). All that will remain are those things that have been done for Christ. One day we all will give an account concerning our lives and our faithfulness.

> **So then each one of us will give an account of himself**
> **to God.**
> **Romans 14:12**

Futility's Remedy

For the believer, usefulness is God's reason for leaving us here rather than bringing us home to heaven (Philippians 1:21-25). God intends for every believer to be fruitful (2 Peter 1:8). Uselessness, how-ever, leads to futility.

> **All that my eyes desired I did not refuse them. I did**
> **not withhold my heart from any pleasure, for my heart**
> **was pleased because of all my labor and this was my**

reward for all my labor. Thus I considered all my activities which my hands had done and the labor which I had exerted, and behold all was vanity and striving after wind and there was no profit under the sun.
Ecclesiastes 2:10-11

Many men reach a time in their lives when they are discontented and disillusioned with life as they know it, especially in their marriages. Some become completely overwhelmed with a sense of futility. As a result, they may seek to change their lives in drastic ways. A total change in appearance, a new sports car and a new woman, unfortunately, are not merely cliches. The world refers to this time as "the mid-life crisis." In actuality these actions are usually the end result of a lack of faithfulness to God, to their wives and to the right goals in life. An exemplary husband will have the right goals and seek to apply them faithfully in his marriage as well as in all that God has given him. These right goals can be summed up as walking with God and bringing Him glory (2 Corinthians 5:9). Are these *your* goals in life and in your marriage?

A Bit of Hope

We must remember that God is willing to give us the grace (help) that is needed to learn faithfulness (Hebrews 4:14-16). He knows that faithfulness will be a process of growth. We *are* being faithful if we are actively pursuing faithfulness. However, we must acknowledge in humility that we cannot do it on our own (John 15:5). We must ask God to teach us and to help us carry out His will. God will be faithful to do this if we are sincere about our desire to walk according to His word (Psalm 27:4-5,8-9).

As we depend on God to do His part we must also prayerfully do our part. Our part is to rid ourselves of any hindrances to good stewardship and to commit ourselves to work diligently toward faithfulness. Ridding ourselves of the hindrances means doing battle with our flesh (our self outlook and independent attitude that does not want to follow God's ways; Romans 8:13; Galatians 5:16). We must be watchful of Satan's schemes to entice our flesh (1 Peter 5:8). Most of all, we must be ready to deny the flesh even when it is painful to do so..

Beloved, I urge you as aliens and strangers to abstain
from fleshly lusts which wage war against the soul.
1 Peter 2:11

Putting Off the Hindrances to Faithfulness

All of the obstacles to faithfulness are fleshly sins that we need to put off. These sins will stand in the way of bringing God glory, of allowing us to be useful, and of our receiving heavenly reward.

That, in reference to your former manner of life, you
lay aside the old self, which is being corrupted in
accordance with the lusts of deceit.
Ephesians 4:22

PUT OFF:	
Sin	*Evidences*
• **Pride**	• Not being dependent on God's help.
	• Not being teachable concerning stewardship areas.
	• Being defensive when approached about unfaithfulness.
	• Not searching God's Word, seeking godly counsel, or getting input from your wife concerning stewardship areas because of a "know-it-all" or "I'm fine" mentality.
	• Giving a false appearance of faithfulness around others.
Before destruction the heart of man is haughty, but humility goes before honor. **Proverbs 18:12**	

- **Selfishness**
  - Caring more about your own desires and preferences than about God's desires and others' needs or wants.

  Do nothing from selfishness or empty conceit, but with humility of mind regard one another as more important than yourselves; do not merely look out for your own personal interests, but also for the interests of others.
  Philippians 2:3-4

- **Idolatry**
  - Sacrificing faithfulness to acquire or serve something that you worship.

  Little children, guard yourselves from idols.
  1 John 5:21

- **Laziness**
  - Not wanting to work at faithfulness.

  - Only doing what is required if it's not hard or you're not tired.

  - Choosing to relax, or sleep rather than to do what you know you should do (when you are able to do it).

  - Procrastination.

  The soul of the sluggard craves and gets nothing, but the soul of the diligent is made fat.
  Proverbs 13:4

- **Irresponsibility**
  - Not being dependable; not keeping your word.

  - Choosing recreation, entertainment, or what you prefer to do instead of what is responsible and faithful.

- Wastefulness.

- Being late (without legitimate reason).

- Not thinking through God's priority that we do good works.

Like a bad tooth and an unsteady foot is confidence in a faithless man in times of trouble.
Proverbs 25:19

- **Man-pleasing**
  - "Keeping the peace" at all cost.
  - Not doing what God wants because some one else may not like it, which may result in conflict or not being accepted or liked.

For am I now seeking the favor of men, or of God? Or am I striving to please men? If I were still trying to please men, I would not be a bond-servant of Christ.
Galatians 1:10

Steps Toward Faithfulness

Once we desire to be the steward God wants us to be, there are some steps we can take to grow in faithfulness. We must put on what is right.

And put on the new self, which in the likeness of God has been created in righteousness and holiness of the truth.
Ephesians 4:24

The first step, of course, is to take stewardship as seriously as God does. It is also important to understand that we must do battle with the flesh in putting on, as well as putting off. You must not follow your selfish feelings or your sinful desires but do what you know is right.

For the flesh sets its desire against the Spirit, and the Spirit against the flesh; for these are in opposition to one another, so that you may not do the things that you please. . . . Now those who belong to Christ Jesus have crucified the flesh with its passions and desires.
Galatians 5:17, 24

We should be aware that beginning to put on faithfulness will not be easy, but it will be rewarding. Here are at least six steps you can take toward putting on faithfulness:

PUT ON:	
Righteousness	*Evidences*
1. **Repentance**	• Pinpoint an area that God has entrusted to you in which you know you need to be more faithful.
	• Begin to search God's Word and seek godly counsel (including your spouse if she is biblically minded) concerning this area.
	Search me, O God, and know my heart; try me and know my anxious thoughts; and see if there be any hurtful way in me, and lead me in the everlasting way. **Psalm 139:23-24**
2. **Study**	• Study and meditate daily on Scriptures that pertain to this area.
	How can a young man keep his way pure? By keeping it according to Your word. With all my heart I have sought You; do not let me wander from Your commandments. Your word I have treasured in my heart, that I may not sin against You. **Psalm 119:9-11**

3. **Prayer**	•	Pray daily that God will help you to change in this area.

Help, Lord, for the godly man ceases to be, for the faithful disappear from among the sons of men. They speak falsehood to one another; with flattering lips and with a double heart they speak.
Psalm 12:1,2

4. **Renewing your mind**	•	Determine what thinking you need to change.

And do not be conformed to this world but be transformed by the renewing of your mind
Romans 12:2a

5. **Planning**	•	Make a specific plan as to how you are going to follow God's principles (a put-off and put-on plan).

The night is almost gone and the day is at hand. Let us therefore lay aside the deeds of darkness, and put on the armor of light. Let us behave properly as in the day, not in carousing and drunkenness, not in sexual promiscuity and sensuality, not in strife and jealousy. But put on the Lord Jesus Christ, and make no provision for the flesh in regard to its lusts.
Romans 13:12-14

6. **Accountability**	•	Obtain accountability from a brother in Christ if you are not making consistent headway.

Brethren, even if anyone is caught in any trespass, you who are spiritual, restore such a one in a spirit of gentleness; each one looking to yourself, so that you too will not be tempted. Bear one another's burdens, and thereby fulfill the law of Christ.
Galatians 6:1-2

Time and Money

Two of the most common areas of difficulty involved in steward-ship are time and money. Managing them can be a very complex chal-lenge and our flesh will wage war against faithfulness in these areas. These areas are crucial because they can affect so many of the other areas. I would like to give some basic guidelines for handling the time and money you have been given.

Stewardship of Time

Being faithful with the time that God has allotted to you means that you will have certain biblical convictions about your time. It also means that you will seek to get a handle on how you should spend it.

Convictions we must have about time:

1. Our days are numbered by God and we will have a mortal end (Psalm 139:16; 90:12).
2. God wants us to spend regular time with Him alone in prayer and meditation of His Word (Matthew 14:23; Psalm 119:148).
3. We should seek to glorify God and be a witness for Him at all times (1 Corinthians 10:31; Act 1:8).
4. We need to make the most of the time we have been given for the glory of God, rather than be slothful (regularly idle) or waste the time God has given us on worthless things (Proverbs 24:30-34, Ephesians 5:15-16).
5. We should not live in chaos but plan our way (Proverbs 16:9a).
6. We have enough time to do what God wants us to do (Ephesians 2:10).
7. Every person needs to exercise the character quality of discipline in the use of his or her time. This means we must go against what we may or may not want to do in order to do what we should do (2 Peter1:5-6).
8. We should consider biblical principles when we plan our time and when we make decisions about what to do as we live, rather than go by our feelings or just take life as it comes (Joshua 1:8).
9. When we have to make choices about how to spend our time, we must consider the people and responsibilities God has given so as not to neglect any of them (1 Corinthians 4:2).

10. We must accept with contentment when God providentially redirects our steps (Proverbs 16:9b).
11. We should get godly counsel if we cannot seem to manage our time for the glory of God (Proverbs 15:22).
12. We should get accountability if we have major relearning to do in how we spend our time (Proverbs 18:1a; Galatians 6:1-2).

Getting a handle on the use of your time:

1. Using a weekly calendar, keep a record of how you actually spend your time for two weeks, then evaluate it or get someone else to help you evaluate it.
2. Make a list of responsibilities and commitments, then a list of your desires.
3. Expect the unexpected. Always allow yourself a buffer of 20-30% of your planned time for the unexpected.
4. Fill out a typical week's schedule and plug in your responsibilities, commitments and desires to see whether or not you have over committed yourself. Not everything has to be done on a weekly basis. You can use a single time slot for two or more things t h a t will be done on different weeks.
5. Use a schedule, even if it is simple, but be flexible if the Lord prov identially makes it impossible for you to follow it. Keep it if at all possible.
6. Have a method of reminding yourself and keeping track of things you need to plan (a note pad, a voice memo device, a dry erase board, etc.).
7. Before you say "yes," pray for wisdom to apply God's principles to the request. Learn to say "no" graciously when you know that there would be something else you are neglecting.
8. Control the phone, the computer, and the television so that you are hardworking and able to be faithful to your responsibilities.
9. Cut back on activities that have no spiritual or relational aspect to them so that your life can be consumed with your relationship with God, your wife and family, and your ministry to others.
10. Generally, don't let others or circumstances *dictate* your use of time. Follow God's principles. When something unexpected comes up, ask yourself, "Can it be done another time?" Or, "Should someone else do this?" If the unexpected thing is also a God-given responsibility, ask yourself, "If I do this now am I grossly neglecting another responsibility I had planned?" As a general

rule, plan to be faithful to the responsibilities God has given you and then keep them!

Stewardship of Finances

Being faithful with the money with which you have been entrusted means that you will have certain convictions about the area of finances. It also means that you will do what you can to get a handle on what you have, on what you can spend, and how you should spend money. There are some very helpful and practical worksheets Appendix Eight to help you act on the following convictions and manage your finances, should you need them.

Convictions we must have about money:

1. Trusting God is key to handling money issues
    (Matthew 6:25-34; Philippians 4:10-20).
    *   When there is a need the first thing we should do is pray.
    *   We should do all we can to provide for our family, be wise with our money, and then trust God for the future.
2. We should work hard to acquire money and items to give to God and to others (2 Corinthians 9:6-15; Ephesians 4:28; 2 Thessalonians 3:6-15). We need to give regularly, generously and cheerfully.
3. Because it is wise and prudent (not out of fear), we should save for the future and the unexpected (Proverbs 6:6-8).
4. It is important to make the most of what God has given us (Matthew 6:19-24; 2 Corinthians 8:7; 9:10-12).
5. We should not owe what we can not *realistically* pay off considering our income now and any emergency plans that are in place should our income end (Romans 13:6-8).
6. God wants us to be orderly (not chaotic) in our affairs (1 Corinthians 14:40; 1 Timothy 3:2).
7. We should be thankful for and content with whatever God has allotted us (1 Timothy 6:6-10).
8. We should ponder every purchase and financial decision to make sure it is in keeping with God's principles (1 Corinthians 10:31; 2 Corinthians 8:1-9:15).
    *   Wise: Can you really use it? How much will you use it?
    *   Unselfish: How can you use this purchase for God and others?
    *   Responsible: Can you afford it? Does it fit your budget?

- Responsible stewardship: Is it the best buy?
9. We should provide well for our immediate family and any parents who can not provide for themselves (Ephesians 5:29; 1 Timothy 5:8).
   - physical needs: food, clothing, shelter
   - medical insurance
   - life insurance—especially on you to provide at least during a transition time should you precede your family in death.
   - disability insurance
   - emergency cash
   - retirement
10. We should get wise counsel if we are not confident in how we are handling our finances (Proverbs 15:22).
11. We should get accountability if we have trouble in the areas of self-control or greed (Proverbs 18:1-2; Galatians 6:1-2).

Suggestions For Taking Control of Your Finances:

> **Know well the condition of your flocks, and pay attention to your herds; for riches are not forever, nor does a crown endure to all generations.**
> **Proverbs 27:23-24**

1. Know what you have and owe.
2. Devise a reasonable (in keeping with your income) budget for you and your family.
3. Track spending until you know where you are misspending and then again until you are confident that you are keeping your budget well.
4. Get out of debt.
5. Keep all receipts for at least two months and records of your income and your expenditures for five years (even if it is just by receipts, paychecks, and bills). There are several inexpensive computer programs you can use.
6. Own your home by age 65 or retirement.
7. Learn to spend less than you earn so you can give and have an emergency fund.
8. Never finance pleasure items.
9. Pay all your bills on time.
10. Look for additional ways to give.

Where The Rubber Meets the Road

Husband, are you seeking to be faithful with whom and with what God has entrusted to you? Are you seeking to invest the things He has given you in His kingdom, or do you want to spend them on your own pleasures (Matthew 6:19-20)? The exemplary husband knows that he has not been given his life, his family, his job, his possessions, or anything else merely for his own benefit but for the benefit of God and others. Being a faithful steward will result in God's glory, our usefulness, and our receiving great heavenly reward. Decide today which stewardship area needs the most attention in your life and commit yourself to working on it.

PART THREE

A HUSBAND'S RESOLVES

Fundamental Commitments of the Exemplary Husband

Chapter Thirteen

A HUSBAND'S RESOLVE
HUMILITY AND SERVICE

You may think that by now you have been sufficiently humbled as a husband. Not a chance, my friend! This is a topic we cannot visit too often. Believe me when I say that we have only touched on the life-producing topic of humility and its fruit.

It is probably safe to say that humility is the one character quality that will enable us to be all Christ wants us to be. We cannot come to God without it. We cannot love God supremely without it. We cannot be an effective witness for Christ without it. We cannot love and serve our wives without it. We cannot lead in a godly way without it. We cannot enjoy physical intimacy the way God intended without it. We cannot communicate properly without it. We cannot resolve conflict without it. We cannot deal with the sin of others rightly without it. We especially cannot resist sin without it. In short, we must embrace and live out humility in order to truly live and be who God means for us to be. It is for this reason that God exhorts us through Paul:

> **Therefore I, the prisoner of the Lord, implore you to walk in a manner worthy of the calling with which you have been called, with all humility and gentleness... .**
>
> **Ephesians 4:1-2**

The Enemy of Humility: Pride

You cannot have humility where pride exists. Pride is the opposite of humility and it is one of the most loathed sins in God's sight.

> **Everyone who is proud in heart is an abomination to the Lord; assuredly, he will not be unpunished.**
>
> **Proverbs 16:5**

Pride is the epidemic vice. It is everywhere and manifests itself in many ways. As much as we may hate to admit it, we all have pride, each and every one of us. The question is not, "Do I have it?" but, "Where is it?" and "How much of it do I have?" We all have the tendency to think too much *about* ourselves and too much of ourselves. Amy Carmichael once said, "Those who think too much of themselves don't think enough." Pride is evidence of foolishness and childishness. Charles Swindoll said, "The world's smallest package is a man wrapped up in himself." Here is what God says about the proud person:

> **Do you see a man wise in his own eyes? There is more hope for a fool than for him.**
>
> **Proverbs 26:12**

Andrew Murray said that pride is "the root of every sin and evil" [12] Murray is right—pride is the beginning of every sin. Despite the fact that it is so widespread, it is perplexing how little has been written on pride in recent years. To read very much on the subject of pride, one must read Puritan literature.

Throughout the Scriptures you see the pride of position (Matthew 23:6), ability (2 Chronicles 26:15-16), achievement (Daniel 4:22), wealth

(1 Timothy 6:17), possessions (Matthew 6:19), knowledge (Isaiah 47:10), learning (1 Corinthians 8:1), spiritual attainment (Luke 22:24), self-righteousness (Romans 10:3), being esteemed or liked (Galatians 1:10), and even pride of spiritual experiences (2 Corinthians 12:7). Our flesh has a bent toward pride. Pride is an easy snare for the devil to use. The Puritan Thomas Watson said, "It is a spiritual drunkenness; it flies up like wine into the brain and intoxicates it. It is idolatry; a proud man is a self-worshiper"[13] Some people try to hide their pride behind spiritual words and actions, but it is there nonetheless.

Some Biblical Terms

Six different Hebrew words are used for pride. All of them convey lifting up, highness, magnification, presumptuousness, or rebelliousness of self. In the Greek language, the words for pride occur in two different categories. One particular word group suggests the idea of "straining or stretching one's neck" (as if to hold one's head up high because of what one thinks he has made of himself or accomplished), "to magnify," or "to be haughty". The other category in the Greek conveys a "blindness" and even suggests the idea of being "enveloped with smoke." Throughout the Scriptures, in both the Greek and Hebrew languages, we find proud people portrayed as having a high view of themselves. While they are "up there" on high in their own thinking, they are blind! They are blinded to their pride, they are blinded to God's truth and, sometimes, even blinded to simple reality. The great Puritan Richard Baxter said, "... [pride is] so undiscerned by the most, that it is commonly cherished while it is commonly spoke against"[14] Biblical synonyms for pride are: vainglory, conceit, boasting, arrogance, loftiness, presumption, haughtiness, being puffed up, high-mindedness, scoffing, and self-seeking.

Some Biblical Examples

We never find the Scriptures saying, "Come on now, you're thinking too poorly of yourself" or "What you need is to consider yourself more." Instead, God has given us many stories and warnings to discourage this very thing. In essence, Scripture tells us to stop focusing on ourselves or on what we want. Illustration after illustration of pride appears in Scripture. The best example of the sin of pride is that of Satan. He voiced the mindset of every proud person when he questioned and denied God (Genesis 3:1-5). Uzziah served God for many years, growing prosperous, famous, and strong, "but when he became strong, his heart was so proud that he acted corruptly" (2 Chronicles 26:16). Nebuchadnezzar's arrogance ruined his life, until he humbled himself before the Most High, praising the One who "is able to humble those who walk in pride" (Daniel 4:37). Belshazzar failed to learn his father's lesson, exalting himself, rather than God, and was destroyed for his pride (Daniel 5:18-30). The Pharisee in Luke 18:10-14 ended up praying only to himself because he considered himself so superior and righteous. Other biblical examples of men who were ruined by their pride include King Saul (1 Samuel 18:7-9), King Herod (Acts 12), and Diotrephes (3 John 9).

We have been given many warnings about the desire to lift up self and serve self. It is also the natural inclination of pride to forget about God or want to be above God. God has been faithful to address the destructive sin of pride with verses like:

> **Pride goes before destruction, and a haughty spirit before stumbling.**
> **Proverbs 16:18**

> **Do nothing from selfishness or empty conceit, but with humility of mind regard one another as more important than yourselves; do not merely look out for your own personal interests, but also for the interests of others.**
> **Philippians 2:3-4**

A Definition of Pride

When someone is proud they are focused on self. This is a form of self-worship. A person is prideful who believes that they, in and of themselves, are or should be the *source* of what is good, right and worthy of praise. They, also believe that they, by themselves, are (or should be) the *accomplisher* of anything that is worthwhile to accomplish, and that they should certainly be the *benefactor* of all things. In essence, they are believing that all things should be *from* them, *through* them, and *to* them or *for* them. Pride is competitive toward others, and especially toward God. Pride wants to be on top. Thomas Watson is quoted to have said, "Pride seeks to ungod God." This phrase certainly describes the arrogant.

But what about those who are caught up in self-pity, who are self-absorbed with a sense of failure? This too is pride. They are just on the flip side of the pride "coin." People who are consumed with self-pity are focusing on their own selves too much. They are not concerned with the glory of God and with being thankful for what good gifts and talents the Lord has given them, but instead are focused on how they think they have gotten a "raw deal," or how they are not "as good as" someone else. Self-pitying people desperately *want* to be good, not for the glory of God, but for themselves. They *want* to do things for and by their own power and might for the personal recognition. They *want* everyone to serve them, like them, and approve of them. When these desires are not fulfilled, a prideful person will become even more inwardly focused and will continue a vicious cycle. The self-focused person who bemoans the fact that they are *not* what they desperately want to be (elevated and esteemed) should not be deceived by thinking they are not proud. Nothing could be further from the truth. To sum it all up, a proud person believes that life is all about *them*—their happiness, their accomplishments, and their worth. From our study we can put together a definition of pride that will help us evaluate our own desires and practices. Pride is:

> **The mindset of self (a master's mindset rather than that of a servant): a focus on self and the service of self, a pursuit of self-recognition and self-exaltation, and a desire to control and use all things for self.**

Manifestations of Pride

As we have said, pride is blinding. This fact is why it is often difficult to see pride in ourselves, and yet so easy to see it in others. Here is a sample list of pride manifestations that can easily clear away the smoke of any self-righteousness.

1. *Complaining against or passing judgment on God.* A proud person in a difficult situation thinks, "Look what God has done to *me after all* I have done *for Him*" (Numbers 14:1-4, 9,11; Romans 9:20).

2. *A lack of gratitude in general.* Proud people usually think they deserve what is good. The result is, they see no reason to be thankful for what they receive. As a matter of fact, they may even complain because they think they deserve better. They tend to be critical, complaining and discontent. The proud person is not in the practice of being thankful toward God or others (2 Chronicles 32:25).

3. *Anger.* A proud person is often an angry person. One's anger can include outbursts of anger, withdrawing, pouting, or frustration. A person most often becomes angry because his "rights" or expectations are not being met (Matthew 20:1-16).

4. *Seeing yourself as better than others.* A proud person is usually on top looking down on others. He gets easily disgusted and has little tolerance for differences (Luke 7:36-50).

5. *Having an inflated view of your importance, gifts and abilities.* Many proud people have a very wrong perception of themselves. They need a loving dose of reality. They need to hear, "What do you have that God didn't give you?" (1 Corinthians 4:7).

6. *Being focused on the lack of your gifts and abilities.* Some proud people may not come across proud at all, because they are always down on themselves. This is still evidence of pride because one is focused on self and wants self to be elevated. Having a "woe is me" attitude is self-pity, which is pride (1 Corinthians 12:14-25).

7. *Perfectionism.* People who strive for everything to be perfect often

do so for recognition. They may do it so they can feel good about themselves. Whatever the reason, this behavior is very self-serving and proud. The basic problem is making things that are less important, more important (Matthew 23:24-28).

8. *Talking too much.* Proud people who talk too much often do it because they think that what they have to say is more important than what anyone else has to say. When there are many words, sin is generally unavoidable (Proverbs 10:19).

9. *Talking too much about yourself.* A person who is proud may center on themselves in conversation. Sharing personal accomplishments and good personal qualities with others can be bragging or boasting (Proverbs 27:2; Galatians 6:3).

10. *Seeking independence or control.* Some proud people find it extremely difficult to work under someone else or to submit to an authority. They have to be their own boss. They might say, "I don't need anyone," or "I don't need accountability for my faith and doctrine." They are often rigid, stubborn, headstrong, and intimidating. They may also say, "It's my way or no way" (1 Corinthians 1: 10-13; Ephesians 5:21).

11. *Being consumed with what others think.* Some proud people are too concerned about the opinion of others. Many of their decisions are based on what others might think. Some are in a continual pursuit of gaining the approval and esteem of others. Focusing on what others think of you or trying to impress others is being a man-pleaser rather than a God-pleaser (Galatians 1:10).

12. *Being devastated or angered by criticism.* Proud people usually struggle a great deal with criticism. Such people cannot bear that they are not perfect or have weaknesses because they cannot accept who they really are (Proverbs 13:1).

13. *Being unteachable.* Many proud individuals know it all. They're superior. They can't seem to learn anything from someone else. They respect no one (Proverbs 19:20; John 9:13-34).

14. *Being sarcastic, hurtful, or degrading.* Proud people can be very unkind people. Those who belittle other people usually want to

raise themselves up above others. Very often this can be quite clev-
erly done through jesting. They may excuse themselves by saying,
"That's just the way I am. That's my personality" (Proverbs 12:18, 23).

15. *A lack of service.* Proud people may not serve because they are not
thinking of others, or because they want to be coaxed to serve and
don't want to continue if there is no praise. Needing recognition
is a sure sign of the wrong motives in service (Galatians 5:13;
Ephesians 2:10).

16. *A lack of compassion.* A person who is proud is rarely concerned for
others and their concerns. They cannot see beyond their own
desires (Matthew 5:7; 18:23-35).

17. *Being defensive or blame-shifting.* You will often hear a proud person
say, "Are you saying it's *my* fault?" or "Well, what about you?"
(Genesis 3:12-13; Proverbs 12:1).

18. *A lack of admitting when you are wrong.* A proud person will make a
great many excuses such as, "I was tired," or "I was having a bad
day" (Proverbs 10:17).

19. *A lack of asking forgiveness.* Proud people rarely admit their sin or
ask for forgiveness of others. They either cannot see their sin
because they are blinded by their pride, or they just can't seem to
humble themselves before someone else and ask forgiveness
(Matthew 5:23-24).

20. *A lack of biblical prayer.* Most proud people pray very little, if at all.
Proud people who do pray usually center their prayers on themselves and their desires, rather than God and others (Luke 18:10-14).

21. *Resisting authority or being disrespectful.* A proud person may detest
being told what to do. We might say he or she has a submission
problem. What they actually have, however, is a pride problem. It
is simply displaying itself in a lack of submission (1 Peter 2:13-17).

22. *Voicing preferences or opinions when not asked.* A proud person might
not be able to keep his preferences or opinions to himself. He will

offer it when it is not asked for. These preferences are usually voiced without consideration for others (Philippians 2:1-4).

23. *Minimizing your own sin and shortcomings.* A proud person typically believes that their sin is no big deal. They think they have a little sin and others have a great deal of it (Matthew 7:3-5).

24. *Maximizing others' sin and shortcomings.* To the proud person, other people are the problem. They may magnify or bring attention to the sin of others by gossiping about the other's sin (Matthew 7:3-5; Luke 18:9-14).

25. *Being impatient or irritable with others.* A proud person might be angry with other people because they are concerned that their own schedule or plans are being ruined. They are often inflexible on preference issues (Ephesians 4:31-32).

26. *Being jealous or envious.* Often when they do not enjoy the same benefits, proud people have a hard time being glad for other's successes or blessings (1 Corinthians 13:4).

27. *Using others.* The proud person usually views others in terms of what those people can do for *them* and *their* interests. Their focus is not on ministering to others. Everything is *for them* and *about them* (Matthew 7:12; Philippians 2:3-4).

28. *Being deceitful by covering up sins, faults, and mistakes.* Some proud people will do just about anything in order for others not to find out negative things about them (Proverbs 11:3; 28:13).

29. *Using attention-getting tactics.* A proud person may try to draw attention to themselves through dress, bizarre behavior, being rebellious, always talking about their problems, etc. (1 Peter 3:3-4).

30. *Not having close relationships.* Proud people often have no use for close relationships, thinking that the trouble outweighs the benefits. They may see themselves as so self-sufficient that they do not need other people (Proverbs 18:1-2; Hebrews 10:24-25).

Here is a way that we can picture our definition and manifestations of pride:

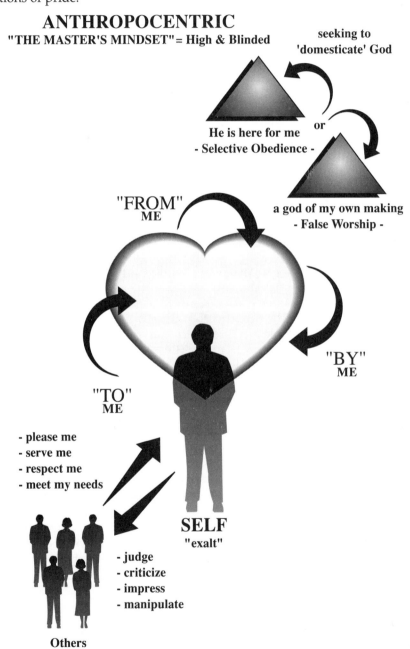

ANTHROPOCENTRIC
"THE MASTER'S MINDSET" = High & Blinded

seeking to 'domesticate' God

He is here for me
- Selective Obedience -

or

a god of my own making
- False Worship -

"FROM"
ME

"BY"
ME

"TO"
ME

- please me
- serve me
- respect me
- meet my needs

SELF
"exalt"

- judge
- criticize
- impress
- manipulate

Others

184

The Attribute of Humility

If pride is the epidemic vice, then humility is the endangered virtue. Humility is so rare because it is unnatural to man. Only a Christian who has the spirit of God can learn humility. The more we learn humility, the more our lives will change. Just as pride is the root of every evil, humility is the root of every virtue.

There are several Old Testament terms translated *humility* or *humble*. Mostly they refer to the action of *bowing low* or *crouching down*. This is what we should do in our hearts. In the New Testament, there are two words used, one meaning *servile, base* or *groveling* and the other meaning *gentle, meek* or *yielding*. These attitudes were very negative concepts in the Greek culture, but Christ revealed them to be virtues.

Our Greatest Example

Of all the biblical examples of humility, the greatest by far is the example of Christ Himself. Christ's very coming to earth was an amazing act of humility. Try to imagine what Christ had in heaven—glory, honor, pure worship and majesty. Then read in Philippians how He humbled Himself:

> **Who, although He existed in the form of God, did not regard equality with God a thing to be grasped, but emptied Himself, taking the form of a bond-servant, and being made in the likeness of men... He humbled Himself by becoming obedient to the point of death, even death on a cross.**
> **Philippians 2:6-8**

Jesus described himself as "meek and lowly in heart" (Matthew 11:29, KJV). Certainly, He knew when to be firm and when to rebuke others for God's glory (Matthew 23), but He was truly humble of heart. While Christ was here on earth, He was in complete submission to the Father's will, even though He Himself was God (John 4:34; 8:28-29). He was devoted to glorifying God (John 17:1, 4). Christ became the servant of men and taught His disciples to do the same (John 13:3-17):

**"For even the Son of Man did not come to be served,
but to serve, and to give His life a ransom for many."
Mark 10:45**

Jesus' perspective is very different from the thinking people often have. In our society, the *first* or the one who is lifted up is the greatest. According to Jesus, however, the *least* is the greatest. The humblest person is the greatest person of all (Mark 10: 43-44). This means that the proud person is last in God's eyes. Jesus' life is just the opposite of what is valued today. God's Word tells us that we must have the perspective of Christ, rather than that of the world (Romans 12:2).

One of Christ's greatest displays of humility was, of course, His act of washing the disciples' feet (John 13:1-17). Though He was God, He wrapped the servant's towel around His waist and cleaned the dirt and perspiration off men's feet. You would think that one could not get any lower than that. And yet, Christ's most amazing demonstration of humility and service was the suffering and death He endured on behalf of sinners like you and me. Since Almighty God was willing to stoop so low and serve mankind in life and in death, we should, therefore, be willing to place ourselves below others. Let's pick up the towel and the basin!

Other Biblical Examples

Other examples of humility in Scripture abound. Abraham gave Lot the first choice when they parted company and divided the land (Genesis 13). Moses is said to be "more humble than anyone else on the face of the earth" (Numbers 12:3). John the Baptist acknowledged that he was not worthy to untie Christ's sandals (Luke 3:16). Mary, the mother of Jesus, submitted herself completely to God's will saying, "Behold the bondslave of the Lord; may it be done to me according to Your word" and "My soul exalts the Lord ... for He has had regard for the humble state of His bondslave" (Luke 1:38, 46, 48). The tax collector beat his breast and prayed, "God, be merciful to me, the sinner" (Luke 18:13). The Apostle Paul was one of the greatest New Testament examples of humility. He told the Ephesian elders, "I was ... serving the Lord with all humility and with tears" (Acts 20:18-19). Paul also referred to himself as, the "chief" of sinners, and the "least of all saints" (1 Timothy 1:15 KJV; Ephesians 3:8). Paul had a right perspective of who he was in respect to God. He said:

> Oh, the depth of the riches both of the wisdom and
> knowledge of God! How unsearchable are His judg-
> ments and unfathomable His ways! For who has
> known the mind of the Lord, or who became His
> counselor? Or who has first given to Him that it might
> be paid back to him again? For from Him and
> through Him and to Him are all things. To Him be the
> glory forever. Amen.
>   Romans 11:33-36

A Definition of Humility

When someone is humble they are focused on God and others, not self. Even their focus on others is out of a desire to love and glorify God. They have no need to be recognized or approved. There is no competition with God or others. They have no need to elevate self, knowing that they have been forgiven and that God's love has been undeservedly and irrevocably set on them. Instead, a humble person's goal is to elevate God and encourage others. In short, they "no longer live for themselves, but for Him who died and rose again on their behalf" (2 Corinthians 5:15). From these truths we can put together a simple definition of humility:

> The mindset of Christ (a servant's mindset): a focus on
> God and others, a pursuit of the recognition and the
> exaltation of God, and a desire to glorify and please
> God in all things and by all things He has given.

Manifestations of Humility

A humble person lives differently than a proud one. How does your life measure up in the area of humility? Here is a sample list to help you evaluate how humble you are.

1. *Recognizing and trusting God's character.* A humble person acknowledges Who God is and rehearses God's character often. Because he does this, he trusts God much more than the proud person. In trials, he will even thank God for the reminder of how much he needs Him and for all the good He is doing through the trial (Psalm 119:66).

2. *Seeing yourself as having no right to question or judge an Almighty and Perfect God.* A humble man thinks of God as his Creator and himself as God's creation. He does not see himself as even remotely qualified to pass judgement on God or what God does. He knows that his perfect and all-wise God can do whatever He pleases, and it will be the best for him (Psalm 145:17; Romans 9:19-23).

3. *Focusing on Christ.* The humble see Christ as their life and their first love. There is no other thing or person that they *must* have. Through the day they talk to and worship Him often (Philippians 1:21; Hebrews 12:1-2).

4. *Biblical praying and a great deal of it.* Humble people want to worship God and they see themselves as totally dependent on God for His enablement. John Owen once said, "We can have no power from Christ unless we live in a persuasion that we have none of our own." Because they see themselves as needy, they pray often (1 Thessalonians 5:17; 1 Timothy 2:1-2).

5. *Being overwhelmed with God's undeserved grace and goodness.* The humble person sees himself as truly deserving of hell. He is immensely grateful to God for forgiving him of so much (Psalm 116:12-19).

6. *Being thankful and grateful in general toward others.* Humble people thank God and others often. They expect nothing, so anything that is received is greatly appreciated. (1 Thessalonians 5:18).

7. *Being gentle and patient.* Humble people want to act like God, and they are not focused on what they want. They also want to love others the way God loves them. They are willing to wait and are not easily irritated (Colossians 3:12-14).

8. *Seeing yourself as no better than others.* A humble person understands

the sinfulness of his own heart. He would never see himself as better than others. This is true no matter who the other person is. He understands that he, in and of himself, is capable of the worst sin. He agrees with John Bradford who said, "but for the grace of God, there I go" (Romans 12:16; Ephesians 3:8).

9. *Having an accurate view of your gifts and abilities.* Humble people do not bemoan the fact that they are not as gifted as others. Neither do they exaggerate their own abilities (Romans 12:3).

10. *Being a good listener.* Humble people consider what others have to say as more important than what they have to say. They take an interest in others by asking questions and listening. Self is not their primary focus (James 1:19; Philippians 2:3-4).

11. *Talking about others only if it is good or for their good.* A humble person will speak well of others, not negatively. He will convey something negative about someone only if he must do so in order to help that person (Proverbs 11:13).

12. *Being gladly submissive and obedient to those in authority.* Humble people are first of all obedient to God, and then the authorities over them (Romans 12:1-2; 13:1-2).

13. *Preferring others over yourself.* Humble people are willing to put others before self without first considering their own rights (Romans 12:10).

14. *Being thankful for criticism or reproof.* Humble people view reproof as good for them and consider that God may be trying to teach them something (Proverbs 9:8; 27:5-6).

15. *Having a teachable spirit.* Humble people realize they don't know everything, and even when they think they are right are willing to consider that they might be wrong (1 Corinthians 4:7). They also know that God can use anyone to teach them, since He was even able to use a donkey to teach Balaam in Numbers 22:22-35. They have many people they admire and respect.

16. *Seeking always to build up others.* Humble people encourage others. They use only words that build up and say what is necessary for

the edification of others. They never cut others down (Ephesians 4:29).

17. *Serving.* Humble people are on the lookout for ways to serve and assist others. They are the first to volunteer for jobs no one else wants. In the area of service, of course, the humble husband will especially serve his wife (Galatians 5:13).

18. *A quickness in admitting when you are wrong.* Humble people have no problem with saying, "I was wrong. You are right. Thank you for telling me." (Proverbs 29:23).

19. *A quickness in granting and asking for forgiveness.* Humble people are eager to forgive because they know how much they have been forgiven. They have no trouble asking for forgiveness because they want to be peacemakers (Colossians 3:12-14).

20. *Repenting of sin as a way of life.* A humble person asks God daily for forgiveness and works toward real change (1 John 1:9; 1 Timothy 4:7-9).

21. *Minimizing others' sins or shortcomings in comparison to your own.* A humble person thinks about his own sin more often than another's sin. He also sees his own sin as more important to deal with than the sin of others (Matthew 7:3-4).

22. *Being genuinely glad for others.* Humble people rejoice with others when good things happen because they are aware that God has blessed them immeasurably and they trust God for what they do not have (Romans 12:15).

23. *Being honest and open about who they are and the areas in which they need growth.* Humble people are open and honest about their growth in the Lord. They ask for help and accountability in the repentance process, knowing they need their brothers and sisters (Philippians 3:12-14; Galatians 6:2).

24. *Possessing close relationships.* Humble people have friends and loved ones because they are friendly and love others (Acts 20:31-38).

Here is a way that we can picture our definition and manifestations of humility:

THEOCENTRIC
"the SERVANT'S MINDSET" = Low & Sober-Minded

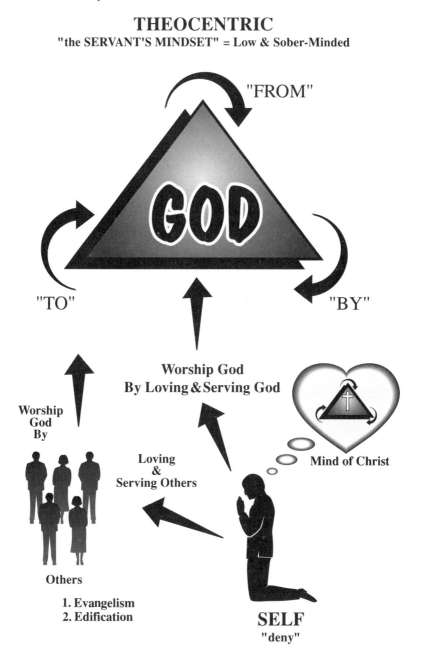

Getting from Here to There

So how do we get from pride to humility? First of all there must be an initial humbling of one's self before God. We are told in the New Testament:

> **Submit therefore to God. Resist the devil and he will flee from you. Draw near to God and He will draw near to you. Cleanse your hands, you sinners; and purify your hearts, you double-minded. Be miserable and mourn and weep; let your laughter be turned into mourning and your joy to gloom. Humble yourselves in the presence of the Lord, and He will exalt you.**
> **James 4:7-10**

Without humility there can be no true repentance (change). In other words we have to humble ourselves before God and then we can *walk* in humbleness. It takes humility to learn humility. That initial humbling of one's self is a response to the work of the Spirit of God. Once we have rightly humbled ourselves before God there are things that we can do (by God's grace) to stay humble.

To remain humble:

1. Pray for God to help you put off pride and to produce humility in you.
2. Read the Psalms and the Prophets often to gain a high view of God and proper self view.
3. Study Jesus (His earthly examples; especially in the Gospels).
4. Ask others if you come across as proud in any way.
5. Spend lots of time worshiping God (e.g. praising, prayer, reading and meditating).
6. Practice the "one-another" principles (Appendix 3).
7. Work to put off pride and put on humility at the level of your thoughts and motives.
8. Work to put off pride and put on humility at the level of your communication.
9. Work to put off pride and put on humility at the level of your deeds.

10. Have the mindset that humility must be a way of life (Philippians 2:3).

Before we conclude, let's review by way of a chart what we have learned thus far:

ATTITUDE	PRIDE	HUMILITY
Outlook:	Epidemic	Endangered
Terms:	High, Lifted Up, Blind	Low, Bowed Down, Sober
Mindset: (attitude of)	Self: The Master	Jesus Christ: The Servant
Source of Good:	From Me	From God
Means of Good:	By/Through Me	By/Through God
Goal of Good:	To Me	To God
Honor:	Self-Imposed	God-Bestowed
Confidence:	Self-Sufficient	Christ-Sufficient
Others:	Conditional/Trading Affection (looked down upon)	Unconditional/Sacrificial (preferred) • Salvation • Sanctification

Get Humble and Keep Humble

It should be abundantly clear that without humility we cannot be the exemplary husbands God has called us to be. In turn, one cannot put on humility if he doesn't first realize areas where he has sinful pride. Pride lies behind every sin and especially behind strife and contention (Proverbs 13:10). If your marriage is characterized by conflict, you must isolate the attitude and the manifestations of pride. Also, if your marriage is characterized as individualistic (two ships that just pass in the night), it is evident you are not humbly ministering to one another.

We just saw in James that "God is opposed to the proud" (James 4:6). We learned in Chapter Seven of this book that this means He is at battle with the proud. God is actively fighting against pride in order that He might capture or win us (Ezekiel 14). Earlier, in this same passage, James says, "He jealously desires the Spirit which He has made to dwell in us" (James 4:5). Husband, if you belong to God, He will deal with your pride if you will not. He will do this because He loves you and because He made you to glorify Him. Spurgeon believed that "every Christian has a choice between being humble or being humbled."

To the humble God promises grace (James 4:6). John MacArthur says, "Humility creates the vacuum that divine grace fills." [15] When we see ourselves rightly in reference to God and others, we will shine with God's glory. Paul tells us in Colossians, "As those who have been chosen of God, holy and beloved, put on a heart of ... humility ..." (Colossians 3:12). This putting on of humility, unfortunately, is not a one-time thing. Pride does not die once, but it must die daily. The Puritan pastor, Thomas Brooks, admonished us well when he said, "Get humble and keep humble."

Chapter Fourteen

A HUSBAND'S RESOLVE
SENSITIVITY

> Husbands, likewise, dwell with them with under-
> standing, giving honor to the wife, as to the weaker
> vessel, and as being heirs together of the grace of life,
> that your prayers may not be hindered.
> **1 Peter 3:7 (NKJV)**

Now that you are equipped with a more lowly mindset, you are ready to put some of your newly-found or renewed humility into practice. The resolve to walk humbly with God and our wives will help us to obey God's command to dwell with them [our wives] in an understanding way. Although we have stressed proper treatment of our wives all along the way, grasping the full meaning of "with understanding" is essential in relating to our wives as we should. For the most part, this chapter is carefully devoted to study and application of Peter's exhortation to husbands in the above verse.

It will become evident that the command to live with our wives in an understanding way is another important ingredient in the making of an exemplary husband.

The Historical Context of the Verse

To gain the full meaning of the verse we are about to look at, we need to understand some of its historical context. Peter's exhortations had great meaning to the churches to which they were given. These churches had both Greek and Roman influences. In the Greek culture wives led difficult lives. Greek men viewed their wives as much lower than themselves. The Greek men usually had many concubines, and their wife's role basically consisted of bearing children and doing housework. The Athenian orator Demosthenes said,

> We have courtesans for the sake of pleasure; we have concubines for the sake of daily cohabitation; we have wives for the purpose of having children legitimately and of having a faithful guardian for all our household affairs. [16]

Unfortunately, the Roman culture was not any better for women. Marriage was basically legalized prostitution and divorcing the wife for various and sundry things was common. [17] Needless to say, women were usually treated very badly.

There were probably some Jewish believers in these churches as well. The Jewish culture could be equally demeaning toward women. Jewish women were treated much like slaves and were given no legal position, and divorce was rampant in the Jewish culture as well. Jewish men viewed women in such low esteem that a typical morning prayer might be, "Blessed art Thou, O Lord our God, who has not made me a... woman.". [18]

At the time Peter wrote, the world's view of women and of being a wife was quite different from God's view. In 1 Peter, he is speaking to men who had been influenced by their cultures. They desperately needed to relate to their wives differently than did the world around them. Though our culture as a whole may not view women in exactly these ways, Peter's exhortation certainly gives us a pattern for how we should treat our wives, and it gives us a caution against letting these demeaning attitudes sneak apply to us, even in small ways.

The Immediate Context of the Verse

The context surrounding 1 Peter 3:7 is also helpful in understanding its meaning. The theme of 1 Peter is that of *righteous submissive living in the face of persecution or difficult circumstances*. Peter begins a specific train of thought in Chapter 2 that he brings right into our verse. He makes the point in Chapter 2 that believers in various circumstances are to honor God even when others make it difficult. He says:

> **Keep your behavior excellent among the Gentiles, so that in the thing in which they slander you as evildoers, they may because of your good deeds, as they observe them, glorify God in the day of visitation.**
> **1 Peter 2:12**

In explanation, Peter first addresses honoring God by obeying foolish authorities (vv. 13-15). Next he addresses the need for slaves to honor God even when their masters treat them badly (v. 18). In the beginning of Chapter 3, Peter tells wives to honor God even when their husbands are disobedient to the Word (v. 1). Then in verse 7 Peter begins, "You husbands in the same way, live with your wife in an understanding way ..." (v. 7). The motivation for all of Peter's exhortations is clearly to bring glory to God before a watching world. Husbands are to honor God in the face of difficulty because this "finds favor with God" (vv. 9-20). Given the historical context of this book, Peter could very well be referring to the scorn that a husband might receive from a culture that did not understand nor embrace the concept of better treatment of one's wife. It is possible that Peter is referring also to the hardship that comes from living with an unsaved or difficult wife. Either way, Peter's point is clear. Husbands *must* honor God in how they treat their wives, regardless of any difficult circumstances inside or outside of marriage.

✓ Understand (/

① honor
② dwell.

The Words in the Verse

Dwelling Together

Another way we can grasp the full meaning of this verse is to look carefully at the some of the key words. Lets begin with the word "live." The word "live" or *sunoikeo* means *to dwell together with.* It is a present active participle that makes the word actually mean *be continually dwelling together with.* However we are to be living with our wives, it is to be a continual, ongoing way of living with them. It is not something we do once or twice or that we do only when we are newlyweds. We are to be doing this all the time, for all of our married days.

Understanding

Now we come to the phrase, "with understanding." This phrase in the Greek is *kata gnosin* and simply means *according to knowledge.* So the meaning of the verse thus far is *be continually dwelling together with your wife according to knowledge.* This knowledge can be anything from the knowledge of one's wife to the knowledge of all Christian principles. The idea here is that a husband must live with his wife *in accordance with the things he should know.* He should live with her while taking into consideration information that is crucial. Remember, at the time this book was written, most men did not know their wives nor Christian principles at all. The concept Peter is talking about here is surely involved in the command for the husband to love his wife. Peter is just walking men through what loving one's wife would mean to a culture that looked down on wives.

Based on what Peter is saying, every husband is responsible to know his own wife well enough to apply God's principles to living with her. If we ignorantly go along in our marriage, we will not do the right things. For example, if a husband does not understand his own wife's capabilities, physical makeup, or what mothering three children requires of her, he could be very unreasonable about how much she should accomplish in a day.

In our culture the word *understanding* might be read as "compassionate" or "sensitive." Certainly, these ideas are implied in the idea of living with your wife in accordance with knowledge. If we are living in accordance with who our wives are and in accordance with Christian principles, we will be treating our wives in a considerate manner. What follows fully supports this idea.

Giving Honor

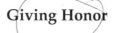

Peter goes on to show what living with your wife according to knowledge would look like. Living with her according to knowledge involves "giving honor." *Honor* carries with it the ideas of showing esteem and thankfulness of the highest degree. Josephus, a Jewish historian, uses the word to describe the honors Titus paid his troops after the destruction of Jerusalem. We see the same kind of honor and gratitude given by the husband to the excellent wife of Proverbs 31:28-30, which says:

> **Her children rise up and bless her; her husband also, and he praises her, saying: "Many daughters have done nobly, but you excel them all." Charm is deceitful and beauty is vain, but a woman who fears the Lord, she shall be praised.**

You can imagine how revolutionary this idea of honoring one's wife was for men of that day. It is interesting to note that in order to give honor sincerely to a wife, one first must know his wife and acknowledge her activities. A husband who is far removed probably will have little honor to offer. Also, a husband who is generally proud will not appreciate his wife.

Peter continues the idea of honoring with a very practical analogy. The two key words in his analogy are *vessel* and *weaker*. The actual word in the Greek for vessel (*skeuos*) means *useful container or instrument*. The word *weaker* actually means *strengthless* or *fragile*. Some take the viewpoint that Peter is saying that the woman is the weaker person in the marriage (physically and/or emotionally). But, if we look at one little phrase, Peter's meaning becomes clearer. That little phrase is *as to*. The Greek word for this phrase is *hos*, which means *in the manner of* or *like*. Peter is still telling us *how* we should honor our wives. We are to treat our wives in the way that we would a very delicate and useful vessel. In other words, we are to esteem her as valuable and handle her *carefully*. Furthermore, it is not clear how the *weaker sex* meaning would tie into giving the wife honor. Wives may or may not be weaker than their husbands in some way, but this is not Peter's point in this passage. His point is that every husband needs to honor his wife by treating her as a delicate and precious possession. Some men I have met over the years treat their wives more like a cheap garbage can. This is atrocious.

Heirs Together

Next we move to the phrase "and as being heirs together of the grace of life." Peter is still telling us how to honor our wives. This time, our little word "as" (*hos*) implies that an actual quality is possessed. There is something specific about who our wife is that we need to know. Peter says that the husband and wife are *sugkleronomos* (fellow-heirs or equal participants) in the *charitos zoes* (the gracious gift of life). Peter is letting us know that a wife is equal to her husband in a significant way.

The gift of life could be marriage, life in general, or eternal life. Since the husband and wife do not have equal functions in the marriage, and since the context of this passage seems to include unequally-yoked marriages (3:1), perhaps the best understanding of this phrase would be *God's gift of being alive*. In this case, the point would be that the wife is just as much a person as the husband, and therefore, she should be treated with the same dignity and human respect as the husband. This certainly fits what these Christians needed to hear. Whatever the *gift of life is*, Peter is trying to get the husband to bring the wife up to his level, rather than to look down on her pridefully because she is a woman. Peter is actually seeking to give men of that day a new and more elevated view of women, particularly their own wives. God has given us this passage today as well. We need to ask ourselves, men, whether we have the right perspective of our own wives.

How Not To Live With Your Wife

Now that we understand what we are to do, what is it we are *not* to do? The opposite of living with our wives in a way that considers her and God's principles is described well in Colossians 3:19:

**Husbands, love your wives and do not be
embittered against them.**

After Paul exhorts husbands to love their wives, he tells them what *not* to do. The word "embittered" (*pikraiuesthe*) carries the idea of being harsh or sharp. We are told that this bitterness will result in action *against* or *toward* one's wife. It also carries the idea of reaching a state that is ongoing. *The New Linguistic and Exegetical Key to the Greek New Testament* by Rogers and Rogers says, "It speaks of the friction that is caused by impatience and thoughtless nagging". [19] This impatience and nagging is how we as husbands are *not* to live with our wives. We are not to be harsh with them. We will not be bitter with them if we are loving them in the ways that Peter exhorts us to. If we choose to live with our wives wrongly, it will affect not only our relationship with our wife, but also our relationship with the Lord Jesus.

The Result of Disobedience

Not living with your wife in a way that pleases God is a very serious offense to Him. In the 1 Peter passage, one reason we are given to live with our wives "according to knowledge" is so that our prayers "may not be hindered"(1 Peter 3:7). Our sin in the area of how we treat our wives will affect our prayers to God. The word for "hindered" is *egkaoptesthai* which means *to be cut into* or *to be impeded*. Our prayers will be interrupted by God. He does not stop loving the believer, but He is apparently not interested in communing with him about other things when such serious sin is going on. We have this same idea communicated in Matthew 5. If a believer remembers, as he is worshiping God, that he has wronged someone, Christ tells us he is to go immediately, get things right, and then come back to worship (Matthew 5:23-24). Christ is communicating that how we relate to others is very important to God, and He does not simply overlook it.

This makes me think of men who convey to others that they have a close walk with God and yet are not living with their wives in an understanding way. How is it that a husband can believe he is serving and walking with God when he is not loving his wife as he should? Such a man is deceived. Living with our wives considerately is a high standard for any of us. We will be fighting with our flesh in order to obey, but we must strive to bring glory to God in how we dwell with our wives if we want our prayers to be unhindered.

How Does This Passage Apply to Us?

Now that we know what God, through the Apostle Peter, is saying, we as husbands know how we must live with our wives. From 1 Peter 3:7, we have learned four things that we must do in order to live with our wives in an understanding way:

- You must gain a knowledge of what attitudes, words, and actions please God.
- You must know your wife so you can live with her in a compassionate and careful way.
- You must esteem your wife as valuable and useful and show your gratitude.
- You must view your wife as an equal person in life.

Many of the topics addressed in this book should help a husband to carry out these things: the need to know God and His standard through the Scriptures, good communication skills, our need to love our wives truly and to possess humility, and the woman's equality as a person. For the remainder of this chapter, I would like to offer some practical suggestions for knowing and honoring our wives better.

How to Know Your Wife Better

There are at least three ways that you can get to know your wife better. If you determine to do these things along the way, you will continually grow in your knowledge of her. Your knowledge will also help you to be more *one* with her and to be a better leader.

Observe her: Look, listen and learn. You can learn a great deal just by being aware of her as a person.

Ask her questions: Don't pester her with lists of questions, but purposefully try to draw information out of her. Not only will you learn more about her, but you will also communicate your interest to her.

- *Experience her world*: As time will allow, try to walk a mile in her shoes. You can and should do some of her responsibilities with her for a day, or enter into a particular task or activity with her (e.g., take care of the children, clean house, etc.) These experiences can be very enlightening and help you to appreciate her and understand what she goes through on a daily basis.

Here are some areas in which you can make observations or ask questions:

- Her likes/dislikes
- Her capabilities/limitations (physical, mental, and skills)
- Her joys
- Her challenges
- Her sorrows
- Her fears
- Her temptations
- Her physical and spiritual needs
- What communicates love to her
- What communicates indifference or dislike to her
- What encourages her/discourages her

It is important to remember that at least some of the information you gather will change in time. Don't think that once you have covered these topics your learning is finished. There are many jokes about the impossibility of fully understanding a woman. The truth is, however, that no one stays the same throughout life—not even *you*. Hopefully, we are all growing. The most important thing to remember about knowing your wife is that you must act on your knowledge. You must *live* according to what you learn! Remember, it is far worse for a wife to know that her husband knows very well how to be considerate and how to prefer her, and yet does nothing, than it is for her to have an ignorant husband. However, before God we do not have the option of remaining ignorant.

Ways You Can Show Honor to Your Wife

God knows if you honor your wife in your heart. On the other hand, your wife will know what she means to you only by your words and actions. Here is a list of ways that you can show honor to your wife:

- Tell her what she means to you and how thankful to God you are for her.
- Tell her specific things you appreciate about her or what she does. Focus on her character.
- Speak kindly to her—the way in which you want to be spoken.
- Do not speak to her or treat her in a condescending way.
- Only say things to her that will build her up (even constructive criticism or admonishment can be done in an encouraging way).
- Say things that build her up to others and when the two of you are with others.
- Do not say things that will belittle her to others or when the two of you are with others. Derogatory jokes and sarcasm are almost always dishonoring.
- Do not treat her as a lowly servant, but serve her instead.

How Are You Dwelling?

Every husband needs to ask himself often, "How am I dwelling with my wife?" It is a very good idea to ask your wife this question as well. Peter has made it clear for us that it really does not matter what our circumstances are—we must honor God in how we live with our wives. Regardless of how our wives treat us or what others will think, we must obey God's command. Husband, are you bringing Christian principles into your relationship with your wife? Do you know your wife and her life well enough to live with her in a considerate way? Are you honoring your wife in how you think of her and treat her? If so, you are exemplifying Christ's love. If not, your prayers are being *cut off* by God and your marriage will suffer. Living with your wife "with understanding" is something you must do as an exemplary husband.

Chapter Fifteen

A HUSBAND'S RESOLVE
HELPING HIS WIFE
DEAL WITH HER SIN

At this point you may be sensing some relief and thinking, "Finally, we have come to something that's not all about me!" On the other hand, I hope that you did not rush to this chapter with much more enthusiasm than the previous ones. If you have not yet read Chapter 1 through Chapter 14, you are definitely in the wrong place! There must be a proper balance to how we deal with our wife's sin, because it is very often misunderstood and mishandled.

All wives sin, just as all husbands sin. There *will* be times when the most loving thing a husband can do is to address his wife's sin. In this chapter, I would like to give some guidelines for what to do when that time comes.

There are two things about this chapter that we must establish before we begin. First, we *must* always speak lovingly to our wife when we address her sin. Secondly, we are *not* talking about conflict in this chapter. We will address both communication and conflict in later chapters (16 and 17). In this chapter we will be talking about those times when your wife has *clearly* sinned and you have not. These truths will also apply to those times when you both have sinned and you have already fully dealt with your sin, but your wife is not able or willing to recognize her own.

A Husband Must Deal With Sin

As your wife's spiritual leader, you must help her with her sin. This is a very important part of loving your wife as Christ loves the church. Although you are not the one who sanctifies, you must be like Christ in your desire to see her sanctified (Ephesians 5:25-27). In *The Family*, John MacArthur writes,

> Jesus gave Himself for the church so that "He might sanctify her, having cleansed her by the washing of water with the Word, that He might present to Himself the church in all her glory, having no spot or wrinkle or any such thing; but that she should be holy and blameless." We learn from this very basic truth: when a man loves someone, *that person's purity is his supreme concern.* ... if a man really loves his wife he seeks that which keeps her feet clean from the dust of this world, doing everything within his power to maintain her holiness, her virtue, and her purity. ... Husbands have the responsibility in the home to provide for their wives every purifying influence that will make them holy. (emphasis mine, pp. 65-66) [20]

Every husband must also deal with his wife's sin because it is expected of him as her brother in Christ. Both husband and wife are required as members of the body of Christ to address one another's sin God's way.

If your brother sins, go and show him his fault in private; if he listens to you, you have won your brother.
Matthew 18:15

Brethren, even if anyone is caught in any trespass,

> **you who are spiritual, restore such a one in a spirit of gentleness... .**
> **Galatians 6:1a**

There is a caution, however, that we must apply to our desire to help our wife with her sin. For the most part we should be focused on our own sanctification.

> **...Each one looking to yourself, so that you too will not be tempted.**
> **Galatians 6:1b**

We need always to remember that dealing with sin is a two-way street. You need her help as much as she needs yours! You should, however, deal with your wife's sin because it is unavoidable and because it would be sinful not to, but not because you are on a mission looking for it. That approach reminds me of the arcade game, "Whack-a-mole," where one looks and waits to hit the emerging mole over the head with a hammer. We should not be waiting or looking for our wife's sin and we certainly should not be hasty or harsh in response to her sin.

Sometimes correcting one's wife will bring pain to her soul. She may even believe that you are setting out to hurt her. Usually, if a husband is careful to love his wife in other ways she will quickly realize that he is only trying to bring her good. Both husband and wife may need to be reminded, "Better is open rebuke than love that is carefully concealed" and " Faithful are the wounds of a friend" (Proverbs 27:5-6).

A Husband Must Be Ready

Though when necessary we surely need to help our wives deal with sin, we have other responsibilities that must come first. There are certain things that an exemplary husband will consider *before he addresses his wife's sin.* He will ask himself some basic questions.

1. Are we a part of a Bible-believing church that preaches the Word, practices the "one another" commands, as well as church discipline (the church leaders confronting those who continue in sin)

and restoration of believers who repent (Hebrews 10:24-25; Matthew 18:15-20)?

2.   Is there any glaring sin in my own life that my wife may see or have against me (Matthew 7:1-5)?

3.   Have I been showing love to my wife and living with her in an understanding way (Ephesians 5:25-33; 1 Peter 3:7)?

4.   Are my goals in addressing my wife's sin *seeking to please God* and *helping my wife to grow in Christ* (Colossians 1:28-29)?

5.   Am I sure that I have all the facts? Never address sin without asking the appropriate questions (Proverbs 18:13, 17)!

A Husband Must Know What to Deal With

One of the most basic things a husband must know before he can address his wife's sin is the answer to the question, "What should I deal with and not deal with?" If you talk to her about things you shouldn't, or react to her too hastily, you can exasperate her. But if you do not deal with your wife's sin when you should, sadly, you are not fulfilling your role as spiritual leader. You are also bringing harm to your wife, and most important, disobeying God.

He Should Deal with Clear Sin

The first thing to determine in answering the question, "What do I deal with?" is whether or not an issue is *clearly* a sin. Any time you think you must talk to your wife about something she has done or is doing, you must be sure that the issue involves *indisputable sin* (plainly prohibited by Scripture and easily recognized by anyone: see Deuteronomy 19:15-21; 2 Corinthians 13:1). We must be careful not to have a standard that is higher than God's, to seek our own preferences, or to presume that we know what are the motives in our wife's heart. These things would be grave sins on our part. Here are some examples of *clear sin* that a husband should deal with and also some examples of *questionable issues* that should *not* be approached as sin.

Examples of Clear Sin	Examples of Questionable Issues
Your wife blatantly lies to you about the finances (Ephesians 4:25).	Your wife goes shopping at a store that is normally more expensive than your budget allows and her purchase may not have been the wisest one.
Your wife screams at you in anger and says "Would you just get out of here and leave me alone?! I'm tired, and you are irritating me" (Ephesians 4:26-29).	While you are trying to explain something to her, you notice that your wife seems to be irritated and does not answer you as nicely as she could.
Your wife repeatedly tells you that she will not have sexual relations with you because she doesn't have desires (1 Corinthians 7:3-5).	Your wife refuses to participate in a certain sexual activity with you until she knows it is right before God.
Your wife watches *all* the soap operas on television *each afternoon* instead of doing her work (Proverbs 18:9; Titus 2:3-5).	Your wife has a favorite television show that she doesn't like to miss, but you think watching television is a waste of time.

Another category of issues that should *not* be dealt with as sin involves certain imperfections that we may not like or that irritate us. This could be anything from forgetfulness to what may appear to be strange quirks. There may be something about your wife that you must simply forebear, realizing that you are not perfect either (Ephesians 4:2). Most assuredly, she has things that she must humbly endure about you as well! These things should not be dealt with as sin, but depending on how much of a hindrance they are to your marriage and to others (it should be significant), it may be good to offer some help. In this chapter we are not dealing with questionable issues or personal irritations, but rather matters clearly defined as sin by Scripture.

He Should Take All Sin Seriously

Before you fall off your chair because of the heading you just read, rest assured that I don't mean that a husband will have to *rebuke* His wife about every sin she commits. I will address this more thoroughly in this chapter. In this section, however, I would like to show you that **God is concerned about every sin and, therefore, we should be too**.

All sin matters to God.

The two questions that we should ask ourselves are, "How does God view sin?" and "How does He deal with it?" The truth is, God sees every sin we commit, and each is grievous and concerning to Him.

> **For My eyes are on all their ways; they are not hidden from My face, nor is their iniquity concealed from My eyes.**
> **Jeremiah 16:17**

> **For the wrath of God is revealed from heaven against all ungodliness and unrighteousness of men....**
> **Romans 1:18a**

Confusion about God's response to sin can arise if we conclude that God's saving grace causes Him not to see our daily sin. While it is true that God *does not* hold the believer's sin against him as far as salvation is concerned, this does not mean that He fails to see and deal with our daily sins. If we are talking about condemnation and punishment, God has forgiven us and has chosen not to remember our sins, that is to use our sin against us in the day of judgment (Jeremiah 31:34; Colossians 2:13-14). But, as far as our sanctification (or daily spiritual growth) is concerned, God *does not* forget about the sins that have not been confessed.

> *If we confess our sins,* **He is faithful and righteous to forgive us our sins and to cleanse us from all unrighteousness.**
> **1 John 1:9 [emphasis mine]**

210

God loves us too much to do *nothing* about our sin. The Lord Jesus prays for us (Hebrews 7:25). His Spirit uses the Scriptures to address our sin (John 17:17; 2 Timothy 3:15-17). He also intends for other believers to address our sin (Romans 15:14). He may use circumstances to make our sin more obvious to us (Luke 5:1-9). Our God even uses fatherly discipline to help us with our sin (Hebrews 12:5). God is concerned about every sin. If we love our wives the way that God loves us, we will be concerned about all sin—hers *and ours*.

I am aware, however, that there are other godly brothers and sisters who believe that God teaches us to "cover" (forget about, not deal with, or choose to overlook) as many sins as we can. In fact, **I taught this view for many years myself**. The basis of what I taught was the more you love, the more you will be able to *cover* or not let it bother you. I also taught that each person must determine for himself what he can truly overlook. It wasn't until I did some careful study of the passages that address this issue, however, that I became unable to reconcile my earlier view with the whole of Scripture. My study showed me that in actuality there are no verses that tell us to forget about *any* clear sin that is not dealt with. (See Appendix Nine for "Love Covers").

I also used to teach that unless someone sins a "big" sin, or unless a sin becomes a regular pattern, we should not address it. The idea was to wait until a person has formed a habit of sin before doing something about it. Otherwise, we are being too picky, judgmental, or playing the role of the Holy Spirit. In addition to finding no Scripture for this view, I also came to realize that this perspective seems to be very unloving and detrimental to others. I say this because it is actually far easier for a person to deal with and avoid sin *before* it becomes a habit. We should not sit around and watch our wives become entangled in sin before we attempt to help them.

Dealing with all sin, then covering it, may still raise some legitimate concerns in your mind. Perhaps it seems as though you would be constantly dealing with sin. This is a very typical thought when seeking to take all sin seriously. In reality this problem is actually not likely. If we deal with sin properly, there is *usually* less and less of it. Dealing with sin God's way has a very purifying effect (1 Corinthians 5:6-8). Just as we are less likely to break the posted speed limit in our cars when we know a police officer is in the area, most Christians are much less likely to sin knowing there is someone around who will hold them accountable. On the other hand, if you are living with a wife who is a professing believer but is not living as one, it is possible that the initial path of dealing with sin could be rocky. But if you persevere in addressing sin God's way, you can give a wife who may not really be saved more of an opportunity to truly come to Christ, in that she will be encouraged to evaluate her commitment to God.

The truth is, when our wife clearly sins, we are not doing her a favor by letting her forget about it. If sin is not dealt with, she will not prosper spiritually.

> **He who conceals his transgressions will not prosper, but he who confesses and forsakes them will find compassion.**
> **Proverbs 28:13**

A Husband Must Know How To Deal With Sin *Graciously*

If we were to stop here, our wives would find they are living with impossible husbands. God is not only concerned about every sin, but He is also gracious and patient in how He deals with our sin.

> **The Lord is compassionate and gracious, slow to anger and abounding in lovingkindness. He will not always strive with us, nor will He keep His anger forever. He has not dealt with us according to our sins, nor rewarded us according to our iniquities. For as high as the heavens are above the earth, so great is His lovingkindness toward those who fear Him. As far as the east is from the west, so far has He removed our transgressions from us. Just as a father has compassion on his children, so the Lord has compassion on those who fear Him. For He himself knows our frame; He is mindful that we are but dust.**
> **Psalm 103:8-14**

In addition to having the right motive of her good, one way of being gracious is to be more focused on what our wife is doing right than what she is doing wrong. God does not overlook the positive things in our lives because we momentarily sin (Revelation 2:1-7). He is often encouraging and appreciating what is right. How much do you encourage your wife about what she is doing right? In our efforts to help our wives with their sin, we must not become totally focused on it.

While some people have an all or nothing mentality in whether they deal with sin or not, others have an all or nothing mentality in *how* they deal with sin. This brings up the second thing we can do to deal with sin graciously. **We should not assume that dealing with someone's sin automatically means that we must confront or rebuke them**. Instead, we should think of dealing with our wife's sin as:

> **A loving and helpful process that** *allows the Holy Spirit the opportunity to work* **and allows your wife the opportunity to take care of her sin on her own initiative.**

A believer should never be *eager* to rebuke another believer at the first sign of sin (Ephesians 4:1-2). This kind of behavior usually stems from a pride issue in which one sees himself as better than others. Sometimes all a husband has to do before his wife acknowledges her sin is pray. In some situations letting a person experience some of the consequences of their sin is enough to bring them to repentance.

There may be a rare time when a husband has to step in and admonish his wife immediately (e.g., if his wife is on a screaming rampage, or is going to do herself or the children harm). Usually, this is not the case. More times than not, giving a pointed rebuke is not even the second or third action a gracious and humble husband will take.

A gracious husband will also deal with his wife's sin reasonably! Though every sin is serious to God, not every sin is a sin of the same magnitude or merits the same response. In the Old Testament, some sins received the death penalty, but not all of them. How we deal with an issue should be in keeping with the level of sin that was committed.

Two Practical Examples

Example One:

Let's assume that you have gathered all the needed facts and are sure that you have witnessed or know about a clear sin that your wife has committed. This is a sin that you have not seen or known your wife to commit before or that has not happened in a long time. This is not a sin of great magnitude. Perhaps she has yelled in anger at the children. Let's walk through a gracious way that you could deal with a wife who has sinned in the above way if she does not deal with her sin of her own accord. Keep in mind that at any point along the way, she might see her sin and repent of it. When you become aware that your wife has sinned a new or a very infrequent sin, you can deal with it *something like this*:

1. To gain a humble and compassionate mindset, ask yourself if you have ever sinned (1 John 1:8). Of course, your answer will be a resounding "yes."
2. Ask yourself if you have the same glaring problem. If you do, confess it and repent before you speak to her about the same thing (Matthew 7:3-5).
3. Pray for her to see her sin (Ephesians 6:18, context is dealing with temptation).
4. Give her a few moments of time.
5. Ask her if she is okay or if you can help her since she seems to be "having difficulty" or "failing to recognize this particular sin." Help her in any way you can. Giving her a hug may even be appropriate.
6. Give her some time to reflect on what happened and on your comment.
7. If she begins to blame others or explain away why she has sinned, pray for her again (Luke 16:15).
8. Acknowledge any real problems she brings up (others or circumstances) and express a desire to help her solve those problems, but also tell her that what you want most is to help her give glory to God. Ask her to please take some time to think through what happened and whether or not she sinned in her thinking or her actions.
9. Pray for her and give her some time alone. Continue to love her—actively and visibly (1 Corinthians 13:4-7).

10. If she does not come back to talk to you, politely ask her what became of her time of reflection.
11. If she acknowledges her actions as sin but does no more about it, gently tell her, "Honey, whatever the circumstances are (and I know they are difficult), because your response was sinful, you must take care of this with God and the children" (1 John 1:9).
12. If she repents and asks forgiveness, those involved should forgive her and cover it (Luke 17:3-4; Ephesians 4:32).

Hopefully, you can see that this gracious way of dealing with sin can be characterized more by **encouragement to do what is right** than by reproof or confrontation. I am not suggesting that every husband must follow these exact steps to deal with his wife's lesser sins. These steps are only a thorough example of how you can help your wife. An easier way to think of this gracious way of dealing with her sin is:

- **Pray**
- **Express concern for her and help her**
- **Give her time**
- **Entreat her**

Most often, somewhere in this process a believing wife will confess and repent of her sin. The wife in this fictional scenario did not continue to resist the help her husband was trying to give her, and she took the opportunity she was given to acknowledge her own sin. She did not choose to be unruly (continue in sin) and, therefore, the situation does not warrant anything stronger. If you think about it, kindly and compassionately is the way you would like others to deal with your sins, too.

Example Two:

Now let's assume that the wife is not yet positively responsive. Perhaps she is resisting her husband's patient encouragement, or even continuing in the sin he is trying to address. A more direct (though loving) admonishment would be needed from the Scriptures. It would also be important for the husband to address at a later time her poor response to his help. One of the worst things a husband can do is to stop short of what is needed (Galatians 6:9-10). This will only cause confusion for your wife and leave issues unresolved. You must love your wife more than you fear the consequences of doing what is right.

Suppose your wife is sinning in a way that has been gently and compassionately addressed several times before, then what? Again, the approach needed now is more pointed. Still, this does not mean that it has to be done immediately and sharply, especially if the wife has not yet conquered an old habit. Perhaps if you pray and give her just a moment's time, she will repent of her own accord. This is often the case when new habits are being learned (Luke 17:4). If she does not quickly repent, a husband can either address his wife on the spot (if he is confident that he can be self-controlled and that he is prepared) *or* he can take the time to plan out what he wants to say. Either way, he must be sure that he can show his wife from the Scriptures what God thinks of her sin and must address it lovingly but directly.

Matthew 18:15-18 and Galatians 6 gives us clear guidelines about what should follow if a wife continues in her sin or is still non-responsive to an admonition. Here is an example of how you can address your wife if she is repeating the same sin over and over, or if she is not responding rightly to your gracious help:

13. Give her a questioning look, pray for her, and give her a few moments. This non-verbal communication can sometimes make her stop and think.
14. If there is no response, compassionately use her name and say, "Honey, you need to think about whether you really want to displease the Lord in this way." Give her some time alone. If her immediate or later response is, "No, I do not want to displease the Lord in this way," ask her if she needs some help in figuring out where she is going wrong and how to put this sin off (Colossians 1:10). See that she gets the help she needs.
15. If you have to go back to her and she argues or gives no response, you can say to your wife something like this, "Honey, I love you, and I would like to talk with you more about this issue. We can talk now or you can tell me when a better time would be." When you talk with her, tell her that you understand how easy it is to sin but God commands her to honor Him in what she does. Express a desire to help her do this. Tell her, "You need to consider (or be reminded of) what God says about   (whatever it is) ." Explain, using the Scriptures (Hebrews 4:12).
16. Ask her, "Wouldn't you like to repent of this sin?" (Psalm 32:5).
17. If she says, "Yes," remind her that repentance means she will confess her sin to God and anyone else involved and ask forgiveness.

Discuss with her that repentance also means that she will determine what to do differently in the future. If this particular sin is a habit, repentance means she will think through a plan of how to stop doing what is wrong and how to start doing what is right (Colossians 3:6-10). If she expresses any need for help in doing these things, see that she gets it.

18. If she says, "No," or makes excuses, explain to her that she needs to repent and that she is sinning against God until she does. Almost always, a wife who is a believer will have turned from lesser sins by this time. Typically, past this point you will only be dealing with sins that are **more major** (e.g. marital unfaithfulness) and a wife who is probably an unbeliever (though you cannot assume she is an unbeliever or treat her as an unbeliever at this point). Tell her that if she wants to repent she must ask forgiveness of God (and anyone else involved) and be willing to do what is right and that you will help her. Tell her that you want to give her time to think about whether she is going to repent or not and that Christ has said, "If you love Me, you will keep My commandments" (John 14:15).

19. Pray for her, continue to demonstrate love for her, and seek godly counsel (Proverbs 12:15; 15:22).

20. If she still does not repent after giving her some time (a week should probably be sufficient), ask one or two believers who know her and love her to talk to her with you. You may want to have one of them be a church leader. Express concern for her and plead with her to repent. If she is not responsive, regretfully warn her of the consequences if she does not repent and then ask her to take some time again to think about what has been said and whether or not she is truly a believer (Matthew 18:16).

21. If she still does not repent, the elders in your church will need to tell the situation to the church so that other members can also plead with her to repent (Matthew 18:17a).

22. If she still does not repent, the elders will put her out of the church and everyone should assume that she is an unbeliever. This does not mean, however, that the husband can put her out of the family (Matthew 18:17b).

23. If at any time she repents, *eagerly* forgive her and help to restore her (Colossians 3:13).

24. If at any time, ever, she tries to harm anyone or engages in illegal activity, the legal authorities should be notified (Romans 13:1-4).

This more direct way of dealing with sin can be summed up as **loving admonishment** or **rebuke,** and is appropriate when you are dealing with someone who is being stubborn or rebellious. Again, not every step of this example is mandated by God. An easier way to think of this process is:

- **Pray**
- **Share God's word**
- **Entreat her in a progressively firm way to repent**

I cannot stress enough that you, as a husband, need to think and evaluate what kind of sin has been committed and whom you are dealing with. You must determine if this is a sin pattern or a rare sin. You must determine how your wife is behaving. Is she fainthearted, is she weak, or is she unruly? We do not deal with each of these people in the same way.

> **We urge you, brethren, admonish the unruly, encourage the fainthearted, help the weak, be patient with everyone.**
> **1 Thessalonians 5:14**

A Husband Must Respond Righteously To His Wife's Sin

Never Respond Foolishly

When your wife is responding in an ungodly way, you must be careful not to get caught up in her foolishness. Instead, you must respond to her foolishness calmly and with the wisdom of Scripture, putting her responsibility back on her. If she mentions anything in the outpouring of her foolishness that you have truly done wrong, acknowledge it as valid, briefly confess and repent of it, promise to talk with her more about your repentance later, and get back to the subject at hand. Make sure your answers are gentle but pointed about her sin and her responsibility.

> **Do not answer a fool according to his folly, or you will also be like him. Answer a fool as his folly deserves, that he not be wise in his own eyes.**
> **Proverbs 26:4-5**

Never Return Evil for Evil

Retaliation for a personal offense is never an option for the Christian. Scripture clearly teaches us to give back *only* good. Jesus Himself is our example.

And while being reviled, He did not revile in return....
1 Peter 2:23a

If we are very careful in this situation to have the right perspective of our wife's sin and focus on the right response, we can keep from returning evil for evil or becoming bitter.

The right perspective about an offense that is against you is:

- Her sin against you is no greater than your sin against God, who *has* forgiven you. Therefore, you should always be willing to forgive her (Matthew 18:21-35).
- Her sin is more against God than it is against you and is a result of her not being in the right place spiritually (Psalm 51:4).
- You, in and of yourself, are capable of the same sin (1 Corinthians 10:12; Galatians 6:1).
- Your love for her is not perfect either (Matthew 5:43-48).
- The greater focus of this sin should not be how it affects you, but how it affects God and her life. There is nothing wrong with letting her know that her sin did affect you and that it does affect your relationship. She needs to know this. Still, if you are more concerned about God and her than you are about you, you will not take up (dwell on) the personal offense and you will be able to maintain a humble and gentle spirit.

The right response to her sin:

- A desire on your part to glorify God no matter what she has done (1 Corinthians 10:31).
- A determination not to be overcome (provoked to sin) by evil in the process of dealing with her, but to exercise self-control and forbearing love (Romans 12:21).
- A willingness to help her spiritually and to keep loving her, which is returning good for evil (Romans 12:17).

- willingness to grant her forgiveness when she repents (Luke 17:3-4).

A Husband Must Understand True Forgiveness

To define forgiveness, a distinction must be made between having a willingness to forgive and actually granting horizontal (to another person) forgiveness. We must always be willing to forgive because God has forgiven us so much (Ephesians 4:31-32). Some call this willingness to forgive "having a forgiving spirit." God **always** wants us to have a forgiving spirit. If we do, we will never refuse to forgive another person who is repentant, and we will not return evil for evil. God has this to say about forgiving others:

> **And forgive us our debts, as we also have forgiven our debtors. ...For if you forgive others for their transgressions, your heavenly Father will also forgive you. But if you do not forgive others, then your Father will not forgive your transgressions.**
> **Matthew 6:12, 14-15**

God always has a willingness to forgive but He doesn't forgive without condition. We are told to forgive others in the same way that God forgives us.

> **Bearing with one another, and forgiving each other, whoever has a complaint against anyone; just as the Lord forgave you, so also should you.**
> **Colossians 3:13**

We know that God grants us forgiveness on the basis of confession and a sincere repentance, which is evidenced by a turning away from whatever sin is being confessed (Psalm 32:1). Since God has this conditional element to His forgiveness, it should be clear that our granting of forgiveness to others should also have a conditional element to it.

> **Be on your guard! If your brother sins, rebuke him; and *if he repents*, forgive him.**
> **Luke 17:3 [emphasis mine]**

> **If your brother sins, go and show him his fault in private;** *if he listens to you,* **you have won your brother. But if he does not listen to you, take one or two more with you, so that by the mouth of two or three witnesses every fact may be confirmed.**
> **Matthew 18:15-16 [emphasis mine]**

However, God's forgiveness is also complete. When a person confesses sin as sin and turns from it, God makes a promise to put that sin out of His mind and never bring it up again (Isaiah 43:25). We, therefore, must also grant complete forgiveness. When sin is confessed and repented of, we must make a promise, also.

When we forgive we make a promise to:

• Never bring that sin up to ourselves without remembering that it has been forgiven, then we must put it quickly out of our mind.
• Never bring that sin up to another person unless the person who sinned needs help in the repentance process.
• Never bring that sin up to the person who committed it unless it is to help them in the repentance process. [21]

It is important to point out that sometimes our wife's words may not be sincere. This insincerity usually becomes evident when there is no apparent desire or action to stop doing what is wrong and start doing what is right. Such a person should be reminded that forgiveness was granted on the basis of their claim of repentance, and since they have not repented, their sin is still not properly dealt with in God's sight. Their guilt remains.

A Husband Must Understand True Repentance

Before a husband can help his wife with her sin (or repent of his own sin for that matter), he must also understand what true repentance is. It is easy to have shallow and/or temporary remorse over one's sin, but true repentance is life-changing. Both husbands and wives need to know the difference between shallow remorse (worldly sorrow which evidences no change) and repentance (godly sorrow which leads to turning away from sin and toward righteousness).

> I now rejoice, not that you were made sorrowful, but that you were made sorrowful to the point of repentance; for you were made sorrowful according to the will of God, so that you might not suffer loss in anything through us. For the sorrow that is according to the will of God produces a repentance without regret, leading to salvation, but the sorrow of the world produces death. For behold what earnestness this very thing, this godly sorrow, has produced in you: what vindication of yourselves, what indignation, what fear, what longing, what zeal, what avenging of wrong! In everything you demonstrated yourselves to be innocent in the matter.
> 2 Corinthians 7:9-11

Shallow remorse can involve:

- Sorrow over getting caught and being found out.
- Sorrow over the consequences of sin or of getting caught.
- Sorrow over the response of others.
- The offering of an apology saying, "I'm sorry" without any mention of repentance or change and without asking forgiveness.
- Trying to do penance by doing unrelated good things to make the consequences go away, to try to cancel out one's wrong-doing, or to appease God.
- Making at least some justification for the sin committed.
- Complaining about the expectation of real change.

Repentance involves:

- Godly sorrow over the sin that has been committed because it is an offense before a holy God (Psalm 51:4).
- A full admission of sin and responsibility for the sin and brokenness with no excuses to God or others (Psalm 51:3).
- An asking of forgiveness from God and others who are involved with the perspective that forgiveness is not deserved (Psalm 51:1-2).
- A hatred for the sin and a desire to avoid it completely (2 Corinthians 7:11).
- A plan and an enthusiasm to make changes (both away from the sin and toward righteousness), whatever it takes (Luke 3:8-18; James 1:22-27)

- A willingness to accept the consequences of the sin and to see justice done (Luke 23:40-43).
- A desire to be in God's Word and with God's people (1 Peter 2:1-3; Hebrews 10:19-25).

A Husband Must Know How to Deal With Bitterness

Sometimes, a wife may become bitter against her husband. Over time, an offense or a series of offenses (real or perceived) may turn into a sinful grudge. God calls this a "bitterness." Like the root of a plant bitterness can grow very deep before the husband or the wife sees it as the serious problem it is. Bitterness can be encouraged by a lack of repentance on the husband's part or happen simply because the wife (or the husband) has not truly forgiven an offense that has been repented of. Bitterness is almost always an issue when the husband and wife have not been dealing with sin properly. When sin is not addressed, there is usually very little repentance (change) happening and this, unfortunately, is the perfect environment for bitterness to grow. A husband and wife need to know how to remove bitterness effectively.

> **Let all bitterness and wrath and anger and clamor and slander be put away from you, along with all malice. Be kind to one another, tenderhearted, forgiving each other, just as God in Christ has forgiven you.**
> **Ephesians 4:31-32 [emphasis mine]**

To remove bitterness, both you and your wife must:

- Work to put off pride and anger because each one of you has sinned before a holy God (Isaiah 6:1-7).
- Work to put on humility and love on the basis that we are all capable of all sin and because God loved us while we were sinners (Ephesians 4:1-2; Romans 5:8).
- Come to an understanding of how you have failed the other spouse. Making a personal sin list and then allowing your partner to add to it is very helpful.
- Acknowledge your failures as sins (Psalm 51:3).
- Confess your sins one by one to God and to your spouse with an enthusiasm to learn what it means to put off that sin and put on

what is right (Psalm 32:5; James 5:16).

- Understand what sins are most grievous to your spouse. It can be helpful to allow your spouse to prioritize your sin list in order of importance (keeping God's perspective in mind).
- Pray for God's help and work to change each item one by one (Hebrews 4:14-16; Ephesians 4:22-24).

Dealing with the Sin of an Unsaved Wife

Obviously, you cannot deal with an unsaved wife in the same way you would deal with a saved wife who has the Spirit of God within her (1 Corinthians 2:14-16). In most cases, she will not even be able to recognize her sin. When she does recognize it, she will not be able truly to repent. Your goals must be different for your unsaved wife. You cannot help in her spiritual growth because she is not saved. Dealing with her sin then means that you will focus first on evangelizing her and second on restraining major sin. Keeping these things in mind, here are some helpful guidelines:

Guidelines For Dealing With an Unsaved Wife's Sin:

1. Pray for her salvation and for major sin to be restrained for God's glory and her good, not your own ease (1 Corinthians 7:14-16).
2. Seek to love her with the love of Christ at all times (Ephesians 5:25-33).
3. Live a godly life before her that is based on a relationship with Christ. Let your light shine. Let her see your good works (Matthew 5:16).
4. Briefly share truth about who God is, who she is, and the way of salvation as often as you have clear opportunity (continue in conversation with her if she desires to hear more: 1 Peter 3:15).
5. Try to draw her into your Christian community in any way you can without pushing her.
6. Expect her to sin and have wrong attitudes and motives often (Titus 3:3; Romans 3:10; 3:23).
7. Do not expect her to be humble or understand submission.
8. Fully deal (to the point of requiring change) only with sin that significantly affects her well-being, the well-being of the children, or the survival of the family.
9. If she is involved in major sin, tell her that you love her but her behavior is wrong before God and destructive to her life. She

might be able to understand this as an unbeliever. Tell her she must stop, and offer to help her in any way you can.
10. Pray for her and give her some time. You can then be gracious and repeat steps 9 and 10 a time or two.

If your unsaved wife becomes rebellious or continually disruptive, deal with the situation in a more serious way. When a wife refuses to stop major sin (adultery, lying, drugs, child abuse, stealing, etc.), withdraws from the relationship, or causes havoc in the home, a husband may have to insist that she reveal her intentions as far as the marriage is concerned. If you find yourself in this situation, the first thing you should do is ask your wife if there is anything in your life that is fueling her bitterness. Then, express your desire to live with her in a peaceful and loving way and your willingness to repent of any sin on your part.

Next, you should seek biblical counsel. If you have no sin that is feeding her aggravation, ask someone from your church leadership or a believer from her family or yours (preferably someone she knows and appreciates) to be present when you speak to her more pointedly about her sin and her commitment to the marriage (2 Corinthians 13:1). Usually, a wife put in this position will either back down from her sin or end the marriage. If she desires to end the marriage, even though it is a grievous thing to your heart, you must let her go without conflict (1 Corinthians 7:15).

Remember that your desire should be for your wife's salvation, but this cannot be your goal (what you must have). Your goal must be only to please and walk with the Lord through whatever happens (2 Corinthians 5:9). We should adopt the attitude of Daniel's friends before Nebuchadnezzar, and of Job in the face of severe trial, saying, "Whether God spares me or not—I will trust Him and obey Him." In other words, God may spare us from bad consequences when we do what is right, but if He chooses not to, we must be committed to obeying Him anyway (Daniel 3:17-18; Job 13:15).

Love Her *All* the Time

Because your wife is not perfect, you will have times when you need to help her with her sin. Helping our wives to deal with their sin is one way that we can love them as Christ loves the church. God wants you to love your wife *all the time*, even when she is sinning. We will have great motivation to love our wives all the time if we remember that we are undeservedly loved by *God* all the time. If you have been in the habit of letting your wife sin freely, I strongly suggest that you sit down with her and discuss your desire to help her more, *before you begin doing so.*

In our efforts to help our wives, we must be more concerned about our own sin and our motives for helping her than about what our wife does or doesn't do. In addition, we must be sure that we are in the habit of loving her in other ways. God is also concerned that we respond His way by helping her with true repentance and by truly forgiving her.

One of the most important things for us to do is practice prayer. We need to utterly depend on God. Husband, be sure that you regularly ask Him to help you to love your wife, to be wise, to have courage and faith, and to use His Word in both of your lives. The most important thing of all is to be an example to your wife in the area of dealing with your own sin. This example will do more to help her than anything. Hopefully, she will see from *your* life what it means to walk humbly with God and deal quickly with sin.

> **He has told you, O man, what is good; and what does the Lord require of you but to do justice, to love kindness, and to walk humbly with your God?**
> **Micah 6:8**

Chapter Sixteen

A HUSBAND'S RESOLVE
GOOD COMMUNICATION

One of the biggest obstacles to a good marriage is poor communication. We could even say that a marriage relationship is only as good as a couple's ability to send and receive the right message. We will see in this chapter, and from Scripture, that good communication from God's perspective is sending a message that is *holy, purposeful, clear* and *timely*.

Communication is the vehicle that is used to accomplish many responsibilities and relational aspects of marriage. Without it a husband can neither lead properly, nor communicate love effectively. One can neither address issues without it, nor resolve conflict without it.

How we communicate with our wives will produce either good or bad consequences. If we communicate poorly, it will have a negative effect on the marriage relationship. (Some of the following is adapted from *Strengthening your Marriage*, by Wayne Mack.) [22]

Some negative effects of poor communication are:

- God will not be honored by a good testimony for Christ.
- The relationship will be superficial and strained.
- Discord and conflict will be common.
- Issues will remain unclear and unresolved.
- Wrong ideas will remain uncorrected.
- Bitterness will begin to set in.
- Wise decision-making will be thwarted.
- The temptation will be great to communicate with another person outside the marriage.

On the other hand, if we communicate in a God-honoring way, it will have a very positive impact on the marriage relationship.

Some of the positive effects of good communication are:

- God is honored by a good testimony for Christ.
- The relationship will be strengthened and be meaningful.
- Companionship and oneness will be enjoyed more.
- Harmony will be present.
- Any disagreement can be handled quickly and without conflict.
- Problem issues can be clarified and resolved.
- Wrong ideas can be corrected.
- Forgiveness and trust will be exercised easier.
- Good decision-making will be enhanced.

Good Communication Is Important to God

Even more important than the fact that good communication is crucial to the marriage relationship is the fact that good communication is extremely important to God. It involves self-control and discipline—character qualities that the Christian must possess. Communication involves ruling our spirit, our tongue, and our body, and going against our feelings when they contradict what we know to be true. Communication involves the heart, which is of the greatest importance to God. He often addresses our communication to expose the heart, because our communication is ruled by what is in our heart. Jesus said:

> **You brood of vipers, how can you, being evil, speak
> what is good? For the mouth speaks out of that which
> fills the heart.**
> **Matthew 12:34**

This area of the Christian life is so important to God that the Bible is full of commands and principles on communication. (See Study Guide for a sample list of Bible verses on communication.)

Perhaps the most crucial element of communication is our speech. It is certainly the most obvious. The Word of God teaches us that if a person can control his tongue he will be a godly man and able to control all of his passions.

> **For we all stumble in many ways. If anyone does not
> stumble in what he says, he is a perfect man, able to
> bridle the whole body as well.**
> **James 3:2**

Being in control of what we say and how we say it is a great virtue in God's sight, and can bring Him great glory. Not being careful about our communication, however, can do a great deal of damage and therefore dishonor God.

> **See how great a forest is set aflame by such a small
> fire! And the tongue is a fire, the very world of iniq-
> uity; the tongue is set among our members as that
> which defiles the entire body, and sets on fire the
> course of our life, and is set on fire by hell.**
> **James 3:5b-6**

A man who communicates in a way that displeases God should not think that he is a godly man. You may be a deacon or a Sunday school teacher in your church, but your communication will reveal the kind of man you really are, because what comes out of your mouth is usually what's in your heart. If you truly desire to exemplify Christ you will seek to become a good communicator. Everything that Jesus Christ communicated was *holy, clear, purposeful,* and *timely.* With a prayer for God's help, let's seek to understand the prerequisites and the mechanics of this kind of communication.

Six Prerequisites to Good Communication

1. *A husband must want to please God more than anything else.* He must want to please God more than to have his own way. He must want to please God more than to be right. He must want to please God more than to be vindicated.

    Therefore we also have as our ambition, whether at home or absent, to be pleasing to Him.
    2 Corinthians 5:9

2. *A husband must be humble.* We have already explored humility in detail but it should be mentioned here that it takes a great deal of humility to communicate for the right reasons, and to not react in pride to something that is being said by the other person. A humble man is a patient man. If a husband is humble he will be patient when what he says is misunderstood, or when he is having trouble understanding what his wife is trying to say to him.

    Therefore I, the prisoner of the Lord, implore you to walk in a manner worthy of the calling with which you have been called, with all humility and gentleness, with patience, showing tolerance for one another in love, being diligent to preserve the unity of the Spirit in the bond of peace.
    Ephesians 4:1-3

3. *A husband must be aware that he is accountable to God for everything he communicates.* God hears our every word and will hold us accountable for them.

    But I tell you that every careless word that people speak, they shall give an accounting for it in the day of judgment.
    Matthew 12:36

4. *A husband must know how to listen.* Good communication is dependent on good listening skills. James says, "everyone must be quick to hear, slow to speak and slow to become angry" (1:19). James means that we need to listen more than we speak.

Unfortunately many of us do just the opposite, especially in the midst of a disagreement. Some of us will not let the other person get a word in edgewise. This talkativeness could be because we believe that only we could have anything valuable to say, because we simply like to hear ourselves talk, or because we are desperately trying to get our own way or be proven right.

If a person is not a good listener, he will most likely jump to conclusions. If he jumps to conclusions he will most likely say or do the wrong thing. We are warned about speaking before we have really heard what others have to say:

> **He who gives an answer before he hears, it is folly and shame to him.**
> **Proverbs 18:13**

Listening well means:

- Concentrating on and carefully considering what the other person is saying.
- Not interrupting (some rare exceptions may apply, e. g., someone who never stops talking, or when someone is out of control).
- Not formulating what you are going to say while the other person is talking.
- Not talking too much, but allowing breaks in the conversation so that another person can have time to process information, formulate what they want to say and then say it to you.
- When you are in an important conversation, always ask for clarification with comments like, "Could you say that again?" or "Could you explain a little more?" or "Is this what you are saying...?"
- Not talking when someone else is speaking. This bad manner is a serious offense.

5. *A husband must know that communication involves more than just words.* Communication involves words, tone of voice, body language, and deeds. It is a well-known fact that the words we speak are only one avenue of our communication. We can say two completely different things by changing our tone of voice and body language. Take the phrase, "Could you please come here?" Put on an angry face, shake your index finger, and put a great deal of emphasis on the word please and you have a harsh comment. Say the

same words, however, with a smile and a warm, coaxing tone of voice, and you have communicated a very different message. We can even cancel out our words if everything else about us says the opposite.

A husband must be very careful about:

- The volume of his voice
- The tone of his voice
- Facial expressions
- Hand gestures
- Sighing, or in some cases, snorting
- Rolling the eyes
- A look of amazement or disgust
- Body posture

Ask your wife to help you recognize any wrong use of these very counter-productive means of communication.

Communication also involves deeds. Sometimes our actions speak louder than our words. Sometimes they speak differently than our words. If we say to our wives "I want to spend time with you today," and then tinker around in the garage or in the yard all day, what are we really communicating? Be sure that your deeds communicate the same thing as your words. Don't just say what is right, do what is right.

> **Therefore, to one who knows the right thing to do and does not do it, to him it is sin.**
> **James 4:17**

6. *A husband must be willing to put forth the effort and spend the time that it takes to communicate.* A husband who is self-serving will most likely not communicate well. We need to talk when we don't want to talk and listen when we don't want to listen. Many husbands find it difficult to talk and listen after a hard day's work, especially if their job is people-oriented. This, however, is where the husband must die to self.

Some husbands may not be gifted in speaking to groups of people, but they must speak to their wives and families in order to love and shepherd them. The less we speak, the harder it will before others to avoid assuming what is going on inside of us. Just because we are ill, tired, or not much of a talker, we are not released from the responsibility to work at good communication.

> Be devoted to one another in brotherly love; give preference to one another in honor; not lagging behind in diligence, fervent in spirit, serving the Lord; rejoicing in hope, persevering in tribulation, devoted to prayer.
>
> Rom. 12:10-12

Biblical Principles of Verbal Communication

Two General Principles

A great deal of our communication involves our speech. We are continually using words to communicate with others. It is very important that we know what God has to say about speech in particular. King David and his son, King Solomon, give us two general principles to remember.

1. **We must truly desire to guard our lips**. We must put great importance on honoring God with our speech. David prayed:

    > Set a guard, O Lord, over my mouth; keep watch over the door of my lips.
    >
    > Psalm 141:3

2. **We must understand that if we <u>do</u> guard our lips, we will avoid all kinds of trouble**. King Solomon, who also told us to "guard our heart" (Proverbs 4:23), said:

    > He who guards his mouth and his tongue, guards his soul from troubles.
    >
    > Proverbs 21:23

With these general principles in mind, we can get more specific about our speech.

Four Specific Principles

We are going to relate our four principles to the qualities of Christ's communication mentioned earlier. His communication was: holy, purposeful, clear, and timely.

1.   Christ's communication was **Holy**:   (truthful and righteous)

What you say must be *the truth..*

> **Therefore, laying aside falsehood, speak truth each one of you with his neighbor, for we are members of one another.**
> **Ephesians 4:25**

Everything Christ said was completely true. As husbands who want to exemplify Him, we must be sure that we are totally honest. This statement means there will be no form of deceit in what we say, and that everything we say will agree with God's truth. We will be very careful that what we say is accurate. God hates lying.

> **There are six things which the Lord hates, yes, seven which are an abomination to Him: .... a lying tongue ....**
> **Proverbs 6:16-17a**

There are many forms of deceit we must guard against.

- An outright lie
  This would be a complete fabrication or contradiction of the truth (e.g., Satan, Genesis 3:4).
- An exaggeration—going further than the truth
  The truth plus a lie always equals a lie (e.g., Esau, Genesis 25:32).
- A half or partial truth— giving only part of the information, so as to lead a person to believe something that is not really true or to cover up the truth (e.g., Abraham, Genesis 12:13)
- An evasion of the truth—changing the subject, not really answering the question, causing another problem to divert attention (e.g., Cain, Genesis 4:9).

How you say it must be *righteous.*

> Let no unwholesome word proceed from your mouth.... Do not grieve the Holy Spirit of God, by whom you were sealed for the day of redemption. Let all bitterness and wrath and anger and clamor and slander be put away from you, along with all malice. Be kind to one another, tender-hearted, forgiving each other, just as God in Christ also has forgiven you.
> **Ephesians 4:29-32**

This principle is where we must rule our spirit and our words, no matter what the other person does. Christ was always in control and holy in how He communicated. You will not be able to control what others say, but by God's grace you can control how you respond.

Our speech must be without:

- Bitterness: a fixed attitude of sharpness or harshness
- Wrath: a temporary outburst of anger
- Anger: a slow burn of indignation
- Clamor: yelling, loud quarreling, harsh contention
- Slander: speaking evil of a person, like name-calling, belittling, attacking the person, etc.
- Malice: speech designed to injure or make someone suffer

Instead, our speech must be with:

- Kindness: gracious, easy, courteous, good, helpful
- Tenderheartedness: compassionate, sympathetic
- Forgiveness: giving up on revenge or a grudge

> **He who is slow to anger is better than the mighty, and he who rules his spirit, than he who captures a city.**
> **Proverbs 16:32**

You must be careful not to enter into sin even if your wife is sinning. Answer her in a godly way and a way that convicts her of her own foolishness. This guideline also applies to answering an angry person or a manipulative person.

> **Do not answer a fool *according to his folly*, or you
> will also be like him. Answer a fool *as his folly
> deserves*, that he not be wise in his own eyes.**
> **Proverbs 26:4-5 [emphasis mine]**

Remember, our actions (in this case our words) are directly connected to our thoughts. If you are going to be successful in practicing right responses, you must begin at the level of your thoughts. Seek to isolate the thoughts that lead to the wrong ways of speaking.

2.   Christ's communication was **Purposeful**:

<u>The reason you say it: Your motivation must be *unselfish.*</u>

For God's glory: **"...Do all to the glory of God." 1 Corinthians 10:31b**

For others' good: **"...Only such a word as is good for edification
according to the need of the moment, so that it will
give grace to those who hear." Ephesians 4:29**

Christ's purposes were God the Father's purposes, and they were always unselfish. If we are not careful we can communicate for the wrong reasons. We should not speak in order to get our selfish or fleshly desires met or to retaliate. Until we are confident that our purpose in speaking is for God's glory and for the other's good, we would do better to remain quiet. Pray for the right motive.

<u>If our motives are right, we will:</u>

*   Act, not react according to feelings or pride
*   Attack the problem, not the person
*   Say only what will accomplish good
*   Be solution-oriented

We need to be aware that this is another area where "the flesh wars against the spirit." Expect your flesh to rear its ugly head but be ready, by God's grace, to deny it and control it. If we want our speech to accomplish good purposes, we will always be gracious in how we speak and we will not use any wrong methods of speech. This idea is explained by Paul in Colossians:

> **Let your speech always be with grace, as though seasoned with salt, so that you will know how you should respond to each person.**
> **Colossians 4:6**

Having gracious speech is likened to something that is seasoned with salt. Salt makes food palatable or tasty and preserves it from corruption. We need to make our words as palatable as possible and as preserving as possible.

Also, our words will not be able to accomplish good purposes if we do not have all the information. Be sure that you have *all* the facts and information and *accurate* facts and information. Ask questions (Proverbs 18:13).

3. Christ's communication was **Clear:**

<u>*The way* you say it must be *straight-forward and appropriate.*</u>

> **But let your statement be, 'Yes, yes' or 'No, no'; anything beyond these is of evil.**
> **Matthew 5:37**

Christ was a master at getting to the heart of the matter when He communicated. Every word He spoke was perfectly suited to the situation. There were times when He spoke in parables for the express purpose of not being understood by those who really weren't interested in following Him or because the time was not right (Matthew 13:10-16). But this approach was taken for God's purposes and is not normally how He spoke to the disciples. Christ was a man of few words. He never said more than what needed to be said. Many words can make a message unclear and also lead to sin.

> **When there are many words, transgression is unavoidable, but he who restrains his lips is wise.**
> **Proverbs 10:19**

The passages above teach clearly that we need to be straightforward (but loving) in our speech, and as brief and appropriate as possible. We need to learn how to get to the heart of the matter wisely, and fittingly. It is impossible to be straightforward, brief, and appropriate, unless we think carefully about what we are going to say.

> **The heart of the righteous *ponders how to answer*, but
> the mouth of the wicked pours out evil things.
> Proverbs 15:28 [emphasis mine]**

<u>If we are going to be clear we will:</u>

- Pray about what to say.
- Think carefully about what needs to be said.
- Speak concisely.
- Refrain from withholding information or frustrating people by saying things like, "I'm not going to tell you. You should know!"
- Discuss mutual definitions. For example, someone might tell you "When you say 'That's different,' what I incorrectly understand is, 'That's stupid,' so don't say that anymore."
- Use no manipulative tactics. Say what you mean. Don't hint or say something to make others feel guilty so they will do what you want.

4. Christ's communication was **Timely**:

<u>*When* you say it the time needs to be *right*.</u>

> **Like apples of gold in settings of silver is a word
> spoken in right circumstances
> Proverbs 25:11**

Christ always communicated at the perfect time. There are two principles concerning when we should communicate. We must communicate *as soon as time and situation will allow* and at *a good time*. We must not put off saying what needs to be said or dealing with a conflict any longer than is necessary. When we wait without good reason, we are giving the devil an opportunity to use the situation for evil.

Choosing the right time to speak will help good communication to take place. It is not being wise to deal with something important when there is really not enough time, when we or the other person are extremely tired, or when we know that the other person is either not in a very good frame of mind or distracted. A wise person will carefully choose his time to communicate.

To be timely we need to:

- Communicate something that needs to be communicated as soon as it is prudent. Don't wait needlessly.
- Have adequate time to communicate what needs to be communicated and give the other person a chance to respond.
- Be sure that the time you choose is the best time for all those involved.

Are You Truly Resolved?

The exemplary husband must be fully resolved to pursue godly communication. It is not easy to create new habits, but with God's help you can continue to improve at communicating His way. Unless you truly desire to honor God in this aspect of your marriage, the relationship will never be what it could be. Furthermore, it is not possible for a husband to fulfill his responsibilities without good communication skills. Communicating in a God-honoring way involves having the right heart (one that is humble and wants to please God), some good listening skills and a willingness to die to self. Then, we must work to make our communication holy, clear, purposeful, and timely.

Chapter Seventeen

A HUSBAND'S RESOLVE
CONFLICT RESOLUTION

It has been said, "Marriage is made in heaven, but so are thunder and lightning." Many marriages are characterized by conflict. For God's people, this should not be so. Any Christian couple can learn to dwell together in unity. I am not saying that Christian couples will always see *everything* eye to eye or even *never* offend one another. What I am saying is that true Christians can learn how to keep from fighting with one another. Even just one partner can keep a conflict from happening (Proverbs 15:18). Every exemplary husband can and must know how to biblically avoid and resolve conflicts with his wife.

Exactly What is a Conflict?

When we talk about conflict we are not talking about having a difference of opinion with someone or disagreeing with someone. We are not even talking about being offended or offending someone. These things can happen without conflict. The Latin word from which we get the word *conflict* means *to strike*. Conflict is a common military term which means to *fight against*. When two people have a conflict they may have a physical fight and/or a verbal fight, but both people are involved and against one another. Conflict, then, is *when both parties sin against one another (in their communication and/or their actions) and are then in opposition to one another.*

What Does God Think of Conflict?

Conflict is a grievous thing to God. He wants His children to have no part in it. The Bible is full of commands about controlling our words and our spirit, full of warnings about strife, and full of instruction on what to do if someone is angry with us or sinning against us. God wants His children to pursue peace:

> **Walk in a manner worthy of the calling with which**
> **you have been called, ... being diligent to preserve**
> **the unity of the Spirit in the bond of peace.**
> **Ephesians 4:1,3**

Most conflicts begin with some sort of offense. God wants us to do everything we can not to offend anyone. Sometimes a person will take offense at the Word of God or even the truth spoken in love. We cannot always avoid offending someone when we love them enough to tell them what they need to hear. What God does *not* want us to do is needlessly or sinfully offend someone. This offense does not bring Him glory. Not offending others is the context of a verse that has been mentioned several times in this book.

> **Whether, then, you eat or drink or whatever you do,**
> **do all to the glory of God. Give no offense either to**
> **Jews or to Greeks or to the church of God.**
> **1 Corinthians 10:31-32**

Not only are we to be careful that we do not offend others, but God tells us to love, pray for, and do good to those who sin against us. We are to return good even to our enemies (Romans 12:21). Taking part in conflict is never an option to God. When we choose to sin in this way we are not acting like His children at all.

> **But I say to you, love your enemies and pray for those who persecute you, so that you may be sons of your Father who is in heaven; for He causes His sun to rise on the evil and the good, and sends rain on the righteous and the unrighteous.**
> **Matthew 5:44-45**

We have already seen what God thinks of the thoughts, words, and actions that are involved in sinful communication. Sinful communication is always involved in conflict. When Christ was addressing His disciples in Matthew 5, He said:

> **You have heard that the ancients were told, "You shall not commit murder" and "Whoever commits murder shall be liable to the court." But I say to you that everyone who is angry with his brother shall be guilty before the court; and whoever says to his brother, "You good for nothing [empty head]," shall be guilty before the supreme court; and whoever says, "You fool [wicked-hearted person]," shall be guilty enough to go into the fiery hell.**
> **Matthew 5:21-22 [explanation mine]**

Here, Jesus puts being angry with someone on the same level as murder. He goes on to show that expressing that anger is even worse! Conflict is a serious thing to God. An exemplary husband will work to rid his marriage of it.

Where Do Conflicts Come From?

Differences

Conflicts can arise out of personal differences and differences of opinion. People are very different from one another. They have different abilities, different amounts of knowledge, different likes and dislikes, and different perspectives. This is something we need to accept as the norm. It is true that the more a couple has in common, the more they will see things in the same way. This does not mean that couples have to have a great deal in common in order to get along. Nor does it mean that they will necessarily have less conflict if they have a great deal in common. A couple can have a great deal in common and still have conflict if they are proud and selfish. Some say there is no hope for couples who are not compatible. This is obviously not God's perspective because when the Bible was written, many couples who married hardly knew each other, if at all (Genesis 24:1-4).

Having little in common does mean, however, that you must work to know one another well, appreciate one another, and see things from one another's perspective. These attitudes are certainly possible to attain, and working on them is a tremendous exercise in real love (Ephesians 4:2-3). I remember one couple in particular who came to see me. They were as different as two people could be and were very disturbed about the frequent conflicts in their marriage. They were a young Christian couple, active in ministry who sincerely loved the Lord. Because of their commitment to their marriage and to the Lord, they began working hard at knowing, appreciating, and trying to understand things from the other's perspective. They now consider this one of the most rewarding times of their lives and are the dearest people in the world to one another. The more you work at knowing, appreciating, and understanding the perspective of your wife, the more you will love her. Husband, *you* must take the lead in this endeavor if there are significant differences between you and your wife. Be encouraged! Spouses who are very different *can* experience companionship and oneness.

One of the things that can help very differing spouses the most is growth in God's Word. The more we have God's Word in common as husbands and wives, the more we will agree. The more each mind is renewed (changed) by Scripture, the more similarly a couple will think (Romans 12:2). One of the worst things a couple can do is work to change one another into each other's likeness. They are to be changed, rather, into Christ's likeness. The more a couple works at love and becoming one, the more differences will be accepted and blended to enhance the marriage.

Offenses

A very serious cause of conflict is a wrong response to an offense or to a sinning spouse. There is no reason an offense or someone else's sin must lead to a conflict in which both parties are sinning. A husband needs to learn how to respond humbly and graciously to his wife's sin and how to follow God's instructions for restoring her. He must control his responses to fit God's rules of communication and the proper handling of sin.

He who restrains his words has knowledge, and he who has a cool spirit is a man of understanding.
Proverbs 17:27

Pride and the Flesh

Whether a conflict arises out of a difference or an offense, it always involves sin. It ultimately stems from self-exalting pride, self-serving lusts, or both. The Proverbs tell us, "an arrogant man stirs up strife" (Proverbs 28:25) and "by pride comes nothing but strife" (Proverbs 13:10; NKJV). We have already addressed pride and humility a great deal (see Chapter 13: "Humility and Service"), but it is important that you as a husband grasp the connection between pride and conflict. A husband must be humble if he wishes to live in harmony with his wife.

Our fleshly lusts are another basic cause of conflict. James rebukes his readers in this way:

What is the source of quarrels and conflicts among you? Is not the source your pleasures that wage war in your members? *You lust and do not have;* **so you commit murder. You are** *envious and cannot obtain;* **so you fight and quarrel. You do not have because you do not ask. You ask and do not receive, because you ask with wrong motives,** *so that you may spend it on your pleasures.*
James 4:1-3 [emphasis mine]

James is telling us that the quarrels and conflicts in which we find ourselves are the outworking or the "deeds" of our fleshly lusts. Paul puts it another way:

> **Now the deeds of the flesh are evident, which are: immorality, impurity, sensuality, idolatry, sorcery,** *enmities, strife, jealousy, outbursts of anger, disputes, dissensions, factions, envying,* **drunkenness, carousing, and things like these, of which I forewarn you, just as I have forewarned you, that those who practice such things will not inherit the kingdom of God.**
> **Galatians 5:19-21 [emphasis mine]**

James' terminology is perfect for understanding the root cause of many conflicts. Several of the Greek words that James uses are military terms, like our term *conflict*. In many contexts, the word for "quarrels" means *military campaigns or chronic states of war*. The word for "conflicts" means *separate conflicts within a war*, or *small battles*. With these words James is conveying the idea of our being in opposition to one another. He goes on to explain exactly what causes this opposition. It comes from the things we intently long for ("lust") or hotly desire ("envy"), but cannot obtain. Conflicts happen when we *must* have something. Our desires may even be good desires in and of themselves, but when they become demands, they are sinful. It is as if we set up a military encampment to obtain whatever it is we want so badly. If we picture our desires and our wife's desires as military tents, the tent pegs become firmly planted and the battle begins.

Encamped Lusts

GOD

1 Peter 5:5 God is opposed to the PROUD

Quarrels and Conflicts

His Lusts*

Her Lusts*

Selfish Desires:
My Way
My Feelings
My Rights
My Expectations
My Needs
My Plans

Selfish Desires:
My Way
My Feelings
My Rights
My Expectations
My Needs
My Plans

PROUD and Fleshly

PROUD and Fleshly

*Lusts = Evil Desires and/or good desires turned lustful

When our goal becomes fulfilling our fleshly desires, we *will* have conflict. If a husband is going to successfully stop participating in battle, he must be able to recognize fleshly lusts.

Some things that are fleshly lusts if pursued for self-gratification are:

- Riches
- Sex
- Food
- Possessions
- Relaxation/comfort
- Enjoyable or extreme experiences
- Recognition/approval

In the midst of a conflict ask yourself, "What is it I am wanting for myself?" If we are to stay out of or resolve conflict, our focus must be the good of others instead of self.

Let no one seek his own good, but that of his neighbor.
1 Corinthians 10:24

A man who is engaged in conflict is focused on self and not on loving his wife and glorifying God. Paul tells us that love "does not seek it's own, is not provoked" and "does not take into account a wrong suffered" (1 Corinthians 13:5)." When we are humble and loving, we will not seek to please self and we will not engage in conflict.

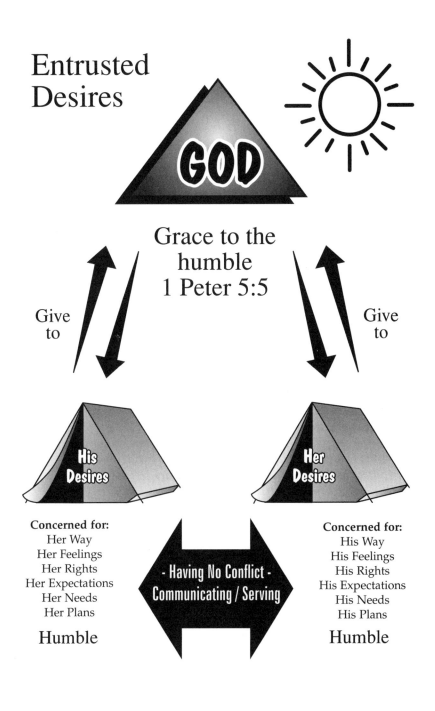

We know that sin begins in one's mind. Our proud and fleshly thoughts can be likened to the seeds of conflict. We must do away with these sinful seeds before they spring up and cause conflict. We must replace proud or fleshly thinking if we hope to avoid conflict. Here are some thoughts that can cause conflict, and replacements for them:

Thoughts that lead to conflict:	Thoughts that avoid conflict:
That's ridiculous! I *will* have my way! How dare she! I will not be treated this way!	She may have a point. I don't have to have my way. I need to pray for her. How can I return good to her?

Can Differences and Disagreements Be Beneficial?

Yes! Differences and disagreements *can* be beneficial. We have already seen that they can be a beginning point to the development of real love, when we purpose to appreciate our spouse despite our differences. Here are some other benefits of differences and disagreements:

- They can encourage us to search the Scriptures (Psalm 119:71-72).
- They can help us think carefully about how and what we think or what we believe (Proverbs 15:28).
- They can help us work harder at communicating effectively (Ephesians 4:25).
- They can produce maturity and endurance (James 1:2-5).
- They can help us sharpen one another (Proverbs 27:17).
- They can strengthen our faith in the truth that God is working all things together for good (Romans 8:28-29).
- They give us opportunity to practice servanthood and preferring one another (Philippians 2:2-3).
- They give us opportunity to love and glorify God (1 Corinthians 10:31-32).

How Do We Avoid Conflicts?

We have seen that there are three sure-fire ways to *start* a conflict: wrong thoughts, wrong words, and/or wrong actions. A good question is, "How can a husband *avoid* one?" This is an important question to ask because there are wrong and right ways to avoid a conflict.

Some sinful ways to avoid conflict:

- *Just keep quiet.* Many husbands choose to avoid conflict in ways that are not acceptable to God. While there may be times that we should keep quiet, avoiding communication as a general rule is sinful. I once read in the newspaper about a couple who were proud of the fact that they had never argued in over 50 years. The husband went on to explain that whenever they disagreed, he would just "keep quiet." Some husbands don't communicate much at all, in order to avoid conflict. We have already discussed why a husband must communicate. He cannot obey God in his role as a husband without really communicating with his wife. It is also very easy for bitterness to grow. When there is little or no communication, eventually bitterness will find a way to express itself (Ecclesiastes 3:7b; Ephesians 4:29-31; Colossians 3:19).

- *Stay away from one another.* Obviously this is not an option for the exemplary husband. Consider God's commands to love, lead, and be one with our wives. We are commanded to be "fervent [stretched out with all intensity] in our love" (John 15:12; 1 Peter 4:8; see also Chapter 4: "Relationships").

- *Change the subject.* This tactic is much like the keep-quiet method, but it also involves deception and manipulation (Proverbs 12:22; Proverbs 24:28).

- *Hide information, sins or bitterness.* This method involves deception, which we know to be sin. There is also no way that a couple can be one when this is going on (Genesis 20:2).

Some God-honoring ways to avoid conflict:

- *Seek to know your wife well, appreciate her and understand her perspective* (1 Peter 3:7).

- *Gather plenty of data before speaking.* Clarify often what you think you heard or understood. Ask lots of questions (Proverbs 18:13,17).

- Pray, study and think about the issue before speaking, if possible (Proverbs 15:28).

- Demonstrate and/or communicate your love and care at the time of a disagreement (Romans 12:9-10).

- Listen more than you speak, but do speak (Proverbs 10:19; 25:11).

- In matters of sin, approach your wife in love (Ephesians 4:15; Colossians 3:19).

- In matters of preference, prefer your wife (Romans 12:10).

- In matters of wisdom and conscience, suggest searching the Scriptures and getting godly counsel (Proverbs 11:14; 2 Timothy 2:15).

- Refuse to sin in your communication (Proverbs 8:6-8).

- Be more interested in God's glory and the other's good, rather than having your own way, or being right (Joshua 22:5; Romans 15:2).

One of the best ways to avoid conflict when another person is angry at you is to give a gentle and caring answer to their angry words. The Proverbs tell us:

> **A gentle answer turns away wrath, but a harsh word stirs up anger.**
> **Proverbs 15:1**

Be careful that your words are the right words as well. I know of husbands who can say something very unkind or condescending in a calm way to further infuriate their wives. What we are really talking about here is returning good for evil. A humble husband will assume that the wife does have a legitimate point underneath her anger, and he will gently express a desire to hear it. When your wife is upset, you can say something like, "I can see you are upset; let's sit down and talk about it. I do love you and want to work this out."

With a firm commitment, a plan, and a prayer for God "to help in the time of need," we can resist the temptation to return the anger that is coming at us (Hebrews 4:16).

We can usually disarm an angry wife quite effectively by a godly response. For those rare times when a wife cannot be disarmed after several tries, the best thing to do is to express your desire to talk when she has calmed down and then walk away. If the situation should ever escalate to physical attack, a couple should seek biblical counseling from their church leadership.

A person who is sincerely and biblically trying to avoid conflict is pursuing peace. Even when there is just one person pursing peace, there will be very little conflict. There may be times when your wife may not be at peace with you, but you can choose to be at peace with her and seek to reconcile with her.

> **If possible, so far as it depends on you, be at peace with all men.**
> **Romans 12:18**

> **So then let us pursue the things which make for peace and the building up of one another.**
> **Romans 14:19**

Resolving Conflicts

"Okay," you say, "but what about when a conflict has already begun or has been fully carried out (but not resolved), then what?" If you know that your wife is bitter against you for any reason, you must make every effort to resolve the situation. By not dealing with her bitterness, you risk having anger, and then bitterness takes root in your own heart. There are right and wrong ways to resolve conflicts. Our method of resolving conflicts needs to be in agreement with God's Word.

Some sinful ways to resolve conflicts:

- *Let time heal it.* Healing alone is not what is needed or what honors God when a conflict has taken place. What is needed is confession, forgiveness, and repentance. Time passes for us but not for God. He wants His children to deal with sin quickly (Matthew 5:23-24; Ephesians 4:26). Usually another's sin and our hurts become bigger (not smaller) with the passage of time. Our memories can become very selective and make the resolution process even more difficult.

- *Try to bury it.* Trying to forget about what happened or stay so busy that you don't have time to think only works for so long. A person who lives this way will most likely accumulate many unresolved issues, which can very easily result in more sin, bitterness, depression, and/or even physical sickness. Many misuse Philippians 3:13 in an attempt to biblically justify this position.

- *Pretend it never happened.* This sinful way to resolve conflict is one way to really irritate your wife! All the pretending in the world does not erase a conflict. A person who does this is not living in reality and will only carry on superficial relationships with other people (Philippians 4:8a).

- *Wait for the other person to initiate the resolution process.* This approach is in direct violation of God's command to go and seek to resolve any problem that someone has with you (Matthew 5:23-24).

- *Punish the other person until they change and take all the blame.* Husbands can do various things to punish their wives until they change and assume the blame. They may give them the silent treatment, refuse to give them money, be harsh with them, or even leave. This method of dealing with conflict is only heaping sin upon sin (Galatians 6:1; Romans 12:9-20).

A biblical way to resolve conflict:

- *Confess any sin that you are aware of to God.* Ask Him to open your eyes to any other sin on your part as you consider His Word. You can start by thinking about your motives, your thoughts, your attitude, your words, and your actions (Psalm 139:23-24; 1 John 1:9-10).

- *Go to your wife, ask forgiveness for each thing you did specifically and discuss your plan not to do those things again* (Ephesians 4:32; James 5:16).

- *Express a desire to resolve the conflict fully and decide together when the best time to do that would be.* Ask her if she would (in the meantime) consider if there is any other way that you have sinned, any sin that she may have committed, and what the issues of the conflict are (Proverbs 15:28).

- *Come together at the appointed time.* Express your desire to honor God and love her by doing everything you can to resolve this issue with both of you on the same team against the problem, not against each other (Psalm 34:14). Think of the problem as not between you but as a challenge for both of you together.

- *Pray together for God's wisdom, self-control, and speech* (Proverbs 16:32; James 1:5).

- *Review God's rules of communication.* Decide on a reminder phrase or sign you can use if there is a violation during your discussion (Ephesians 4:15, 26-32; James 1:19).

  1. Be a good listener
  2. Speak the truth.
  3. Speak in a righteous way—in love.
  4. Speak with the right purposes: God's glory and the other's good.
  5. Speak as clearly as possible.

- *Each one should take a turn to confess any sin that has not been confessed (to God and spouse), and ask forgiveness.* Each should ask for the other's input (Ephesians 4:32; James 5:16; 1 John 1:9).

- *Begin discussing the issues that precipitated the conflict.* Let me suggest maybe spending only 30-40 minutes trying to reach a point of unity concerning the issue (at least come up with a plan). After that, decide on another time to come together again. Seek to love one another in the meantime.

- Decide what you can agree upon (each takes a turn).
- Decide what you do not agree upon (each takes a turn).
- Decide what kind of issue(s) you are dealing with (each offers input).

  Is it a preference issue? Discuss ways to prefer one another (Philippians 2:3-5).

  Is it a sin issue? Discuss a repentance plan (Ephesians 4:22-24).

  Is it a conscience issue? Study and get counsel but do not ask the other to go against their conscience until the thing in question can be done in faith (Romans 14:23).

  Is it a wisdom issue? Gather facts, study, get counsel, and have each spouse give input. Then you are to make a biblical leadership decision as the husband (see Chapter 11 for information on biblical decision-making). At this point the wife should submit and trust in God's sovereignty, unless the husband is asking her to sin (Proverbs 2:3-6; Proverbs 12:15; 2 Timothy 2:15).
- Decide on specific steps to resolve the issue (each offers input).
- Together begin carrying out the appropriate steps to resolve the issue.
- Decide if and when you need to discuss the issue again.
- End your time together with prayer and an expression of love.

This resolution process encourages both husband and wife to remain humble, self-controlled, and solution-oriented. It is especially good for couples who are just starting to resolve issues biblically. Though it may take more than one time, it should help to resolve any issue. If you as a couple should be unsuccessful in reaching a point of unity after three tries, the wisest thing to do is enlist another godly couple to assist you. They should be able to determine what is keeping you from resolving the issue.

Avoiding conflict and resolving conflict will take repeated practice for those of you who have already created bad habits in this area. The good news is, if you persevere through the learning process, you will begin to enjoy the fruit of your labor. Handling personal differences, differences of opinion, and conflict God's way will cause love and unity to grow in your marriage, and both of you to grow in wisdom.

Who among you is wise and understanding? Let him show by his good behavior his deeds in the gentleness of wisdom. But if you have bitter jealousy and selfish ambition in your heart, do not be arrogant and so lie against the truth. This wisdom is not that which comes down from above, but is earthly, natural, demonic. For where jealousy and selfish ambition exist, there is disorder and every evil thing. But the wisdom from above is first pure, then peaceable, gentle, reasonable, full of mercy and good fruits, unwavering, without hypocrisy. And the seed whose fruit is righteousness is sown in peace by those who make peace.

James 3:13-18

PART FOUR

A HUSBAND'S REGRETS

Fatal Sins to the Exemplary Husband

Chapter Eighteen

A HUSBAND'S REGRET
ANGER

Our responsibility is to depend on God as we work toward becoming more like Him every day. Sometimes, there is a life-dominating sin that will greatly hinder a man from becoming more like Christ. In this section of the book, I want to offer some biblical help for three such sins. In marriage counseling over the years, I have seen these problems again and again in the lives of husbands. Even if we say we do not have a serious problem in these areas, we all have had experience with them and give way to them from time to time. We all need to be on guard against these sins and know how to deal with temptation when it comes. We need to avoid them as the detrimental sins they are.

For each one of these sins we need a clear *definition*, an *explanation*, a method of *examination*, and a path of *transformation*.

Sinful Anger Displeases God

Many men consider themselves possessed by the "anger demon" and think that they are victims of an anger attack. They themselves feel as if their anger is something they cannot control. These men talk about years of turmoil, and spend much of their time regretting the pain (sometimes even physical) and fear that they have caused their loved ones. Others see anger as a basically harmless vice because they do not hit anyone and their anger is short-lived, though powerful. We saw in Matthew 5:21-22 that Christ put sinful anger on a par with murder. God also has this to say about anger:

> Cease from anger and forsake wrath; do not fret; it leads only to evildoing.
> **Psalm 37:8**

As exemplary husbands we must put off sinful anger. When we are angry we are being foolish. This foolish behavior dishonors the Lord and it will cause great difficulty in your marriage.

> He who is slow to anger has great understanding, but he who is quick-tempered exalts folly.
> **Proverbs 14:29**

Definition

There are two kinds of anger mentioned in the Bible: *righteous anger* and *unrighteous anger*.

Righteous anger is indignation for holy reasons. This kind of anger is consumed with the desire for righteousness or with God's will, reputation, and honor. When God is angry, He has this kind of anger. It may be possible for man to have this kind of anger. Paul seemed to be righteously angry when he heard about those who were "led into sin" (2 Corinthians 11:29). Paul says in Ephesians 4:26, "Be angry and yet do not sin." This could be a reference to righteous anger or it could be a reference to the initial inclination or provocation to be angry. To be sure, righteous anger is extremely rare among men. Anyone who is righteously angry is not sinning, is not thinking of himself, and is in complete control. When Jesus cleared out the temple, He exemplified righteous and controlled anger (Mark 11:15-18).

> **God is a righteous judge, and a God who has indigna-**
> **tion every day.**
> **Psalm 7:11**

Unrighteous anger takes two basic forms. One is explosive and reactionary and involves venting one's feelings (Proverbs 15:28; Ephesians 4:31). Sometimes this kind of anger is easily seen and heard and is usually called "wrath" in the Bible. The other kind of anger is more of an inward slow burn. This kind of anger is simply termed "anger" in the Bible. Both of these kinds of anger are of man and are very ungodly. Here are some typical evidences of these kinds of anger.

Vented Anger	The Slow Burn
Yelling/screaming	Clamming up/moodiness
Slamming things around	Being frustrated
Cursing	Being irritated
Telling someone off	Being disgusted
Attacking verbally/name-calling	Glaring
Hitting	Huffing/snorting

> **But now you also, put them all aside: anger, wrath,**
> **malice, slander, and abusive speech from your mouth.**
> **Colossians 3:8**

Identifying Sinful Anger

Before we can talk about changing, we need to know more about what is involved with unrighteous anger and where it comes from. Sinful anger is a deed of the flesh.

> **Now the deeds of the flesh are evident, which are:**
> **immorality, impurity, sensuality, idolatry, sorcery,**
> *enmities, strife, jealousy, outbursts of anger, disputes, dissen-*
> *sions, factions....*
> **Galatians 5:19,20 [emphasis mine]**

<u>Here are some important facts about sinful anger:</u>

1. *Anger is natural to the fallen human heart.* It has been said, "The heart of the problem is a problem of the heart." Our hearts are desperately wicked. But for the grace of God every evil thing would come out of them. Before we can rid ourselves of anger we must admit that it is a sin problem and not blame it on a personality type, an inherited trait, or a chemical imbalance (Genesis 6:5; Jeremiah 17:9; Matthew 15:18-19 and Titus 3:3).

2. *Anger always involves thoughts and intentions.* Our hearts consist of our thoughts and our intentions or motives and more. Sinful anger begins in the mind. Because this is true, anger is a willful and deliberate choice. Though the reaction of anger may be such a well-worn path that it happens very quickly, thoughts and intentions are always involved (Proverbs 4:23 and Ephesians 4:17-18).

3. *Anger is caused by not being able to attain our prideful and/or selfish goals.* In other words, anger stems from our lusts. If you ask yourself when you are angry, "What is it I am wanting?" you will get to the root of your anger. The thing that you are wanting so badly could actually start out as a good desire, but at some point it becomes a goal or something you *must* have. Anger is an excellent tip-off that we are focused in the wrong direction. When something happens to block what we must have, we become sinfully angry (Read James 4:1-3).

4. *Anger never accomplishes God's righteous ends.* Though our anger will at times enable us to attain what we are after, it never accomplishes the righteousness of God. It never accomplishes anything worthwhile. If we are going to win the battle over anger, we must first accept the fact that when we become sinfully angry we are headed in the wrong direction. This doesn't necessarily mean that we must completely abandon a desire, but it does mean that we must do an about-face concerning our goal and how we attain it, or consider whether we even need to attain it. Read Proverbs 11:23 and James 1:20. Below is a way to picture what happens when we become sinfully angry.

The Cause of Anger

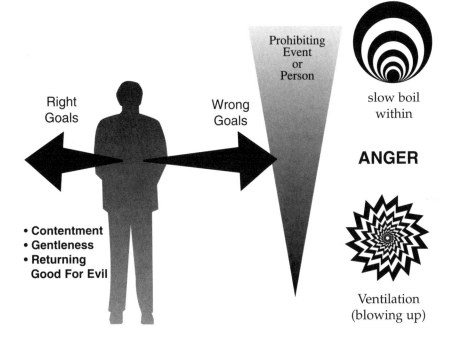

Right Goals
- Respond to problems in God's way or accept them as from God
- Uphold God's reputation/care what God thinks of me
- Serve others/help others, but leave them in God's hands
- Do what God wants me to do
- Pile up treasures in heaven
- Trust in God's control

Wrong Goals
(Wicked desires or desires turned to goals)
- Others doing right
- No difficulty (self-focus)
- Problem removed (self-focus)
- Good treatment/respect (from Others) (pride)
- Personal rights observed
- Others good opinion/ approval (pride)
- Wealth/material thing (selfishness)
- Control (self-focus/pride)
- Being better/being best or right (pride)
- Fulfilling a desire or plan/ getting my way (selfishness)
- Immediate results/actions

5. *Anger sometimes points to something good and right that should be done about a problem instead.* Sometimes we become angry when we have a situation or a problem that we need to do something about. Sometimes we become angry because there doesn't seem to be anything else we can do. Unfortunately, when we are in this mode of thinking we are being problem-oriented rather than solution-oriented. We must discover and learn to choose God's way of dealing with problems. Even then, we must be very careful to seek the right solution for the right reasons and to leave the outcome to God or we might become angry all over again. Some examples of when you need to do something right about a problem might be: when a person sins against you, when you have an overwhelming responsibility, when your schedule has been thwarted, etc. (Psalm 119:4, 9, 15, 16 and Proverbs 14:8)

6. *Anger is expressed in our thoughts, body language, speech, and actions.* Many men who struggle with anger don't see the seriousness of their problem because they may not take full action on their anger. We must remember that God sees the heart, and it is what goes on in there that makes up who we are. Even if we think we are angry only in our mind, we are still sinfully angry before God and that anger comes out in subtle but destructive ways we may not recognize. Even if it evidences itself only in a lack of communication, this is still a serious problem. In order to control our anger, we are going to have to be more aware of our thoughts, body language, and speech, not just major actions. Do not think, "It's all right if I just yell at her because I'm not hitting her." (Psalm 19:14 and Romans 6:12-13)

7. *Anger involves a lack of self-control.* People who struggle with anger lack self-control in their thoughts and often their deeds. They may find that they have trouble controlling themselves in other ways as well: time management, money management, lust, etc. Many times a self-control problem has been present for years. Perhaps the angry person has not controlled himself from childhood. Not controlling ourselves and merely following our initial inclinations is a choice that becomes easier and easier. While the basic problem of anger is not a lack of self-control, it will take self-control to redirect wrong thinking and learn new habits. (Proverbs 17:27; 25:8; 29:11 and 2 Peter 1:6)

8. *Anger is always accompanied by other sins when it is tolerated.* We have already mentioned some of these sins. Being aware of these sins will make us more aware of anger as a true anger problem. Look for sins such as: a critical spirit, withdrawal, gossip, slander, vengeance, unwholesome words (of the mind or of speech), rejoicing in someone's misfortune, and self-pity (Proverbs 29:22).

9. *If not dealt with, anger will turn into something worse.* Anger will usually follow the progression of bitterness, stubbornness, hate, rebellion, and can even lead to depression and/or suicidal tendencies (Job 4:8 and Ezekiel 18:30).

Examination

Before we discuss how to conquer anger, let us take serious inventory of our own lives. The first step to solving a problem is admitting that you have one. One of the worst things you can do when you are angry is tell yourself or someone else, "I'm not angry." Be careful of renaming anger as being "frustrated, miffed, ticked, stressed," etc. It is also important to pinpoint specific times and situations when you typically become sinfully angry. We all have times when we become angry. Answer the following questions to determine when, how often, and in what manner you become sinfully angry.

Search me, O God, and know my heart; try me and know my anxious thoughts; and see if there be any hurtful way in me, and lead me in the everlasting way.
Psalm 139:23-24

1. Is there anyone I am presently angry with?
2. What am I angry with them about?
3. How have I dealt with and responded to that person (or those persons)?
4. What do I typically do when I am angry? How might God be trying to reveal an anger problem to me?
5. What have been some results of my anger?
6. Do others see me as a critical or impatient person? (Ask them!)
7. When were the last five times I was angry?
8. What was my thinking at the time?
9. What kinds of things provoke me to anger?

10. Do I need to keep track in the next few weeks of when and why I become angry ? (When you feel irritated and frustrated, as if you are churning inside or ready to blow up, write down what you are thinking)

11. How many of these situations are precipitated by something else I am doing wrong? (My irresponsibility, laziness, poor time or money management, wrong treatment of others, etc.)

Transformation

Now that we understand anger, we can talk about what it takes to put it off and put on its righteous counterpart. Instead of anger we are to put on gentleness, patience, and humility (Ephesians 4:2, 32). Here are some things that you can do to change your angry ways:

Before anger hits again:

1. Confess your past sins of anger to God and others who have been aware of it. Explain your intentions to be gentle, patient, and humble in the future and ask for forgiveness (Matthew 5:23-24).

2. Ask God to work in this area of your life and help you to put forth full effort toward Christlike change (2 Corinthians 9:8).

3. Come up with the right thoughts to combat the wrong ones you typically have. Write them out. Use Scripture or scriptural concepts in your new thoughts. Include thankfulness in your new thoughts. Put your new thoughts in prayer form whenever you can (Romans 12:2).

Thoughts That Lead to Anger	Thoughts That Lead to Gentleness and Patience
I can't believe she is running late again! I hate being late. I insist on being on time! I'm not going to stand for this anymore!!	I don't like to be late but love is patient. I will show love to her by being patient. How can I help her to be on time more for her good? Thank you, Lord, that she takes the time to look nice.

How dare she talk to me like that! I deserve more respect than that. I will not be treated this way!	I'm not going to let my pride flare up. Lord, you didn't sin when you were not respected. What is she trying to say? I'll deal with her sin later. I'm thankful to be made aware that I have done something wrong.
Why can't the kids just do right and leave me alone! I'm tired and want to watch this TV show. They're going to get it!	Dealing with the children is my job as a parent and it pleases you, Lord. I'm tired but just give me the grace to help the children to learn. Thank you for them, Lord, and for the opportunity to teach them.

4. Memorize some verses on anger and some verses on gentleness, patience, forgiveness, or humbleness (Ephesians 4:23).

5. Since anger always involves pride, selfishness or both, seek to put on loving and humble thoughts and actions daily. Make a list of times and ways you can show love and humility (John 13:35 1 Corinthians 13:4-7; 1 Peter 5:5).

6. Determine what godly desires and goals you should be fixed on in situations in which you typically become angry (Psalm 40:8; 1 Corinthians 10:31).

7. Do a study on the patience and long-suffering God has with you (Numbers 14:18; Psalm 145:8, 2 Timothy 2:15; *The MacArthur Topical Bible* under God's patience, longsuffering, and grace).[23]

8. Be alert, ready to exercise self-control and to change your thinking. Watch out for the situations and thoughts you have discovered. Make a concise list of each one (1 Peter 1:13).

9. Ask others to hold you accountable for your anger (Galatians 6:1-2 Hebrews 10:24-25).

10. Do not associate with angry individuals, unless they are seeking to change (Proverbs 22:24).

At the time you are tempted to become angry or are beginning to become angry:

1. Pray for God's help (Hebrews 4:16).

2. Put off being angry (Proverbs 14:17).
   - Ask yourself, "What is it I am wanting so badly?" Let go of it as something you must have. The only desire you must have is to glorify God!
   - Ask yourself, "What am I thinking that is wrong?"

3. Put on gentleness, patience, and humility (Proverbs 16:32; James 1:19).
   - Ask yourself, "What should I be thinking?" Use your new thoughts and Scripture.
   - Ask yourself, "What is the right goal?"
   - Ask yourself, "How can I be patient and think of others?"
   - Ask yourself, "What do God and others want?" and "How can I serve them?"
   - Ask yourself, "Is there something right that I should do about the problem or issue?" (Address someone's sin in the right way, plan a solution, get counsel, etc.)

If you fail and become sinfully angry:

1. Ask yourself, "How did I sin?" Be specific.
2. Ask yourself, "If I had this to do over again, what should I think and do differently?"
3. Take care of your sin of anger as soon as possible (Ephesians 4:26).
4. Confess and ask forgiveness of God and anyone else who may have been aware of or the recipient of your sinful anger. Be specific about how you were sinfully angry: wrong thinking, wrong actions, lack of love, etc. (Psalm 32:5; James 5:16).
5. Tell God and others what you plan to do in the future instead of becoming sinfully angry (Psalm 119:59-60).

6.   Be on guard once again (1 Peter 5:8).

It is important that you not entertain the thinking, "This is impossible!" or "I'll never be able to change!" If you practice the principles above, you will see your anger become less and less frequent. With God's grace, God's Word, and your sincere efforts, you *will* be able to change (1 Corinthians 10:13). Remember that being tempted is not a sin, but following through with sinful anger is. Do not grow weary in "well-doing" and you will see the fruit of your efforts (Galatians 6:9). If God can change one of "the sons of thunder" (the Apostle John) into the apostle of love, He can change you (Mark 3:17; 1 John 4:7-21). A husband who wants to exemplify Christ must be "slow to anger" and "abounding in lovingkindness."

> **The Lord is compassionate and gracious, slow to anger and abounding in lovingkindness.**
> **Psalm 103:8**

Chapter Nineteen

A HUSBAND'S REGRET
ANXIETY AND FEAR

From the time we were little boys we were told, "Be brave!" "Show no fear!" And yet we live in a society where anxiety and fear are rampant. Even though we, as Christians, should not and need not worry, we still find reasons to be anxious and fearful. Many men experience more worry than they care to admit, living in a state of anxiety and rarely having a sense of peace. Some have trouble sleeping nights and try to manage their worries and fears with medication. Still others suffer what our society labels as debilitating "panic attacks" or even worse, "nervous breakdowns."

Husbands have great potential for worry because they have such great responsibility. We all face pressures and problems in life to one degree or another. The good news is that God speaks a great deal about anxiety and fear in His Word. He knows the difficulties we face. He has also given the Christian everything he needs to trust Him and find peace of mind. The problem is that many of us don't understand anxiety and fear, or how to combat them.

Definition

Anxiety and ungodly fear are like "kissing cousins." Though they are not exactly the same, where you see one, you often see the other because they are so very closely related. Anxiety usually involves worrying about what could possibly happen. Fear goes a step further and is more convinced that what is dreaded will really happen. When someone experiences *apprehension* that does not stay within biblical bounds, there is definitely a lack of peace and trust. Concern and fear are not always wrong. Both the words *concern* and *fear* are used in the Bible to refer to right and wrong responses. There is a godly concern and an ungodly concern (anxiety). There is a godly fear and an ungodly fear.

Godly concern is caring about important things for the right reasons. It is also accompanied by a trust in God's ultimate control and faithfulness. This kind of concern helps you to be responsible to God and does not send you into a confused state. It will involve a focus on *the responsibilities of today, eternal goals*, and *others*. Paul talks about the unmarried person being only "concerned" about the things of the Lord and the married person needing to be "concerned" also about pleasing his wife (1 Corinthians 7:32-33). In the New Testament reference is made to Paul's "concern for all the churches" and Timothy's "concern" for the Philippians' "welfare" (2 Corinthians 11:28; Philippians 2:20). These are examples of godly concern. For your concern to be the right kind of concern you must be focused on what is true and helpful from God's perspective.

So that there may be no division in the body, but that the members may have the same care for one another.
1 Corinthians 12:25

Ungodly concern (anxiety) goes beyond reasonable concern and involves worry about mere possibilities. When we are anxious, we are not focused on God and what is true and helpful. When we are anxious, we are often concerned that something *we want* to happen may not happen. Therefore, we are focused *on difficulties of the future, temporal matters*, and *self*. In Matthew 6 we are told not to worry about tomorrow and about "what we will eat," or "what we will wear for clothing" because unbelievers "eagerly seek these things" (Matthew

6:31-32). Instead, we are to concern ourselves with obeying God *today*. We are commanded not to be anxious for anything, but to trust God in everything.

Be *anxious* for nothing.
Philippians 4:6a

Godly fear has two parts: *the fear of God* and *reasonable fear of danger or difficulty*. When our fears fall into these two categories, we are not sinning.

- *The fear of God*: This fear is an acknowledgment of and an awe of who God is, which causes either full and glad submission to His loving will or terror of His judgment. We are all commanded to fear God (Deuteronomy 13:4). The one who loves God and delights in His will fears God as he should. This kind of fear is holy and wise and will keep us from ungodly fear.

  Praise the Lord! How blessed is the man who fears the Lord, who greatly delights in His commandments. ...He will not fear evil tidings; his heart is steadfast, trusting in the Lord, his heart is upheld, he will not fear.
  Psalm 112:1,7,8a

- *Reasonable fear of danger or difficulty.* There is a fear of danger and difficult circumstances that is reasonable. We would not be living in reality if we did not even consider how an upcoming situation might affect us. God wants us to live in reality, but at the same time He wants us to bring Him into the picture. It is reasonable to respond to danger and disaster. God has equipped us with a bodily response—an increase in adrenalin production—that can help us when physical danger is imminent. This increase can cause other bodily responses: pounding heart, muscle tension, heightened awareness, dry mouth, perspiration, and butterflies in the stomach. As long as we do not let our fear or our feelings keep us from doing what is right, and we turn to God in our fear, that fear is not ungodly. We are all going to feel afraid sometimes. Don't make the mistake of equating courage with a lack of feeling afraid. The most courageous men are those who feel afraid but place their trust in God and do what He says to do. The question is what do we do when we are afraid?

> **When I am afraid, I will put my trust in You.**
> **Psalm 56:3**

Ungodly fear is a certain kind of fear that we are commanded not to have (John 14:1, 27). Ungodly fear is an intimidating and often paralyzing fear. It takes many forms. Any time we cease to focus on God and others because of fear we are experiencing ungodly fear. When we do this we are focused on self. Any time we fail to do what we should do just because we are afraid of what might happen to us, we are being fearful in an ungodly way (Matthew 25:14-26; 1 Peter 3:6). We are also being fearful in a way that displeases God when we, without basis, are convinced that something dreadful will happen. Finally, when we give in to ungodly fear, we are calling God a liar (Numbers 23:19).

> **You who fear the Lord, trust in the Lord; He is their**
> **help and their shield.**
> **Psalm 115:11**

Explanation

Since anxiety always involves a certain amount of fear, for the remainder of this chapter we primarily will address fear. There are several key things we must know about ungodly fear.

1. *Ungodly fears are directly related to what we are thinking.* We have already seen that feelings come from what we think and believe. This means that what we choose to tell ourselves will either calm our fears or feed them. We must pay careful attention to our thoughts and be sure that they are "true,... honorable,... right,... pure,... lovely,... of good repute (noteworthy),... excellent,... and worthy of praise." (Proverbs 4:23 and Philippians 4:8)

2. *When sinfully fearful, we are focused on the circumstances rather than on God.* Ungodly fear and the failure to do what is right is inevitable, if we look at our circumstances without adding God and His truth into the picture. We must not only add them into the picture, but we must also dwell on them. We must fix our mind and heart on

them. (Genesis 32:7-12; Numbers 13:25-14:5; Psalm 55:22; Psalm 77:4-14 and Mark 4:35-41)

3. *When we are fearful we are focused on self.* Ungodly fear is selfish and therefore the opposite of love. When one continues in fear he is always focused on self and what self does or doesn't want without consideration of God and others. When we are afraid we must put on love for God and others. Love will help to dispel selfish fear. (Deuteronomy 7:17-18; Isaiah 51:12-13 and Philippians 2:4)

4. *When we are engaged in ungodly fear we are fearing something else more than we fear God.* This situation usually means that we want something or love something more than we want or love God. When we fear something more than God we always forget about Him and His Word (promises) and we usually disobey Him in other ways as well. We are unfaithful to God. Read the following verses and determine what fear they were fearing more than they feared God: Job1:13-20; 3:25; Proverbs 14:26-27; 29:25; Matthew 6:31-33; 10:28; Galatians 1:10; 2:12; Hebrews 13:5-6 and 1 Peter 3:13-14.

Things we may fear more than God:	Things we may want or love more than God:
Man	*Man's approval*
Unwanted circumstances	*Life of ease/comfort with no pain*
Losing something or someone dear	*Money, health, a person, things*
Bodily harm	*Safety, no pain*

5. *Ungodly fear will most likely motivate us to commit other sins.* When we give way to ungodly fear we will be tempted to sin in other ways also. We might lie, follow the crowd, be inconsiderate of others, or even deny the Lord and His Word. (Genesis 26:7; 1 Samuel 15:24; Matthew 26:69-70; and Galatians 2:12)

6. *Ungodly fear accomplishes absolutely nothing worthwhile.* Anxiety and

fear have been compared to rocking in a giant rocking chair. It involves a great deal of work but doesn't get you anywhere. Worrying (sinning) never accomplishes anything but trouble. (Proverbs 13:15; NKJV, and Matthew 6:27)

7. *Not being right with God can lead to fear and anxiety.* When a person does not know God as Savior there is often fear of death and judgement—and rightly so! Even a Christian who is sinning usually experiences fear and anxiety about getting caught, the discipline of God, and the consequences of their sin. (Psalm 38:17-18; Proverbs 14:32; Proverbs 28:1; and Hebrews 9:27)

Fear can reach paralyzing proportions when it is allowed to grow. The more a person acts on his fears instead of going against them or pushing through them, the more afraid he will become. We must be willing to endure fear if we have to in order to obey God, to be responsible, and to love others. (2 Timothy 2:3-4 and 1 Peter 4:1)

Examination

Now it is time to consider your own life. The first thing you must do is admit your sins of ungodly fear and anxiety. You will have to stop calling your sin "being stressed out," "concerned," "part of my personality," or "a sickness," and certainly not talk about your worry as if it were a virtue. The second thing you must do is to put some thought into how and when you become fearful. Answer the following questions to evaluate where you are with this sin:

1. Is there anything that you are presently fearful about?
2. Recall the last 5 times you were fearful. Explain the situation that was involved. Did the situation come about due to other sins of yours?
3. What was your thinking for each of the situations in #2? Were you thinking about tomorrow? Were you concerned about temporal things or eternal things? Was your focus on unfounded possibilities? What were you fearing more than God? How were you focused: on self or not loving others?
4. How did you respond to your fear? What did you do or not do?
5. What were the results of being sinfully fearful (if you were)?
6. How were you not trusting God?

7. What have you done about those things, situations or fears since?
8. What kinds of things typically contribute to your anxiety or fear?
9. What sins do you tend to commit due to fear or anxiety? Do you lie? Do you fail to do what God wants? Are you irresponsible? Do you choose not to think of others or love others?
10. Do you need to keep track of when and why you become anxious or fearful in the next few weeks?
11. Are you sure that you are in good standing with God because you are in Christ? Are you confident that you are God's child? On what do you base your confidence?
12. Do you have any unconfessed sin in your life?

Transformation

Having come to a better understanding of ungodly fear and our own involvement with it, we can now learn exactly how to change in this area. Instead of anxiety and fear, we want to put on the fear of the Lord and trust in God's promises, love, and responsibility.

> **Be anxious for nothing, but in everything by prayer and supplication with thanksgiving let your request be made known to God. And the peace of God, which surpasses all comprehension, will guard your hearts and your minds in Christ Jesus. Finally, brethren, whatever is true, whatever is honorable, whatever is right, whatever is pure, whatever is lovely, whatever is of good repute, if there is any excellence and if anything worthy of praise, dwell on these things. The things you have learned and received and heard and seen in me, practice these things, and the God of peace will be with you.**
> **Philippians 4:6-9**

Before fear hits again:

1. Be sure that your salvation is settled and repent of any other known sin (Psalm 32:5; 1 John 5:10-13).
2. Confess and repent of your sins of ungodly fear to God and others whom your fear may have affected (Psalm 51:1-4; Matthew 5:23-24).

3. Ask God to work in this area of your life and help you to put forth full effort toward change (2 Corinthians 9:8).
4. Determine right thoughts and actions to combat the ones you usually have (see your answers above). Make your thoughts thankful, hopeful, trusting, and loving. Include Scripture in them. Try to put your new thoughts in prayer form (Psalm 119:59-60).

Fearful Thoughts	Thankful, Hopeful, Trusting and Loving
Oh no! I just know this plane is going to crash. I can't do this. I don't want to die!	Thank you Lord, that I am in your hands. I am just as safe up here as I am on the ground. You are in control of all things. I can trust you to help me with whatever happens.
My job is ending soon and I don't have another one yet. What am I going to do? We're going to be in the poor house!	I thank you Lord, that you know our needs. I will do all I can to find another job, but I know you will help us through whatever happens. Please help me find another job. You are in control of all things. I will trust you and be content with what you provide.
If I confront her sin, she is going to get really angry, and I don't know what else she will do, but it will be really bad.	If I confront her she may be angry, but I will endure it in order to do what you want, Lord. I ask you to help her respond well, but I will trust you with whatever the outcome is.

5. Memorize some helpful verses from this chapter to help renew your mind (Romans 12:2).

6. Do a study of God's sovereignty (Isaiah 46:9-11; Genesis 50:20; Jeremiah 32:27; Romans 8:28) *

7. Do a study of God's presence and care: (Joshua 1:9; Psalm 27:1-14; Psalm 23:4). *

8. Do a study of God's sufficient grace (help) in times of trouble (Isaiah 41:10; 2 Corinthians 12:9; Hebrews 4:16).*

9. Increase your fear of God. Study, pray, and commit to love God with all your heart (Deuteronomy 10:12,20; Psalm 119:2).

10. Be alert, ready to use self-control and do battle with your thoughts (1 Peter 1:13).

During the time of fear:

1. Earnestly seek the Lord and His help (Psalm 34:4; Psalm 46:1-3).

2. Put off being sinfully fearful (Isaiah 12:2; Ephesians 4:22).
   - Ask yourself, "What am I fearing more than God?"
   - Ask yourself, "Are my thoughts headed in the wrong direction?" Are they:
     - On the future?
     - On temporal things?
     - On untrue things?
     - Focused on me?
     - Void or deficient of God and His truth?

3. Put on trust, responsibility, and love.
   - Focus most on God and His promises (Psalm 18:1-2).
   - Make yourself dwell on right thoughts and your memory verses (Ephesians 4:23).
     - Stay in the present
     - Think about eternal things and things that God is concerned with
     - Think true thoughts
     - Think profitable thoughts

   - Ask yourself, "How can I now do what is right?"
     - What is the responsible thing to do right now?
     - What is a loving thing I can do right now?
     - What constructive thing would God want me to do about this problem?

* The MacArthur Topical Bible is an excellent reference for study. See Endnotes.

4.   Be willing to endure the temptation to fear if you must in order to love God and others (2 Timothy 2:3-4).

If you fail and give way to anxiety or ungodly fear:

1.   Ask yourself, "How did I sin?" Be specific about thoughts and actions.
2.   Ask yourself, "If I had this to do over again, what would I think and do?"
3.   Confess and ask forgiveness of God and anyone else who was affected by or who witnessed your sinful fear (James 5:16; 1 John 1:9).
4.   Tell God and others what you plan to do in the future instead (Psalm 40:8).
5.   Be on guard once again (1 Peter 5:8).

Fear does not have to control you. In fact, you are commanded to control fear. If you are a believer, God has given you all the resources to do this. Through practice of His principles you can conquer a pattern of anxiety or ungodly fears. If God could turn a man who denied Him three times because of fear into a courageous apostle (Peter), He can change you, too.

**The steadfast of mind You will keep in perfect peace,
because he trusts in You. Trust in the Lord forever, for
in God the Lord, we have an everlasting Rock.
Isaiah 26:3-4**

Chapter Twenty

A HUSBAND'S REGRET
LUST

One of the most destructive sins for the husband and the family is that of sexual lust. This sin opens the door to all kinds of degradation. In a society that is obsessed with sex, it can be very difficult to gain victory over the sin of lust and the many forms of sexual sin to which it leads. Based on the counseling I have done in the church, I would say that most men find it difficult to remain pure in this area. From the media we are taught that lust is acceptable and normal. This portrayal is very different from how God views lust. Husband, you must conquer sexual lust before you will be able to exemplify Christ!

It can be difficult to see this sin as clearly as God does. A great number of men are involved in sexual sin in one way or another regularly. It doesn't take long to see it take its toll in a man's life and in his relationships. This sin *can* and *will* destroy a man's life and his marriage relationship as no other. Let me emphasize my point by repeating the previous sentence. This sin can and will destroy a man's life and his marriage relationship as no other. Men who would never physically hurt their wives will deeply hurt them within through their use of pornography and through extra-marital affairs.

Because the flesh loves the pleasure of sexual sin so much, many men don't really want to give up their lust. They may hate the guilt and the consequences but not really hate the sin. When one becomes regularly involved with lust and what follows, it can seem impossible to stop. The good news is, however, that all things are possible with God! A person who struggles with lust and other sexual sin, *can* have victory (1 Corinthians 6:9-11). Even if you have allowed yourself to become entangled with this sin, you *can* learn new habits and learn to view the sexual area in a wholesome way, if you really want to please God. It will take work to apply God's principles, but perseverance will enable you to overcome your sinful habit. There is great hope, men. The question is, Are you ready to do what God says?

Definition

Most men are familiar with lust, but they may not fully understand what it is and where it comes from. All sexual sin begins with the sin of lust. We need to know what it really is so that we can take full responsibility for it.

The word "lust": The major Greek word for lust is *epithumia*. This word simply means *to have a strong desire that is focused on satisfaction or attaining what is desired*. This Greek word can be used in a good sense. In the Greek septuigent it is used in reference to the "desire of the righteous" (Proverbs 10:24). Jesus "earnestly desired" to eat the Passover with His disciples before He died (Luke 22:15). Paul had a "great desire" to see the Thessalonians (1 Thessalonians 2:17). God even gave instruction to the church concerning the man who "desires" the office of overseer (1 Timothy 3:1). The Bible also uses this word in a bad sense, however. When the word is used negatively, it is usually termed "evil desire" or "lust".

The lust of the flesh is a sinful desire and is quite different from a righteous desire. The desire of the flesh (our unredeemed humanness) is evil of every kind. Lust is nothing more than evil desire looking for fulfillment. It is only looking for *self*-satisfaction. The lust of the flesh can involve any of the bodily appetites and members, but the eyes are usually the initial agent for men. We are commanded not to have "lustful passion, like the Gentiles who do not know God" (1 Thessalonians 4:5). We are also told to "flee youthful lusts and pursue righteousness" (2 Timothy 2:22). Lust is welcoming and continuing in the evil desires of the flesh, rather than resisting them and fleeing from them by turning to God and what is right.

> **For the grace of God has appeared, bringing salvation to all men, instructing us to deny ungodliness and worldly desires and to live sensibly, righteously and godly in the present age.**
> **Titus 2:11-12**

Lustful thinking is a grave sin in God's sight, but, if it is tolerated, it is only the beginning of our lust. Unless our inward thoughts are disciplined, they *will* progress to more outward sin. Sexual lust is usually not satisfied until physical sexual sin achieves selfish fulfillment. Even though it may take days of mental episodes before lust requires complete fulfillment, the flesh does not give up until it is either satisfied or mortified (put to death by saying "no" to it's desires, and by putting on righteousness) (Romans 8:13; 13:12-14; Colossians 3:5).

If tolerated, lustful thoughts will progress to actions such as:

- Using one's wife for selfish sex.
- Masturbation (usually using pictures, adult movies, telephone sex calls, Internet chat rooms and sex web sites, or "window watching" for arousal and preliminary enjoyment).
- Sex with a woman other than your wife.
- Sex with another man.
- Sex with a child.
- Sex with an animal.

These sins are the outworking of a regularly lustful heart, and they are abominable to God. A person who commits sins such as these has already given himself over to evil desire long before he carries out the deed. So these *deeds* can also be thought of as lust. Furthermore, we can think of mental lust as very similar to the deeds of lust. Both are following evil sexual desires. Both are sexual sin. Now we can understand why Christ said:

> "You have heard that is was said, 'You shall not com-
> mit adultery;' but I say to you that everyone who looks
> at a woman with lust for her has already committed
> adultery with her in his heart."
> **Matthew 5:27-28**

Explanation

Before a man can have victory over lust, he must embrace and act upon certain truths. Just understanding what lust is will not be enough to prepare him for the battle that rages within.

> Finally then, brethren, we request and exhort you in
> the Lord Jesus, that as you received from us instruc-
> tion as to how you ought to walk and please God (just
> as you actually do walk), that you excel still more. For
> you know what commandments we gave you by the
> authority of the Lord Jesus. For this is the will of God,
> your sanctification; that is, that you abstain from sex-
> ual immorality; that each of you know how to possess
> his own vessel in sanctification and honor, not in lust-
> ful passion, like the Gentiles who do not know God;
> and that no man transgress and defraud his brother in
> the matter because the Lord is the avenger in all these
> things, just as we also told you before and solemnly
> warned you. For God has not called us for the purpose
> of impurity, but in sanctification. So he who rejects
> this is not rejecting man but the God who gives His
> Holy Spirit to you.
> **1 Thessalonians 4:1-8**

1. Lust involves listening to and believing lies. Some examples are:
    - "This is just a small sin. It doesn't matter. It won't hurt anyone."
    - "But I need to."
    - "I deserve some enjoyment."
    - "I can't resist it. I'm only human."
    - "This activity will be so pleasurable."
    - "I'll never be able to change, so why try? I'll never win

against this."
- "No one will know."
- "I won't keep doing this. This will be the only or the last time. I don't really have a problem."

But I am afraid that, as the serpent deceived Eve by his craftiness, your minds will be led astray from the simplicity and purity of devotion to Christ.
2 Corinthians 11:3

2. There really is no small sin. Sin is not small in God's eyes, and it is a lie of Satan that a little sin doesn't matter. Any sin that is tolerated is a serious matter to God because it always leads to more sin. Lust follows a progression of entanglement. It does not become a life-dominating sin overnight, but it will happen, and in a much shorter time than your flesh wants you to believe. Here is a general progression of the sin of lust.

   a) Failure to worship God (Romans 1:21)
   b) An ungrateful heart (Romans 1:21)
   c) Introduction to sexual sin (Proverbs 3:31,32)
   d) Experiencing sexual sin (Proverbs 10:23)
   e) Repeating the experience of sexual sin (Proverbs 26:11)
   f) Developing a routine or a ritual for your sexual sin (Proverbs 6:18)
   g) Domination by your sexual sin (2 Peter 2:14, 18-19 NKV)
   h) God gives you over to your sexual sin (Romans 1:21-24)
   i) All kinds of degradation (Romans 1:28-32)

A little sin is a very dangerous thing. If you believe this fact, you will avoid sin all the more (Proverbs 5: 3, 8-9,22-23; Proverbs 29:6; and James 1:13-16).

3. Satan wants to destroy you. He is your enemy and will certainly make the most of your fleshly desires. You must be alert and wise to his schemes (1 Peter 5:8-9 and Ephesians 6:10-11; 2 Corinthians 2:11).

4. Sin always has a price. There are always consequences to sin. There is a spiritual consequence—sin always darkens the heart and one's judgement and prevents fellowship with God. There is the consequence of guilt and the effects of guilt (depression, fear,

and illness). There are also very often physical consequences such as a difficult life, an unwanted pregnancy, sexually transmitted diseases, the destruction of a relationship, financial difficulties, church discipline, and even criminal conviction. Most important, however, there are eternal consequences that God will carry out if there is no repentance (change). For the Christian, this can include turning him over to death, and for the unbeliever, eternal hell. (Proverbs 21:17; Proverbs 22:8; Matthew 18:17-18; Matthew 19:3-9; Romans 13:2-4; 1 Corinthians 5:5 and 1 Corinthians 6:9-10)

5. There is a war raging. Every husband must be aware that there is a spiritual war raging in his own members (body) and going on around him. Within him, the Spirit wars against the flesh and the flesh wars against the Spirit. If a husband does not prepare for the fight, get into the battle and stay alert, he will be taken captive by the flesh. If we are not walking in the Spirit (being mindful of God, His Word and His righteous path), it is as if we are letting the enemy walk right into our camp. When we are not in total pursuit of righteousness, it is as if we are trying to make friends with the enemy. We will then be easy prey, and we will soon join with the enemy in the fight against the Spirit and all that is righteous. There is also a spiritual war raging against good and evil involving God   and His angels and Satan and his angels. But Satan is no match for God, or for you if you are a believer who is dependent on God and pursuing righteousness. (Romans 7:21-25; 2 Corinthians 10:3-6; Galatians 5:16-17; Ephesians 6:12-17; and 1 John 4:4)

6. Expect the battle to be more severe when you first begin to fight If you are serious about having victory over your sin, you must be ready for a difficult fight. The good news is that you can win, and the more you fight the easier the battle becomes. Victory is sure if you do what God says and endure to the end. (Galatians 6:9; 2 Tim 2:3-4; 1Peter 5:6-10; 1 John 5:4; and Jude 24-25)

7. Lust must be nipped in the bud. The only way to win against the flesh is to not give it a chance. The old saying "give him an inch and he takes a mile" is certainly true of our flesh. It is very important to flee temptation from the outset. We must flee from it to the Lord and to what is righteous instead. Sexual thoughts must be forsaken *immediately* and replaced with righteous ones. (Genesis 39:7-12; 1 Corinthians 10:13; and Romans 13:11-14).

8. Radical action must be taken. The flesh must have no opportunity. This basic truth will often mean taking what may seem to other people to be drastic measures. You must starve the flesh to loosen its grip. You may need to cut out television, movies, and even certain routes of travel for awhile. You may need to graciously cut certain people out of your life. You may need to move. You may need to change jobs. You must figure out how you can make no provision for the flesh by not even allowing it a remote opportunity. Christ was clear that we must take radical action against dominating sin. One of the most important ways of making no provision for the flesh is to make yourself accountable to your wife and a godly man (or men) in your church who can help you stand strong. You should definitely seek their counsel about any drastic changes you think are necessary. (Mark 9:42-48; 1 Corinthians 15:33; and Colossians 3:5-11)

9. The opposite of lust is love. Any man who hopes to rid himself of lust must learn to pursue love with fervency. Lust is purely selfish and often involves taking from or using someone else. One of the best things a man can do to rid himself of lust is to look for ways to show real love (giving), especially to his wife. He needs to give generously to others on a regular basis, but especially when temptation comes. A great way to *start* is to pray for any person who is a temptation for you. Pray for their spiritual condition or that God would teach and bless them. Be sure that you pray for them briefly (in order to turn your selfishness into love) and then move on to other responsibilities and serving. To continue to dwell on them may give you more opportunity to lust after them. (Matthew 22:39; Romans 12:9-13; 13:8-10 and Ephesians 5:1-4)

10. You must walk in the Spirit to avoid the deeds of the flesh. The best way to win against the flesh is to fix your mind on God and His Word. This is walking in the Spirit. You cannot walk by the flesh and walk in the Spirit at the same time. They are diametrically opposed to one another. The more you walk in the Spirit the more you will do the deeds of the Spirit. (Romans 8:6-8; Galatians 5:16-20; Galatians 6:7-8 and James 1:21-22,25)

11. Lust usually involves other kinds of sin. When a person is living in lust he will most likely commit other sins in order to accomplish his lustful sin. Deceit is almost always involved in sexual sin. One

may try to manipulate other people into helping him accomplish his sin, or even enter into it with him. Also, when one is confronted with his sin, he will very likely blame-shift and make excuses for it. A person involved in habitual sexual sin will also sin in other ways simply because he is walking in the flesh. (Proverbs 4:19 and James 3:14-16)

12. A dominating sexual sin *cannot* remain a secret. More than likely, you are only kidding yourself by thinking that you can handle this problem on your own. Lust never really is secret. Even when sin seems secret, it's not. God sees it. Secrecy is helping you to sin. Sin loves isolation. As awful as it may seem to come clean by telling someone who can help, it doesn't compare to the alternative of continuing in your sin, which will only lead to more darkness and degradation. If you want to win against sin, you must let others into your life. Read Numbers 32:23; Psalm 51:4; 69:5; 90:8; Proverbs 15:3 and Jeremiah 16:17.

At this point, I would like to make it clear that you *should* let your wife (the one who is supposed to be 'one' with you) know about your basic struggle and how she can help, but do so with *caution*. You should be honest about your struggle, but it is not necessary to give her all the details. She needs enough information to know how to pray for you, what tempts you, and how she can help hold you accountable, but you don't need to tell her every time you are tempted, or even about every time you have a lustful thought. While she can be a part of your accountability, she should not bear the brunt of the accountability that you need. You *must not* in any way give her the impression that your success or failure is dependent on her. Be sure that you convey to her that the Lord, you, and whoever is helping you are working very hard on the situation, and that *she* does not have to. You and your wife may need to sit down with another godly couple if she is having a very difficult time dealing with the situation, becomes bitter, begins policing you, or refuses to help or deal with the situation at all.

Sexual sin by its very nature leads to isolation. A man who is engaged in "secret" sin will distance himself from others. This distance is because of guilt, the fear of being found out, and the desire to keep sinning. A man who wants to continue in sin will not want to be close to righteous people. A lustful person may also not be a very likeable person because he is selfish, proud, and often angry. He may be somewhat isolated for this reason also. Still, if you struggle with sexual lust as a believer, it is of the utmost importance that you make a friend whom you can tell about your sin problem, and who will help you apply God's principles to it. (Proverbs 18:1 and Proverbs 27:17)

13. Lust can be an idol or a refuge. For many, sexual sin is nothing more than the idol of pleasure. They worship the temporary pleasure their sin brings, rather than worshiping God. They are intent on having worldly pleasure and will sin to get it. For others, sexual sin is more of a refuge in times of trouble or when they cannot have what they are worshiping. They turn to sexual pleasure as a bit of relief from their misery. (Jeremiah 13:25; Romans 1:25; Colossians 3:5 and Psalm 62:5-8)

14. There is more to life than sex. When a man's life is dominated by this sin, everything relates to it. It becomes everything to him. Instead, he must repent of this attitude and find other good things to focus on and do. If you are married, sex should only be a small aspect of your marriage and life. If you are not married, you must forsake the idea altogether. Contrary to what those who are in bondage think, sexual pleasure does not equal happiness—only knowing, walking with, and serving God does. (Psalm 1:1-2; Colossians 3:1-3; and John 15:7-11)

15. Sex can be holy and pure. If you are married and struggle with lust you must begin to think of sex in a new way. You must plan to take a different path of thinking when you are having intimacy with your wife. It should be an opportunity to bring pleasure to your wife. Sex as God intended it is holy and pure and should be enjoyed. If you seek to give instead of to get, you will enjoy this God-given blessing in a totally new way—a pure and holy way. Read Chapter 11 of this book again.

16. You can bring glory to God and have a useful life for Him by truly forsaking sin and turning to God. When we lust, God fades from view, and when God fades, we will lust even more. Your heart must be set on God. From Kent and Barbara Hughes' *Liberating Ministry:*

Lay this maxim to heart: *When lust takes control, God is unreal to us.* What a world of wisdom there is in this! When we are in the grip of lust, the reality of God fades. The longer King David gazed, the less real God became. Not only was his awareness of God diminished, but in the growing darkness he lost awareness of who David was— his holy call, his frailty, and the sure consequences of sin.

That is what lust does. It has done it millions of times. Lust makes God disappear, at least in the lust-glazed eyes of those involved. Here, fellow servants, we must once again ask some questions: Is God fading from view? Were you once walking closely with him, but now, because of creeping sensuality he seems but a distant phantom? If so, you must take decisive steps to guard your heart. You must terminate the intake of lustful words and images—whether they be gotten from reading, or the media, or an acquaintance. If you do not, God will fade and you will fall. [24]

Your sin can be forgiven and made powerless in your life. You will no doubt face temptation, but you can lead a new way of life. Read Isaiah 38:17; Psalm 25:4-9, 18; Psalm 51:9; Acts 3:19 and 1 Corinthians 6:9-11.

Examination

The first step to overcoming your sin problem is to admit that you have one. The second thing you must do is to take full responsibility for it. No one else has caused this problem—not God or anyone who has influenced you. Your sinful heart has chosen to take whatever opportunities you were given because your heart (without God) is utterly wicked. You must be brutally honest with yourself in order to begin on the path of righteousness. Answer the following questions honestly:

Search me, O God, and know my heart; try me and know my anxious thoughts; and see if there be any hurtful way in me, and lead me in the everlasting way.
Psalm 139:23-24

1. Are you regularly worshiping and communing with God?
2. Are you regularly thankful and grateful to God?
3. Are you content with God alone and His spiritual blessings?
4. Are you focused on loving others?
5. How are you regularly serving others?
6. How are you using your gifts in the church?
7. Do you have sexual thoughts?
8. Do you change sexual thoughts immediately?
9. Have you ever entertained a sexual thought for any length of time?
10. Have you repeated entertaining sexual thoughts?
11. Have you exposed yourself to sexually explicit material?
12. Have you committed any sinful sexual deeds?
13. Have you repeated any sinful sexual deeds? How many times?
14. What do you do when you are down or troubled? Where do you go?
15. Do you regularly commit sexual sin (in thought or deed)?
16. Is there a pattern or a ritual to your sexual sin?
17. How often do you think about sexual things and/or sexual satisfaction?
18. How much is your life ordered around your sin?
19. Would you say that you are in bondage to your sexual sin?
20. Do you view sex as self-satisfaction?
21. Is your sin a secret?
22. What are the effects of your sin?
23. In what other ways are you following the flesh?
24. What other interests do you have?

And He was saying to them all, "If anyone wishes to come after Me, he must deny himself, and take up his cross daily and follow Me. For whoever wishes to save his life will lose it, but whoever loses his life for My sake, he is the one who will save it."
Luke 9:23-24

Transformation

Friend, if you are sinning by committing sexual sin (in thought or deed), God says you must repent (Acts 26:20). The question is, are you really willing to repent? Are you at a place in your life where you hate and grieve over your sin because of the offense it is to God? The Puritan Thomas Watson once said, "We are to find as much bitterness in weeping for sin as we ever found sweetness in committing it"[25] Are you willing to take full responsibility for your sin problem and make no excuses? Are you ready to do whatever it takes to put off this sin and put on righteousness? Without a heart of true repentance you will never be able to change. But if you are willing to humble yourself and turn from your sin, you can glorify God with a changed life.

> **May it never be! How shall we who died to sin still live in it? ...Therefore do no let sin reign in your mortal body so that you obey its lusts, and do not go on presenting the members of your body to sin as instruments of unrighteousness; but present yourselves to God as those alive from the dead, and your members as instruments of righteousness to God. ...Do you not know that when you present yourselves to someone as slaves for obedience, you are slaves of the one whom you obey, either of sin resulting in death, or of obedience resulting in righteousness?**
> **Romans 6:2, 12-13, 16**

Before temptation hits again:

1. Confess your sins of lust to God and to any others you have sinned against in the process (who are aware of your sin). Explain your willingness to give yourself fully to repentance (putting off your sin and putting on what is right). Then ask for forgiveness (Psalm 51:1-4; Matthew 5:23-24).

2. Daily, even several times a day, ask God to work in this area of your life and help you to put forth full effort toward change (2 Corinthians 9:8).

3. Begin to cultivate a passion for God and regular (daily) worship and Bible meditation/study. Study God's attributes and what Christ has done for you. Learn to walk through your day being mindful of God and His Word (Matthew 22:37; Chapter 7: "Worshiping Christ Alone").

4. Tell your wife and someone who can be a help to you in your struggle so that you will have accountability. No more secrets (Hebrews 10:24-25).

5. Make a list of helpful verses and truths from this study to meditate on regularly and use when you are tempted (Romans 12:2).

6. Make a list of righteous and loving *thoughts* to put on when lustful thoughts come into your mind. Especially prepare loving thoughts and prayers to apply to those you are tempted to lust after (Ephesians 4:23). For example:

    -   "Lord, I pray that this person will come to know you."
    -   "Lord, bless this person today. Help them in whatever way is needed."
    -   "They are God's creation. I will not use them but serve them. How can I serve this person?"

7. Make a list of ways to show love to your wife (Ephesians 5:25).
8. Make a list of ways to show love to others (Philippians 2:3-4).
9. Make a covenant with God about your eyes (Job 31:1; Psalm 101:3).
10. Take whatever radical steps are needed to make no provision for your flesh (Romans 13:14).
11. Think through the times and situations in which you are normally tempted. Avoid them if at all possible. Prepare for them and get accountability for them if you cannot avoid them (Psalm 119:59-60).
12. Think through your schedule and your normal routine of sin, and think of ways to reorder your life (different places, different activities, a different schedule) as much as possible.
13. Write out a prayer that you can pray when the battle is raging.
14. Write out a prayer that you can pray before times of intimacy with your wife.
15. Find a way to serve in your church (1 Corinthians 12:4-7).
16. Develop other interests and activities that have an element of giving or serving to them. Don't be idle!

At the time of temptation: (F.L.E.E. from sin to God).

1. Flee! Act quickly to run away from sin. Acknowledge your complete allegiance to God and put on loving thoughts and actions. Get out of or vary the situation immediately (2 Timothy 2:22).
2. Lean on God. Call on Him for strength to honor Him. Draw near to God and He will draw near to you (Psalm 37:5; James 4:8).
3. Entertain the right thoughts (Philippians 4:8-9). Rehearse those things for which you are grateful and thankful.
4. Eagerly continue to pursue love and righteousness. Don't look back. Look to your "ways to love and serve" lists for ideas if necessary. Engage yourself in giving (Proverbs 21:21).

If you fail and commit sexual sin (in thought or deed):

1. Do not engage in panic, self-pity, or giving up! These attitudes are just what Satan is hoping for, but this is not acceptable to God because it is not in keeping with true repentance, and it will not get you anywhere! Get up and get back on the path to victory if you are still serious about repentance. You probably will not be flawless in putting off old habits. It takes time to change. It is a serious matter to choose to sin, but all is not lost if you return to a righteous path and refuse to give up (Proverbs 24:16).

2. Ask yourself what God says about your sin and determine how it was *taking* or *using* instead of *giving* and *loving*.

3. Ask yourself, "If I had this to do over again, what would I do?" and "Am I really grieved over my sin because it is against God and because I want to love and serve Him?" Am I really serious about giving full effort to change?

4. Confess your sin to God as abominable before Him, share your desire to repent, and ask forgiveness. Tell Him your plan to keep this from happening again (Psalm 32:5; James 5:16).

5. Thank Christ for already paying the penalty for that sin and for His ability to change you (Romans 7:24-8:1).

> **Therefore, having been justified by faith, we have peace with God through our Lord Jesus Christ.**
> **Romans 5:1**

How much do you want to honor Christ with your life? Are you willing to do what God requires? Determination, with dependence on God, is the key. You are assured victory if you *practice* God's principles and depend on His power. Yes, it will be hard work. Is it worth it to you? The hard work required will actually be a good deterrent to turning back to sin. God knows what He is doing by not zapping us out of our sinful habits. The process that you must go through and the discipline you will learn will serve your Christian growth in many ways.

You *can* change. Many have gone before you. As impossible as it may seem now, you must make the commitment to give it everything you've got because you believe God's promises. I can assure you that if you are only partially committed to the task or only willing to do part of what it takes, you will *not* succeed. Repentance is an all or nothing commitment. Give it everything you have, and God will give you His power to cooperate with Him in the change process.

Men, the consequences of this sin are so harmful to your relationship with God and so devastating to your family, that if you do not deal with this sin through repentance, you will regret it. **Do not be deceived.**

> **Therefore we do not lose heart, but though our outer man is decaying, yet our inner man is being renewed day by day. For momentary, light affliction is producing for us an eternal weight of glory far beyond all comparison.**
> **2 Corinthians 4:16-17**

Chapter Twenty-One

WHEN ALL IS SAID AND DONE

In the introduction, I wrote that the overall purpose of this book was to *assist husbands toward purposeful and lasting Christlikeness for the glory of God*. Now that we have reached the end of the book, we should ask the question, "How can we sum up Christ's life?" The answer to that question should be how we want to have our lives summed up as well. It is common for me to pass one of the men in our church and ask, "How's it going?" The predictable reply is usually, "Whew, I'm busy. Really busy." I think to myself, "I'm busy too. Hopefully we are busy about the right things." Being busy is not necessarily a bad thing. Christ was busy—not crazy and frantic, but he was busy. Being busy, however, about the wrong things is definitely a bad thing. Can you say that as a husband you are busy in ways similar to Christ? Christ summed up all of Scripture, as well as what should be our two greatest priorities in the first and second greatest commandments.

> **And He said to him, "You shall love the Lord your God with all your heart, and with all your soul, and with all your mind." This is the great and foremost commandment. The second is like it, "You shall love your neighbor as yourself." On these two command-**

ments depend the whole Law and the Prophets.
Matthew 22:37-40

As you can see, these two commands are both relational. Practically speaking, Christ's life was all about His relationship to God the Father first, and then about loving and serving others—even to the point of sacrificing Himself for our sins. What each husband must ask himself at the end of this book is, "Now that all is said and done, does my life really revolve around my relationship with God first and then loving and serving others in my sphere second (especially my wife)?" Even in the non-relational things we must do, we can have a relational reason for doing them. Are Christ's two priorities really our priorities, or are we just interested in making money, gaining prestige, being in control, or pouring ourselves into some hobby such as our car or sports? We will not be the husband we should be unless we truly adopt Christ's two greatest priorities.

All that we have learned (and hopefully have begun to implement) about being a godly husband depends first of all on our greatest priority—our relationship with God. Before you can even begin to become an Exemplary Husband, you *must* be a Christian. You must not only be a Christian, but you must truly worship God and be maturing into Christlikeness.

You *Must* be a Christian

There are men who are deceived into thinking they are Christians because they go to church and do good deeds. It is not, however, until they look into the mirror of God's Word that they really begin to see who God is. It is God and His Word that cuts through deceptions and shows you what you really are like. I know one man who thought he was a believer until he read what the Scripture had to say about being a husband. He thought, "I can be that husband." But quickly he realized that he could not be the husband God wanted him to be because he did not really know God personally. Christians know God. They have been reconciled to Him. Christians have God's empowering help. Their greatest heart's desire is to give God glory and to be used by Him as He pleases.

Think about it. How would you fill in the blank in the following sentence? For me to live is _____. If your answer is anything other than Christ, you ought at least to question your salvation and examine yourself to see if you really are in the faith. Any husband can turn over a new leaf or pull himself up by his boot straps and determine to do better, but only a Christian can make the inward and the outward changes that please God, that give Him glory, and that are lasting. Only a Christian has been given the Spirit of God, and only a Christian can be filled with the Spirit (which is living in accordance with God's Word and God's presence). You must be a Christian if you are going to be a godly man and a godly husband.

You *Must* be Worshiping

Men, the need to be worshiping the Lord Jesus Christ must grip your soul! It should be your very life, the occupation of your heart. It should happen all day, every day, and with everything that you think and do. Anyone or anything that takes priority over God has become an idolatrous lust in your heart. Remember, an idol does not necessarily have to be something bad in and of itself (Chapter 7). Some things become sinful when we firmly set our heart on them. Certainly none of us will ever perfectly worship the Lord in this life, but our worship of the Lord Jesus Christ should always be increasing. If it is, our longing for other earthly things should be decreasing. Worshiping Christ should not only be a Sunday morning activity, but also an all day, every day heart preoccupation.

What do you think about as you go through your day? What is your greatest desire? What *is* on your mind? Are lustful scenarios sinfully filling your mind? Are you playing over and over in your thoughts ways your wife has hurt you? Or, are you worshiping God by praying and talking to Him as your day progresses? Is He everything to you? Are you grateful to Him? Are you content? Only our Lord is worthy of this kind of adoration and devotion.

You *Must* be Maturing

Many of the men I have counseled have told me that they desire to grow as a Christian and have repeatedly asked the Lord to take their sin away and heal their marriage, but they never see any lasting change. Growing and maturing as a Christian is not simply a matter of praying and "letting go." It is a dependence on God while striving toward godliness. You are responsible to work at not "carry[ing] out the desire of your flesh" and at "disciplining yourself for the purpose of godliness" (Galatians 5:16, adaptation added; 1 Timothy 4:7). You may have heard of the man who prayed "Give us this day our daily bread" and then he sat down to wait for the bread to drop from heaven. God's Word does tell us to pray but it also tells us to get to work (2 Thessalonians 3:10). That's what we need to do with our marriages—pray *and* work at becoming an exemplary husband. It is an ongoing process "'til death do you part."

This world has taught us that we should focus on loving ourselves, that real love is sexual lust, and that we should be served. It is easy to be conformed to the thinking of this world. Unfortunately, our thinking is often more sinful than we realize, but by God's grace our minds can be renewed and we can learn to deal with our selfish flesh every day. With God's help we can work hard to put on love. We *can* grow and mature as Christians and as godly husbands.

You *Must* Love Your Wife

When you married your wife you made a vow before God to love her and that is precisely what God expects you to do. In fact, your love for your wife should be even greater today as it should be maturing and becoming more and more in line with God's blueprint. It is a love that sees beyond her fading physical beauty and is faithful even in sickness. As you know, God is very much concerned that our love for our wives reflect His love for the church. A husband who has Christ's kind of love will care for his wife, will put his wife first, and will be an understanding but deliberate leader.

Conclusion

Men, we could sum up this entire book with these two points — love the Lord your God with all your heart, and lovingly lead and cherish your wife for the glory of God. Now that you have just beheld God's perfect standard for a godly husband, are you a husband who exemplifies and glorifies Christ? Are you willing to evaluate yourself in regard to the biblical mandates to the husband? Does your life really exemplify Christ, and is your marriage a picture of Christ and the church? How hard are you willing to work at this? And for how long? Now that all has been said and done, what do you say?

- Oh, well. No one is perfect.
- I'm only human.
- I gave it my best shot.
- There is no use trying.
- My wife isn't any better.
- I'm too old to change.
- Compared to other men, I'm not that bad.
- I'm too tired to press on.
- Maybe I'll work at it after the kids are gone.
- I'm just too busy to work on it.
- My wife will need to change first.
- I can take a break because I'm really not that far from the model of Christ (This is impossible!).

What we should say:

- I've not arrived (not by a long shot).
- I thank God for His mercy and grace.
- I thank God for my wife.
- I will confess my sin(s) to God and my wife.
- I will ask for forgiveness from God and my wife.
- I will make a plan of change to turn away from sin and turn toward righteousness, and I'll share it with my wife.
- I will seek to serve faithfully in a Bible-believing church, and in time (under the supervision of the church leadership) help other men to be faithful in this most godly duty of marriage (2 Timothy 2:2).
- By God's grace I will press on (exercise myself unto godliness) to be like Jesus my Savior and Lord, the Great Bridegroom of the Church until He returns for me or I die and go to be with Him.

I want to thank you for reading this book. I have made a commitment to pray for all who read it and who want to apply these biblical principles in their life and marriage. I wholeheartedly agree with what the Scriptures have so fervently taught us: that knowledge which does not lead to piety (practical holiness) is useless and a great sign that we are off course (1 Corinthians 8:1). My prayer for you (and I hope your prayer for me) is based on Colossians 1:28-29:

> **And we proclaim Him, admonishing every man and teaching every man with all wisdom, so that we may present every man complete in Christ. For this purpose also I labor, striving according to His power, which mightily works within.**

Endnotes

1. J.B. Phillips, *Your God is Too Small* (Chicago: MacMillan Publishing Co., 1953).
2. Wayne Grudem, *Systematic Theology* (Grand Rapids, MI: Zondervan Publishing House, 1994), p. 201.
3. J.C. Ryle, *Walking with God* (London: Grace Publications, 1996), p.93.
4. A.W. Tozer, *The Knowledge of the Holy* (New York: Harper & Row, 1961), p.9.
5. George Barna, *The Future of the American Family* (Chicago: Moody Press, 1993), p.44.
6. Robert Jamieson, Volume 1: *Genesis* (Grand Rapids, MI: Wm. R. Eerdmans Co., 1948), p.21.
7. John Murray, *Divorce* (Phillipsburg, NJ: Presbyterian and Reformed Publishing Co., 1987), p.31.
8. Jay Adams, Marriage, *Divorce and Remarriage in the Bible* (Grand Rapids, MI: Ministry Resources Library, 1980), pp.18,88-89.
9. Alexander Strauch, *Men and Women Equal Yet Different* (Littleton, CO: Louis and Roth Publishers, 1999), p.23.
10. Gary Friesen, *Decision Making and the Will of God* (Portland, OR: Multnomah Press, 1980), p.130-131.
11. J.C. Ryle, *Walking with God* (London: Grace Publications Trust, 1996), p.47.
12. Andrew Murray, *Humility* (Springdale, PA: Whitaker House, 1982), p. 10.
13. Thomas Watson, *The Godly Man's Picture* (Carlisle, PA: The Banner of Truth Trust, 1992), p. 85.
14. Richard Baxter, *A Christian Directory* (Morgan, PA: Soli Deo Gloria Publications, 1996) p. 192.
15. John MacArthur, School News Publication, The Master's Seminary Mantle, Winter, 2000, p.1.
16. John MacArthur, *The Family* (Chicago: Moody Press, 1982), p.21.
17. John MacArthur, *Different by Design* (Wheaton, IL: Victor Books, 1994), p.53.
18. John MacArthur, *The Family* (Chicago: Moody Press, 1982), p. 20.
19. Linguistic Key to the Greek New Testament (Grand Rapids, MI: Zondervan Publishing House, 1998), p.574.
20. John MacArthur, *The Family* (Chicago: Moody Press, 1982), pp. 65-66.
21. Jay Adams, *From Forgiven to Forgiving* ((Amityville, NY: Calvary Press Publishing, 1994), p. 25.
22. Wayne Mack, *Strengthening Your Marriage* (Phillipsburg, NJ: Presbyterian and Reformed Publishing Co., 1977), p.60.
23. John MacArthur, *The MacArthur Topical Bible* (Nashville: Word Publishing, 1999).
24. Kent and Barbara Hughes, *Liberating Ministry From the Success Syndrome* (Wheaton, IL: Tyndale House Publishers, 1987), p.89.

Biographical Sketch of Stuart Scott

Dr. Stuart Scott was born in Philadelphia, and raised in New York and Illinois. His Dad was a scientist, and then a college Bible professor and pastor. His mother was a homemaker and an elementary school-teacher and principal. He has three brothers: Ray, Tom, and Richard, who is with the Lord. Although Stuart heard the gospel growing up in his Christian home, it wasn't until age eighteen that he repented and trusted in Jesus Christ as his Lord and Savior,

After salvation, Stuart had a burning desire to be useful and fruitful in the kingdom of God. He began biblical studies at Columbia Bible College, (B.A. - now Columbia International University), then attended Grace Theological Seminary, (M.Div.) after which he went on to Covenant Theological Seminary, (D.Min.). He received some training in biblical counseling at the Atlanta Biblical Counseling Center, and then pursued his Fellow status with the National Association of Nouthetic Counselors (a recognized fellowship of Christian men and women who are trained to serve in the local church, and committed to the sufficiency of Scripture for both salvation and sanctification.)

Stuart has served as staff and senior pastor for over twenty years in Indiana, South Carolina, Florida, and Southern California. He directed a biblical counseling center for three years in Columbia, SC. For eight years he served as Associate Pastor over the Discipleship Counseling Ministry at Grace Community Church in Sun Valley, CA. He served full time as an associate professor of biblical counseling at the Master's College and was an adjunct professor at the Master's Seminary.

Currently Stuart is Associate Professor of Biblical Counseling at Southern Baptist Theological Seminary, and Professor and Dept. Co-ordinator of Biblical Counseling at Boyce College in Louisville, KY. He enjoys ministering to churches both here in the US, and in other countries, speaking at conferences for men, couples, and pastors on marriage, parenting and biblical counseling issues.

Stuart and his wife, Zondra, have two adult children and two grandchildren.

APPENDIX

Taking Thoughts Captive

1. What happened and what was your response? (actions and thoughts)

2. What is the basic thinking that needs change or addition?

3. What is God's truth on this subject(s)? (Write out verses from your study or the counsel of others concerning God's character, promises, or precepts.)

4. What is a concise prayer/thought you will pray/think the next time the original thought arises? (begin with thanksgiving - end with request) Include Scripture.

5. What is any action you need to take considering your circumstance or thinking? (always includes repentance for thinking contrary to God's truth)

God's Process of Change Explained

Even though God gets all the credit for our growth, He has chosen to work *along with* the Word and our efforts. Read what God's Word says about how we change:

> **So then, my beloved,...work out your own salvation with fear and trembling. For it is God who is at work in you both to will and to work for His good pleasure.**
> **Philippians 2:12-13**

> **How can a young man keep his way pure? By keeping it according to Your word. With all my heart I have sought You; Do not let me wander from Your commandments. Your word I have treasured in my heart, that I may not sin against You.**
> **Psalm 119:9-11**

Most sincere Christians are grieved at their sinful choices. Many believers also are bewildered when prayer alone does not take care of their failure to change. The fact is, we need to do more than just pray. True repentance will result in growth and will involve two things: *renewing the mind* and actively *putting off and putting on.* This dual responsibility in dealing with our sin is often ignored by professing Christians.

1. Renewing the Mind

Repentance according to God is a change of direction. The Greek word repentance in Luke 17:3 *(metanoia)* connotes "a change of mind that results in a change of direction." Change must begin in the mind. For this reason, God places great emphasis on the mind in the Scriptures. Even when God addresses the heart he is actually addressing the mind. The heart and mind are used synonymously in the Scriptures.

> **But some of the scribes were sitting there and *reasoning in their hearts.***
> **Mark 2:6 [emphasis mine]**

God knows that we cannot live the new life He has given unless we are renewing our mind (Ephesians 4:23). Having experienced immediate changes at salvation, many Christians think that God will somehow mystically continue to change them into Christ's likeness. This is *not* His plan. Instead, God expects us to be transformed "by the renewing of our minds" (Romans 12:2). This can happen only as God's Word *dwells in us*. We must have God's Word consistently before us and purposefully implanted in our minds (i.e., meditation and memorization).

> **Let the word of Christ richly dwell within you, with all wisdom teaching and admonishing one another with psalms and hymns and spiritual songs, singing with thankfulness in your hearts to God.**
> **Colossians 3:16**

It is not unusual for new believers (and even believers who are older in the Lord) to be oblivious to the fact that there is anything wrong with their thinking. Christians, along with society, have become very undisciplined and permissive in their minds. We need a greater awareness of the fact that our minds are fallen and that our thinking can *often* be unbiblical. It is too bad that we cannot simply change heads at salvation! The stark reality is, how we think greatly determines how we live. Thinking affects desires, feelings and actions.

> **Watch over your heart with all diligence, For from it flow the springs of life.**
> **Proverbs 4:23**

God is saying that we will not act biblically unless we think biblically, therefore, the first act of repentance (change) is to examine the thinking that is behind our actions and renew our minds with God's truth.

> **We are destroying speculations and every lofty thing raised up against the knowledge of God, and we are taking every thought captive to the obedience of Christ.**
> **2 Corinthians 10:5**

We must replace sinful (wrong motive, selfish, anxious, void of God) thoughts with *righteous, thankful, hopeful and trusting* alternatives. In dealing with sinful thought patterns that have become a part of us, it is very helpful to come up with specific new thoughts so that we are ready for battle the next time the old thinking arises. We often have to work at this change in spite of our feelings.

Each time we choose to change a thought to a more scriptural one we are *renewing our mind*. Before long, you will notice that certain biblical thoughts come more naturally and certain biblical choices are made easier. See Appendix One to help you renew specific thoughts.

> **Therefore, I urge you, brethren, by the mercies of God, to present your bodies a living and holy sacrifice, acceptable to God, which is your spiritual service of worship.** *And do not be conformed to this world, but be transformed by the renewing of your mind,* **so that you may prove what the will of God is, that which is good and acceptable and perfect.**
> **Romans 12:1-2 [emphasis mine]**

2. Putting off and Putting on

True repentance also includes determining what needs to be *put off* and *put on* and then specifically planning how and when you are going to do just that. Many times we don't become aware that our thinking is wrong until it affects our behavior. Even when we have worked on our thinking, true repentance (change) has not taken place until we obey the command to *put off* sinful actions and *put on* righteous actions in their place.

> **That, in reference to your former manner of life,** *you lay aside the old self,* **which is being corrupted in accordance with the lusts of deceit, and that you be renewed in the spirit of your mind, and** *put on the new self,* **which in the likeness of God has been created in righteousness and holiness of the truth.**
> **Ephesians 4:22-24 [emphasis mine]**

In order to obey God's put off and put on commands, there must first be a clear understanding of exactly *what* should be put off. Still, knowing what to put off is not enough for lasting change either. Many Christians exert a great amount of effort trying to stop doing what displeases God. Unfortunately, they make little headway when *putting off* is the focus of their efforts.

It just doesn't work to concentrate on putting off *alone*. We are never told to *break* habits, but rather to *replace* them (i.e., Ephesians 4:25, 28-32). So, God intends for us to pursue putting on the righteous alternative to whatever sin we are trying to put off.

For instance, if we know that we need to put off anger and put on gentleness, this is a good start. Next, we have to think through our daily situations and decide three things: We must decide *when* we typically get angry, *what* thinking needs to be renewed, and *how* the temptation first begins.

But put on the Lord Jesus Christ, and make no provision for the flesh in regard to its lusts.
Romans 13:14

Once we have done these three things, we will know what to do when temptation begins and when the situations arise in which we usually get angry. The more we *prayerfully practice* substituting the right for the wrong, the more we will develop new, God honoring habits. Here again, we see a way that we can "exercise ourselves unto godliness" (1 Timothy 4:6-7).

As we are serious about doing our part to repent , we can know that God will answer our prayers for His transforming power (John 9:31; 14:13-17). We should *never* pray, expecting *Him* to do it all. But, if we are ready to obey and do our part, and we pray according to God's will, we know He will answer our prayer and help us grow. This fact is true because it is *always* His *will* that we grow (e.g. 1 Thessalonians 4:3; 2 Peter 3:17-18).

This is the confidence which we have before Him, that, if we ask anything *according to His will*, He hears us.
1 John 5:14 [emphasis mine]

A Sample of Relationships God Addresses in the Bible

- Husbands to wives (Ephesians 5:25-33)

- Wives to husbands (Ephesians 5:22-24

- Parents to children (Ephesians 6:4)

- Children to parents (Ephesians 6:1-3)

- Masters to slaves (Ephesians 6:9)

- Slaves to masters (Ephesians 6:5-8)

- Christian to Christian (Romans 12:9-16)

- Christian to non-Christian (I Peter 2:12-17

- Church leaders to flock (I peter 5:1-4)

- Flock to Church leaders (Hebrews 13:7)

- Elder to younger (I Timothy 5:1)

- Younger to elder (I Timothy 5:1)

- Young man to young woman (I Timothy 5:2)

- Young woman to young man (I Timothy 5:2)

- Citizen to government (Romans 13:1-7)

- Government to citizen (Romans 13:1-7)

- The weak in faith to the strong in faith (Romans 14:1-23)

- The strong in faith to the weak in faith (Romans 14:1-23)

Daily Reminder of How to Treat One Another

DAY	ONE ANOTHER	SCRIPTURE	MAIN IDEA
1	PREFER	Romans 12:10	Prefer, "outdo" one another in honor
2	DEVOTED	Romans 12:10	Be devoted to one another in brotherly love
3	SAME MIND TO	Romans 12:16	Have a modest opinion of yourself toward one another
4	BUILD UP	Romans 14:19	Pursue that which makes for peace and building up one another
5	ACCEPT	Romans 15:7	Accept one another as Christ also accepted us to God's glory
6	ADMONISH	Romans 15:14	Full of goodness, knowledge and able to admonish one another
7	SUE "NOT"	1 Corinthians 6:7	Do not have lawsuits with one another; no one really wins
8	CARE FOR	1 Corinthians 12:25	Have the same care for one another which averts division
9	ENVY "NOT"	Galations 5:26	Do not envy one another, but manifest a spirit of contentment
10	TRUTHFUL TO	Ephesians 4:25	Speak truthfully in every matter to one another
11	KIND TO	Ephesians 4:32	Be kind, pleasant and tender-hearted to one another
12	SUBJECT TO	Ephesians 5:21	Be subject to those in authority over you (wives to husbands and children to parents – Ephesians 5:22-24, 6:1)

13	REGARD	Philippians 2:3	Don't be conceited, but regard one another as more important than yourself
14	LIE "NOT" TO	Colossians 3:9	Do not lie to one another since you have put that habit away
15	BEAR WITH	Colossians 3:13	Bearing with and forgiving one another as the Lord forgave
16	TEACH	Colossians 3:16	Teach and admonish one another with the words of God
17	LOVE	1 Thessalonians 3:12	May the Lord cause you to increase in love for one another
18	COMFORT	1 Thessalonians 4:18	Comfort one another since the Lord will return for his people
19	ENCOURAGE	1 Thessalonians 5:11	Encourage one another, especially as to your faith in the Lord
20	PEACE WITH	1 Thessalonians 5:13	Live in peace or harmony with one another
21	SEEK GOOD FOR	1 Thessalonians 5:15	Seek after that which is good for one another and for all men
22	PRAY FOR	1 Timothy 2:1	. . . prayers . . . made for all men
23	STIMULATE	Hebrews 10:24	Consider was to stimulate one another to love and good deeds
24	SPEAK "NOT" AGAINST	James 4:11	Do not speak slander-ously against one another
25	COMPLAIN "NOT"	James 5:9	Don't complain against one another that you may not be judged
26	CONFESS	James 5:16	Confess your sins to one another (to those you have sinned against)

27	HOSPITABLE TO	1 Peter 4:9	Be hospitable to one another, generous and without complaint
28	SERVE	1 Peter 4:10	Use God's gracious gifts to serve one another
29	HUMBLE TOWARD	1 Peter 5:5	Be humble to one another, knowing God is opposed to pride
30	GREET	1 Peter 5:14	Greet one another in a caring and loving manner
31	FELLOWSHIP WITH	1 John 1:7	We have fellowship with one another as we walk with God

The Biblical Position on

DIVORCE AND REMARRIAGE

The Elders' Perspective

PREFACE

Recognizing that the Bible is the very Word of the Living God to man, and understanding the priority of knowing and obeying its truths, the elders of Grace Community Church are deeply committed to studying and teaching Scripture with diligence and authority. Thus, the central ministry of our church is the continuous imparting of biblical truth to the people of God that they may know and serve Him in worship, ministry, and evangelism. Through their years of study, training, and teaching, the elders have come to convictions regarding the major truths of the Bible. This booklet presents one of those truths that reflects the heart of our teaching here at Grace.

—John MacArthur, Jr.

SECTION ONE

God hates divorce, because it always involves unfaithfulness to the solemn covenant of marriage that two partners have entered into before God, and because it brings harmful consequences to those partners and their children (Malachi 2:14-16[1]). Divorce in the Scripture is permitted only because of man's sin. Since divorce is only a concession to man's sin and is not part of God's original plan for marriage, all believers should hate divorce as God does and pursue it only when there is no other recourse. With God's help a marriage can survive the worst sins.

In Matthew 19:3-9[2], Christ teaches clearly that divorce is an accommodation to man's sin that violates God's original purpose for the intimate unity and permanence of the marriage bond (Genesis 2:24[3]). He taught that God's law allowed divorce only because of

---

[1] Malachi 2:14-16 - "Yet you say, 'For what reason?' Because the LORD has been a witness between you and the wife of your youth, against whom you have dealt treacherously, though she is your companion and your wife by covenant.15 "But not one has done so who has a remnant of the Spirit. And what did *that* one *do* while he was seeking a godly offspring? Take heed then, to your spirit, and let no one deal treacherously against the wife of your youth.16 "For I hate divorce," says the LORD, the God of Israel, "and him who covers his garment with wrong," says the LORD of hosts. "So take heed to your spirit, that you do not deal treacherously."

[2] Matthew 19:3-9 - "And *some* Pharisees came to Him, testing Him, and saying, "Is it lawful *for a man* to divorce his wife for any cause at all?"4 And He answered and said, "Have you not read, that He who created *them* from the beginning MADE THEM MALE AND FEMALE,5 and said, 'FOR THIS CAUSE A MAN SHALL LEAVE HIS FATHER AND MOTHER, AND SHALL CLEAVE TO HIS WIFE; AND THE TWO SHALL BECOME ONE FLESH'?6 "Consequently they are no longer two, but one flesh. What therefore God has joined together, let no man separate."7 They *said to Him, "Why then did Moses command to GIVE HER A CERTIFICATE OF DIVORCE AND SEND *her* AWAY?"8 He *said to them, "Because of your hardness of heart, Moses permitted you to divorce your wives; but from the beginning it has not been this way.9 "And I say to you, whoever divorces his wife, except for immorality, and marries another woman commits adultery."

[3] Genesis 2:24 - "For this cause a man shall leave his father and his mother, and shall cleave to his wife; and they shall become one flesh."

"hardness of heart" (Matthew 19:8). Legal divorce was a concession for the faithful partner due to the sexual sin or abandonment by the sinning partner, so that the faithful partner was no longer bound to the marriage (Matthew 5:32[4], 19:9; 1 Corinthians 7:12-15[5]). Although Jesus did say that divorce is permitted in some situations, we must remember that His primary point in this discourse is to correct the Jews' idea that they could divorce one another "for any cause at all" (Matthew 19:3) and to show them the gravity of pursuing a sinful divorce. Therefore the believer should never consider divorce except in specific circumstances (see Section Two), and even in those circumstances it should only be pursued reluctantly because there is no other recourse.

SECTION TWO

The only New Testament grounds for divorce are *sexual sin* or *desertion by an unbeliever.*

The first is found in Jesus' use of the Greek word *porneia* (Matthew 5:32, 19:9). This is a general term that encompasses sexual sin such as adultery, homosexuality, bestiality, and incest. To support the fact that sexual sin is a legitimate grounds for divorce, in the Old

---

[4] Matthew 5:32 - "But I say to you that everyone who divorces his wife, except for *the* cause of unchastity, makes her commit adultery; and whoever marries a divorced woman commits adultery."

[5] 1 Corinthians 7:12-15 - "But to the rest I say, not the Lord, that if any brother has a wife who is an unbeliever, and she consents to live with him, let him not send her away.13 And a woman who has an unbelieving husband, and he consents to live with her, let her not send her husband away.14 For the unbelieving husband is sanctified through his wife, and the unbelieving wife is sanctified through her believing husband; for otherwise your children are unclean, but now they are holy.15 Yet if the unbelieving one leaves, let him leave; the brother or the sister is not under bondage in such *cases,* but God has called us to peace."

Testament God Himself divorced the northern kingdom of Israel because of her idolatry, which He likens to sexual sin[6] (Jeremiah 3:6-9[7]). When one partner violates the unity and intimacy of a marriage by sexual sin-and forsakes his or her covenant obligation-the faithful partner is placed in an extremely difficult situation. After all means are exhausted to bring the sinning partner to repentance, the Bible permits release for the faithful partner through divorce (Matthew 5:32; 1 Corinthians 7:15).

The second reason for permitting a divorce is in cases where an unbelieving mate does not desire to live with his or her believing spouse (1 Corinthians 7:12-15[8]). Because "God has called us to peace" (v. 15), divorce is allowed and may be preferable in such situations. When an unbeliever desires to leave, trying to keep him or her in the marriage may only create greater tension and conflict. Also, if the unbeliever leaves the marital relationship permanently but is not

---

[6] On the other hand, God did not give a bill of divorce to Judah, illustrating that an unfaithful partner can be forgiven.

[7] Jeremiah 3:6-9 - "Then the LORD said to me in the days of Josiah the king, "Have you seen what faithless Israel did? She went up on every high hill and under every green tree, and she was a harlot there.7 "And I thought, 'After she has done all these things, she will return to Me'; but she did not return, and her treacherous sister Judah saw it.8 "And I saw that for all the adulteries of faithless Israel, I had sent her away and given her a writ of divorce, yet her treacherous sister Judah did not fear; but she went and was a harlot also.9 "And it came about because of the lightness of her harlotry, that she polluted the land and committed adultery with stones and trees."

[8] 1 Corinthians 7:12-15 - "But to the rest I say, not the Lord, that if any brother has a wife who is an unbeliever, and she consents to live with him, let him not send her away.13 And a woman who has an unbelieving husband, and he consents to live with her, let her not send her husband away.14 For the unbelieving husband is sanctified through his wife, and the unbelieving wife is sanctified through her believing husband; for otherwise your children are unclean, but now they are holy.15 Yet if the unbelieving one leaves, let him leave; the brother or the sister is not under bondage in such *cases*, but God has called us to peace."

willing to file for divorce, perhaps because of chosen lifestyle, irresponsibility, or to avoid monetary obligations, then the believer is in an impossible situation of having legal and moral obligations that he or she cannot fulfill. Because "the brother or sister is not under bondage in such cases" (1 Corinthians 7:15), that is he or she no longer needs to remain married, divorce is acceptable without fearing the displeasure of God.

SECTION THREE

Remarriage is permitted for the faithful partner only when the divorce was on biblical grounds. In fact, the purpose for a biblical divorce is to make clear that the faithful partner is free to remarry, but only in the Lord (Romans 7:1-3[9]; 1 Corinthians 7:39[10]).

Those who divorce on any other grounds have sinned against God and their partners, and for them to marry another is an act of "adultery" (Mark 10:11-12[11]). This is why Paul says that a believing woman who sinfully divorces should "remain unmarried, or else be

---

[9] Romans 7:1-3 - "OR do you not know, brethren (for I am speaking to those who know the law), that the law has jurisdiction over a person as long as he lives? 2 For the married woman is bound by law to her husband while he is living; but if her husband dies, she is released from the law concerning the husband.3 So then if, while her husband is living, she is joined to another man, she shall be called an adulteress; but if her husband dies, she is free from the law, so that she is not an adulteress, though she is joined to another man."

[10] 1 Corinthians 7:39 - "A wife is bound as long as her husband lives; but if her husband is dead, she is free to be married to whom she wishes, only in the Lord."

[11] Mark 10:11-12 - "And He *said to them, "Whoever divorces his wife and marries another woman commits adultery against her; 12 and if she herself divorces her husband and marries another man, she is committing adultery."

reconciled to her husband" (1 Corinthians 7:10-11[12]). If she repents from her sin of unbiblical divorce, the true fruits of that repentance would be to seek reconciliation with her former husband (Matthew 5:23-24[13]). The same is true for a man who divorces unbiblically (1 Corinthians 7:11). The only time such a person could remarry another is if the former spouse remarries, proves to be an unbeliever, or dies, in which cases reconciliation would no longer be possible.

The Bible also gives a word of caution to anyone who is considering marriage to a divorcee. If the divorce was not on biblical grounds and there is still a responsibility to reconcile, the person who marries the divorcee is considered an adulterer (Mark 10:12).

SECTION FOUR

Believers who pursue divorce on unbiblical grounds are subject to church discipline because they openly reject the Word of God. The one who obtains an unbiblical divorce and remarries is guilty of adultery since God did not permit the original divorce (Matthew 5:32; Mark 10:11-12). That person is subject to the steps of church discipline as outlined in Matthew 18:15-17[14]. If a professing Christian violates the marriage covenant and refuses to repent during the process of

---

[12] 1 Corinthians 7:10-11 - "But to the married I give instructions, not I, but the Lord, that the wife should not leave her husband, 11 (but if she does leave, let her remain unmarried, or else be reconciled to her husband), and that the husband should not send his wife away."

[13] Matthew 5:23-24 - "If therefore you are presenting your offering at the altar, and there remember that your brother has something against you, 24 leave your offering there before the altar, and go your way; first be reconciled to your brother, and then come and present your offering."

[14] Matthew 18:15-17 - "And if your brother sins, go and reprove him in private; if he listens to you, you have won your brother.16 "But if he does not listen to you, take one or two more with *you*, so that BY THE MOUTH OF TWO OR THREE WITNESSES EVERY FACT MAY BE CONFIRMED.17 "And if he refuses to listen to them, tell it to the church; and if he refuses to listen even to the church, let him be to you as a Gentile and a tax-gatherer."

church discipline, Scripture instructs that he or she should be put out of the church and treated as an unbeliever (v. 17). When the discipline results in such a reclassification of the disobedient spouse as an "outcast" or unbeliever, the faithful partner would be free to divorce according to the provision for divorce as in the case of an unbeliever departing, as stated in 1 Corinthians 7:15. Before such a divorce, however, reasonable time should be allowed for the possibility of the unfaithful spouse returning because of the discipline.

The leadership in the local church should also help single believers who have been divorced to understand their situation biblically, especially in cases where the appropriate application of biblical teaching does not seem clear. For example, the church leadership may at times need to decide whether one or both of the former partners could be legitimately considered "believers" at the time of their past divorce, because this will affect the application of biblical principles to their current situation (1 Corinthians 7:17-24[15]). Also, because people often transfer to or from other churches and many of

---

[15] Corinthians 7:17-24 - "Only, as the Lord has assigned to each one, as God has called each, in this manner let him walk. And thus I direct in all the churches.18 Was any man called *already* circumcised? Let him not become uncircumcised. Has anyone been called in uncircumcision? Let him not be circumcised.19 Circumcision is nothing, and uncircumcision is nothing, but *what matters* is the keeping of the commandments of God.20 Let each man remain in that condition in which he was called.21 Were you called while a slave? Do not worry about it; but if you are able also to become free, rather do that.22 For he who was called in the Lord while a slave, is the Lord's freedman; likewise he who was called while free, is Christ's slave.23 You were bought with a price; do not become slaves of men.24 Brethren, let each man remain with God in that *condition* in which he was called."

those churches do not practice church discipline, it might be necessary for the leadership to decide whether a member's estranged or former spouse should currently be considered a Christian or treated as an unbeliever because of continued disobedience. Again, in some cases this would affect the application of the biblical principles (1 Corinthians 7:15[16]; 2 Corinthians 6:14[17]).

Any believer who is in a divorce situation that seems unclear should humbly seek the help and direction of church leaders, because God has placed those men in the Body for such purposes (Matthew 18:18[18]; Ephesians 4:11-16[19]; Hebrews 13:17[20]).

---

[16] 1 Corinthians 7:15 - "Yet if the unbelieving one leaves, let him leave; the brother or the sister is not under bondage in such *cases*, but God has called us to peace."

[17] 2 Corinthians 6:14 - "Do not be bound together with unbelievers; for what partnership have righteousness and lawlessness, or what fellowship has light with darkness?"

[18] Matthew 18:18 - "Truly I say to you, whatever you shall bind on earth shall be bound in heaven; and whatever you loose on earth shall be loosed in heaven."

[19] Ephesians 4:11-16 - "And He gave some *as* apostles, and some *as* prophets, and some *as* evangelists, and some *as* pastors and teachers, 12 for the equipping of the saints for the work of service, to the building up of the body of Christ; 13 until we all attain to the unity of the faith, and of the knowledge of the Son of God, to a mature man, to the measure of the stature which belongs to the fullness of Christ.14 As a result, we are no longer to be children, tossed here and there by waves, and carried about by every wind of doctrine, by the trickery of men, by craftiness in deceitful scheming;15 but speaking the truth in love, we are to grow up in all *aspects* into Him, who is the head, *even* Christ,16 from whom the whole body, being fitted and held together by that which every joint supplies, according to the proper working of each individual part, causes the growth of the body for the building up of itself in love."

[20] Hebrews 13:17 - " Obey your leaders, and submit *to them*; for they keep watch over your souls, as those who will give an account. Let them do this with joy and not with grief, for this would be unprofitable for you."

SECTION FIVE

Salvation indicates that a person has begun a new life. That new life is defined by a pattern of obedience to what God has revealed about every area of life-including marriage and divorce. According to 2 Corinthians 5:17[21], the believer has become a "new creature" when he believes in Jesus Christ. This does not mean that painful memories, bad habits, or the underlying causes for past marital problems will no longer exist, but it does mean that Christ begins a process of transformation through the Holy Spirit and the Word. A sign of saving faith will be a receptivity and a willingness to obey what God has revealed about marriage and divorce in His Word.

According to 1 Corinthians 7:20-27[22], there is nothing in salvation that demands a particular social or marital status. The Apostle Paul, therefore, instructs believers to recognize that God providentially allows the circumstances they find themselves in when they come to Christ. If they were called while married, then they are not required to seek a divorce (even though divorce may be permitted on biblical grounds). If they were called while divorced, and cannot be reconciled to their former spouse because that spouse is an unbeliever or

---

[21] 2 Corinthians 5:17 - "Therefore if any man is in Christ, *he is* a new creature; the old things passed away; behold, new things have come."

[22] 1 Corinthians 7:20-27 - "Let each man remain in that condition in which he was called.21 Were you called while a slave? Do not worry about it; but if you are able also to become free, rather do that.22 For he who was called in the Lord while a slave, is the Lord's freedman; likewise he who was called while free, is Christ's slave.23 You were bought with a price; do not become slaves of men.24 Brethren, let each man remain with God in that *condition* in which he was called.25 Now concerning virgins I have no command of the Lord, but I give an opinion as one who by the mercy of the Lord is trustworthy.26 I think then that this is good in view of the present distress, that it is good for a man to remain as he is.27 Are you bound to a wife? Do not seek to be released. Are you released from a wife? Do not seek a wife."

is remarried, then they are free to either remain single or be remarried to another believer (1 Corinthians 7:39[23]; 2 Corinthians 6:14[24]).

SECTION SIX

In cases where divorce took place on unbiblical grounds and the guilty partner later repents, the grace of God is operative at the point of repentance. A sign of true repentance will be a desire to implement 1 Corinthians 7:10-11[25], which would involve a willingness to pursue reconciliation with his or her former spouse, if that is possible. If reconciliation is not possible, however, because the former spouse is an unbeliever or is remarried, then the forgiven believer could pursue another relationship under the careful guidance and counsel of church leadership.

In cases where a believer obtained a divorce on unbiblical grounds and remarried, he or she is guilty of the sin of adultery until that sin is confessed (Mark 10:11-12). God does forgive that sin immediately when repentance takes place, and there is nothing in Scripture to indicate anything other than that from that point on the believer should continue in his or her current marriage.

---

[23] 1 Corinthians 7:39 - "A wife is bound as long as her husband lives; but if her husband is dead, she is free to be married to whom she wishes, only in the Lord."

[24] 2 Corinthians 6:14 - "Do not be bound together with unbelievers; for what partnership have righteousness and lawlessness, or what fellowship has light with darkness?"

[25] 1 Corinthians 7:10-11 - "But to the married I give instructions, not I, but the Lord, that the wife should not leave her husband, 11 (but if she does leave, let her remain unmarried, or else be reconciled to her husband), and that the husband should not send his wife away."

SECTION SEVEN

Obviously, the church has a responsibility to uphold the biblical ideal of marriage, especially as exemplified by its leadership. First Timothy 3:2, 12 says that leaders must be "the husband of one wife" (lit. "one-woman man"). That phrase does not mean that an elder or deacon is only to have or have had one wife, but that he be solely and consistently faithful to his wife in an exemplary manner. It says nothing about the past before his salvation, because none of the other qualifications listed refer to specific acts in the past (prior or subsequent to salvation). Rather, they all refer to qualities which currently characterize a man's life.

The Pastor's marriage should be a model demonstration of Ephesians 5:22-29[26], the relationship of Christ to His church. In cases where a potential pastor, elder, or even deacon has been divorced, the church must be confident that he has given evidence of "ruling his family well" and proven his ability to lead those close to him to salvation and sanctification. His family is to be a model of faithful and

---

[26] Ephesians 5:22-29 - "Wives, *be subject* to your own husbands, as to the Lord.23 For the husband is the head of the wife, as Christ also is the head of the church, He Himself *being* the Savior of the body.24 But as the church is subject to Christ, so also the wives *ought to be* to their husbands in everything.25 Husbands, love your wives, just as Christ also loved the church and gave Himself up for her; 26 that He might sanctify her, having cleansed her by the washing of water with the word, 27 that He might present to Himself the church in all her glory, having no spot or wrinkle or any such thing; but that she should be holy and blameless.28 So husbands ought also to love their own wives as their own bodies. He who loves his own wife loves himself; 29 for no one ever hated his own flesh, but nourishes and cherishes it, just as Christ also *does* the church."

righteous living (1 Timothy 3:4-5[27]; Titus 1:6[28]). It would be necessary to carefully examine the circumstances surrounding his divorce (whether it was before or after salvation, on what grounds, etc.) and any consequences still remaining that may affect his reputation-because God desires the pastors of His church to be the best possible models of godliness before men. If he truly desires to be "above reproach" (1 Timothy 3:2), a potential leader will be willing to undergo such scrutiny.

For further study on this subject, see the following materials:

John MacArthur — tape series *On Divorce;* commentary sections on Matthew 19 and 1 Corinthians 7

Jay Adams — *Marriage, Divorce, and Remarriage in the Bible*

John Murray — *Divorce*

Thomas Edgar — Essays in *Divorce and Remarriage: Four Christian Views,* edited by H. Wayne House

---

[27] 1 Timothy 3:4-5 - "*He must be* one who manages his own household well, keeping his children under control with all dignity5 (but if a man does not know how to manage his own household, how will he take care of the church of God?)."

[28] Titus 1:6 - "If any man be above reproach, the husband of one wife, having children who believe, not accused of dissipation or rebellion."

Bi–weekly/Monthly Leadership Worksheet
A Tool for Greater Understanding and Establishing New Habits

When a Christian husband leads his wife and home like Christ he can glorify God, see God work (answers to prayer), and be fulfilled. This worksheet not only lists the areas of leadership that you need to think through, but it also helps you get started by having you chose the regular times for preparation and discussion once or twice a month. With time, one should become more spontaneous - not so structured. Answer the * questions prior to meeting with your wife.

LEADING IN THE MARRIAGE RELATIONSHIP

☐ Set times for preparation and meeting

On what day and at what time will you prepare?

On what day and at what time will you meet with your wife?

☐ Complete the following exercises:

*1.   Things I appreciate about her:

*2.   Ways I can show sweetheart love to my wife:

*3.   My own confessions and personal changes to make:

*4.   When I will seek to spend time with her:

5.   Things we can do together:

6.   My plan to pray with her daily:

7.   My plan for intimacy (Next time: transfer what stays the same
        and add anything new):

•   *A prayer to pray beforehand:

•   * Thoughts to think at the time:

•   Things to say at the time (ask):

•   Ways to prepare her (ask):

•   Ways to please her (ask):

8.   Concerns my wife has about the relationship:

*9.   Concerns I want to share about the relationship:

10.   Spiritual input/direction to share regarding concerns after considering all of it prayerfully:

LEADING MY WIFE
(same preparation time, same meeting time)

☐   Complete the following exercises:

*1.   Encouragement to give her:

*2.   My own confessions and personal changes to make:

3.   Praises from her:

4.   Update on delegated areas (finances, children during the day, etc.):

5.   When I can spend time in the Word with her regularly:

6.   Questions and requests from her:

7.   Concerns and prayer requests from her:

8.   Ways I can serve her:

9.   Tentative plans of hers (freedom whenever possible):

*10.   Observations of patterns:

•   Are there any observed sin patterns to lovingly and respectfully talk with her about?

•   Is more instruction/help/accountability needed?

•   If she is a believer, and is not repenting at all, what believer can I bring in that knows and loves her?

•   Do I need to bring in a church elder?
                Who?
                When?

*11.   Spiritual input and direction to her:

12.   Biblical concerns from her about my leadership or life:

PROTECTING AND LEADING OUR HOME
(same preparation time, same meeting time)

☐   Complete the following exercises:

*1.   Am I being the greatest servant in my home in attitude and action? How? If not, where, how, and when can I change?

*2.   Am I providing food, clothing, shelter, and safety for my family to the best of my ability? Any changes I can pray about and work toward without compromise of Biblical principles?

*3.   Is there anything affecting the home adversely (compromises, T.V., schedules, people, reading materials, etc.)?

*4.   My own confessions and personal changes to make:

5.   Input from wife:

6.   Is the home basically and usually operating in order or in chaos? Any specific areas of need?

7. Does my wife believe she is totally equipped to run the home (under my direction)? Is she overwhelmed?

•   Items needed:

•   Training needed:

•   Weekly help needed (due to training, physical limitations, home–schooling, multiple births, etc.):

•   Ways I can help:

•   Accountability needed:

*8. Thoughts or tentative plans to share about decisions/ directions that affect my wife/family:

9. Input from my wife about thoughts or tentative plans/ decisions:

10. Final decisions/directions to share that affect wife/family. (If affect whole family will have a family meeting. Date:_____)

LEADING MY CHILDREN

☐ Set times for preparation and meeting

On what day and at what time will you prepare?

On what day and at what time will you meet with your children?

☐ Complete the following exercises:

*1. Ways I can show love to him/her:

*2. When I will spend time with him/her:

*3. My own confessions and changes to make:

*4.   Encouragement to him/her:

5.   Praises from him/her:

6.   Questions or requests from him/her:

7.   Concerns or prayer requests from him/her:

8.   Tentative plans of his/hers (give freedom when possible):

9.   Observations of patterns and needs:

•   Are there any observed sin patterns to lovingly and
       respectfully talk with him/her about or instruct him/her in?

- Is discipline needed? (If so, what?)

- Is more instruction/help/accountability needed?

- If he/she is a believer, and he/she in not repenting at all, what believer can I bring in who know and loves him/her?

- Do I need to bring in a church elder?
  Who?
  When?

10. Direction and spiritual input to him/her:

11. Information or delegation to wife:

12. Biblical concerns from him/her about my leadership or life:

PERSONAL SCHEDULE FOR _____

RESPONSIBILITIES	TIME	Sun	Mon	Tues	Wed	Thurs	Fri	Sat
	5:00							
	5:30							
	6:00							
	6:30							
	7:00							
	7:30							
	8:00							
	8:30							
	9:00							
	9:30							
	10:00							
	10:30							
	11:00							
	11:30							
	12:00							
	12:30							
	1:00							
	1:30							
	2:00							
	2:30							
	3:00							
	3:30							
	4:00							
	4:30							
	5:00							
	5:30							
	6:00							
	6:30							
DESIRES	7:00							
	7:30							
	8:00							
	8:30							
	9:00							
	9:30							
	10:00							
	10:30							
	11:00							
	11:30							
	12:00							

ACCOUNTABLE TO: _____

JAMES W. RICKARD
THE STEWARDSHIP SERVICES FOUNDATION
21726 PLACERITA CYN. RD.
SANTA CLARITA, CA 91321
(661) 254-4370

FINANCE SEMINAR

DO WE KNOW WHAT GOD'S WORD SAYS?

1. We are to be found faithful stewards.
   1 Corinthians 4:1-2

2. Surrender daily all decisions, problems, or successes.
   Proverbs 3:5-6

3. Be willing to accept God's direction.
   Philippians 4:6

KEY FINANCIAL PRINCIPLES

1. **GIVE TO GOD FIRST.**
2. Learn to be a saver.
3. Learn to spend less than you earn.
4. Cash in emergency fund.
5. Don't finance pleasure items.
6. Protect the family with adequate life insurance.
7. Retirement plan in progress by age 40.
8. Own your home by age 65 or retirement.

THINGS TO THINK ABOUT

Less than 30% of credit card holders pay off entire balance each month. Family with credit cards will spend 30-40% more than if only made purchases with cash.

Typical symptom treatments for larger problem:
Consolidate bills with new loan
Put wife to work
Can't stand pressure so go out and buy something expensive

In 95% of families, majority of debt comes from husbands. Women have a basic fear of debt. As a result women take families into debt in little increments, men take families into debt in giant leaps.

Of people with financial problems
> 60% have borrowed more money than they can realistically repay during their lifetime
> 40% have borrowed more money than they can even make payments on

We will never handle anything less significant than money, nor more outwardly indicative of our inward spiritual condition.

It is virtually impossible to be obedient and impatient at the same time.

Children today want their living standard to start or even be superior to that enjoyed by their parents.

It's not the high cost of living that gets us, but living high.
It's not how much you make, but how well you want to live.

If you go shopping with a friend, you spend 10% more
If you go shopping with children, you spend 12% more
If you go shopping with your husband, you spend 20% more.

In 85% of divorces, the reason has something to do with money.

Whenever you value something too much, whatever happens to it happens to you; e.g., car breaks down, you break down.

Debt – Delinquent financial obligation.
Obligation – Money borrowed and repaid according to agreement.

Two worldly attitudes regarding money:

1. Keep God out of things
2. Our ego is supreme and should rule

BUDGETING

A budget plan shouldn't take more than 4 hours initially to set up, and 30 minutes a week to maintain.

It will take 7-9 months for the budget plan to work efficiently.

A budget is not a plan for a husband to punish his wife.

Common budgeting errors:
Don't use it
Make it so difficult you can't live with it

People should fix <u>maximum</u> level of spending and not just keep readjusting for income increases.

GENERAL GUIDELINES FOR YOUR BUDGET

BUDGET ITEMS	SUG. %	BUDGET ITEMS INCLUDE
Giving*	11%	
Housing	30-36%	utilities, taxes, insurance, mortgage payment, and repairs
Food	14-16%	
Auto	13-16%	insurance, gas, maintenance, payments
Insurance	2-4%	life insurance (health insurance-fringe)
Entertainment	2-5%	put money in envelope and don't mix with other funds
Clothing	5%	
Medical/Dental	5%	
Savings	5%	also unexpected emergencies
Credit	5%	the cut-up credit card sent to a creditor really impresses them (the goal should be 0%)
Household/Misc.	4-8%	haircuts, cosmetics, piano lessons, & gifts

All percentages are from take-home pay except your giving, which is based on gross income.

Listed below are major budget categories and possible minor subcategories. Choose subcategories to fit the needs of your family. Also feel free to add subcategories (as indicated by _____) and place subcategories under different major headings according to the needs of your family.

OFFERING TO THE LORD

HOUSING
Mortgage / Rent
Homeowner's / Renter's Insurance
Property Taxes
Homeowner's Association dues
Repairs and Maintenance
Home Improvements
Furnishings
Supplies
Cleaning Expenses
Yard Maintenance
_____

UTILITIES
Electricity
Gas
Water / Sewer
Garbage
Telephone
Cellular Phone
Online / Internet Service
_____

FOOD
Groceries
Restaurants and Carry Out
_____

AUTOMOBILE
Principal and Interest
Auto Insurance
License Fees
Gas and Oil
Maintenance
_____

LIFE INSURANCE

MEDICAL
Doctor
Dentist
Eye Care
Prescriptions / Drugs
Medical Insurance Premiums
_____

LOANS
Bank
Credit Companies
_____

EDUCATION / CHILDCARE
Tuition
Books
Music / Other Lessons
Childcare
School Supplies
_____

ENTERTAINMENT / RECREATION
Babysitters
Magazines / Newspapers
Cable TV
Vacation
Health Club Fees
Clubs / Activities
_____

CLOTHING
Husband
Wife
Children
Dry Cleaners / Laundromat
_____

GIFTS
Birthdays
Anniversaries
Christmas
_____

GROOMING
Toiletries / Cosmetics
Hair Care
_____

MISCELLANEOUS HOUSEHOLD
Allowances
Animal Food / Veterinary Care
Home Office Supplies
_____

SAVINGS / INVESTMENTS

BUDGET WORKSHEET

INCOME	MONTHLY	ANNUAL
Salary Net (After Tax)	$ _____	$ _____
Interest and Dividends	_____	_____
Other Income	_____	_____
TOTAL INCOME	$ _____	$ _____

EXPENDITURES	MONTHLY	ANNUAL
Offering to the Lord	$ _____	$ _____
Housing		
Mortgage / Rent	_____	_____
Insurance	_____	_____
Property Taxes	_____	_____
Homeowner's Assoc. Dues	_____	_____
Repairs and Maintenance	_____	_____
Home Improvements	_____	_____
Furnishings	_____	_____
Supplies	_____	_____
Cleaning Expenses	_____	_____
Yard Maintenance	_____	_____
_____	_____	_____
Utilities		
Electricity	_____	_____
Gas	_____	_____
Water / Sewer	_____	_____
Garbage	_____	_____
Telephone	_____	_____
Cellular Phone	_____	_____
Online / Internet Service	_____	_____
_____	_____	_____
Food		
Groceries	_____	_____
Restaurants and Carry Out	_____	_____
_____	_____	_____
Automobile		
Principal and Interest	_____	_____
Auto Insurance	_____	_____
License Fees	_____	_____
Gas and Oil	_____	_____
Maintenance	_____	_____
_____	_____	_____
Life Insurance	_____	_____
Medical		
Doctor	_____	_____
Dental	_____	_____
Eye Care	_____	_____
Prescriptions / Drugs	_____	_____
Insurance Premiums	_____	_____
_____	_____	_____

Loans
   Bank
   Credit Companies
   _____

Education / Childcare
   Tuition
   Books
   Music / Other Lessons
   Childcare
   School Supplies
   _____

Entertainment / Recreation
   Babysitters
   Magazines / Newspapers
   Cable TV
   Vacation
   Health Club Fees
   Clubs / Activities
   _____

Clothing
   Husband
   Wife
   Children
   Dry Cleaners / Laundromat
   _____

Gifts
   Birthdays
   Anniversaries
   Christmas
   _____

Grooming
   Toiletries / Cosmetics
   Hair Care
   _____

Miscellaneous Household
   Allowances
   Animal Food / Veterinary Care
   Home Office Supplies
   _____

Savings

TOTAL EXPENDITURES $ _____ $ _____

INCOME $_____ MINUS OUTGO $_____ = UNALLOCATED $ _____

When a man's outgo exceeds his income his upkeep becomes his downfall!!

EXPENSE RECORD

Date	Category	Where	What	Cash	Check	Credit	Amount Spent

This expense tracking worksheet can be tailored to meet your needs. Simply fill the category column with your major categories and any minor categories that you wish to track.

EXPENSE TRACKING SHEET

Category	Jan	Feb	Mar	Apr	May	Jun	Jul	Aug	Sep	Oct	Nov	Dec

ARE YOU AN OVERSPENDER?

Many people who spend too much have common personality characteristics. To isolate these Money magazine asked 15 credit counselors
and financial planners to draw up this checklist. True or false:

T   F

____ ____ 1. You spend money on the expectation that your income
             will rise.

____ ____ 2. You take cash advances on one credit card to pay off another.

____ ____ 3. You spend over 20 percent of your income on credit-card bills.

____ ____ 4. You often fail to keep an accurate record of your purchases.

____ ____ 5. You have applied for more than three cards in the past year.

____ ____ 6. You regularly pay for groceries with a credit card because you
             need to.

____ ____ 7. You often hide your credit-card purchases from your family.

____ ____ 8. Owning several credit cards makes you feel richer.

____ ____ 9. You pay off your monthly credit-card bills but let others slide.

____ ____ 10. You like to collect cash from friends in restaurants, then
             charge the tab on your credit card.

____ ____ 11. You almost always make only the minimum payment on your
             credit-card bill.

____ ____ 12. You have trouble imagining your life without credit.

SCORING

*More than 2 true answers: You must stop. It's time to draw up a budg-
et, pay off bills and re-evaluate spending habits.*

*More than 5 true answers: You may be wise to consult a financial
counselor for help in changing your habits.*

SHOPPING TIPS

Millions upon millions of dollars are spent each year by manufacturers to study our shopping habits for the purpose of influencing our thinking to attract us to their product. No regard is given to whether we need the product or not. This decision is ours. The decision of whether or not to buy lies solely with us. However, we must keep in mind that we are fighting a professional army of sales people every time we turn on the T.V., radio, read the paper or magazines, or go to the store. For this reason, we must develop smart shopping habits and a strong defense against the worldly traps set by Satan to take away that which God has given us.

Please note the following list of suggested aids for your use in developing smart shopping habits:

1. Do not buy on impulse alone!
    a) Allow only one purchase at a time that is not a part of your planned budget.
    b) Never buy impulse items with credit.
    c) Stay out of the store unless it's necessary.

2. Do not overextend finances for gift items.
    a) Keep a calendar of gift-giving events and plan ahead.
    b) Do not buy gifts on credit.

3. Good grocery buying habits.
    a) Always use a written list of needs.
    b) Never go grocery shopping when hungry.

SUMMARY

1. Control credit cards.

2. Evaluate your standard of living.

3. Have short- and long-range goals for your family.

4. Guard your financial integrity.

"There is nothing wrong with looking at your life and feeling good about a job well done for God!"

LUKE 16:10,11

WARNING SIGNS OF DEBT

1. Bills are consistently paid late
2. You pay only the minimum amount on your credit cards
3. Collection agencies have contacted you
4. Your credit card limits have been reached
5. More of your income is being spent on debt payments
6. You need overtime or a second job to pay your bills
7. Your spouse needs to work in order to pay bills
8. Losing your job would be financially catastrophic
9. You regularly "rob Peter to pay Paul"
10. Money is constantly on your mind

A HANDLE ON YOUR DEBTS

	Interest Rates	Monthly Payment	Outstanding Balance
Auto Loans	%	$	$
Personal Loans	%		
Tuition Loans	%		
Home Equity Loan	%		
Other Loans	%		
Credit Cards	%		
Bank	%		
Store	%		
Airline	%		
Gas	%		
Other	%		
Other	%		
Other	%		
TOTAL		$	$

SET A TARGET DATE TO GET OUT OF DEBT

Installment loans **EXCLUDING** mortgage should be less than 10% of take-home pay. Your goal should be to eliminate all installment debt.

Mortgage payment including insurance and taxes should not exceed 33% of take-home pay.

Consolidation loans work only if you change your habits and stop careless spending.

HOW TO GET OUT OF DEBT

Step 1:

Stop all new indebtedness immediately.

Step 2:

Promise to put all extra income into debt retirement.

Step 3:

Sell all depreciating items for which you are now in debt.

    a) Replace with less expensive item.
    b) Get out from under all monthly payments.
    c) Sell all items with maintenance and upkeep costs first.

Step 4:

Closely examine food costs. You should be able to make a 15% minimum cut.

Step 5:

Begin immediately to "do it yourself" instead of paying for services.

Step 6:

Set a challenging goal for debt retirement on a pay-period basis, and make all the necessary sacrifices until you are out of debt.

Step 7:

Make getting out of debt a family effort. Let every member participate with his own resources.

ESTATE PLANNING

"Stewardship is not just money, time, or talent. Stewardship is all of these and more. Stewardship is the very life God has given us and some day we shall be responsible to give an account of it all to Him."

Two Precious Freedoms

    A. Right to accumulate
    B. Right to distribute before and after death

Two hundred fifty million dollars per week goes into probate court undesignated.

20 – 25% of adults have a will written correctly.

Less than 10% of adults have done any estate planning.

Eleven of twelve women will become widows and will be widows for an average of 11+ years.

Why spend 40 years acquiring, 10 years conserving but <u>not</u> 2 hours on distribution?

Principles of inheritance:
1. Give it while you're alive so that you can help them manage it (e.g. prodigal son).
2. Evaluate their handling of a little so that you can see if they can handle much.
3. Don't do for them what God wouldn't do. Don't buffer them or set them up; it may do more harm than good.

You should have:
1. An inventory of holdings and possessions updated annually.
2. A will drawn up by an attorney making certain your wishes, assets and the law all mesh together.
3. Contingency cash for spouse.
4. A plan of action for spouse (location of assets, record of ownership, etc.)

MISCELLANEOUS

Several years ago the IRS received $300 cash in the mail with an anonymous note attached which read, "Some time ago I cheated on my income tax return and haven't had a good night's sleep since. My hope is that now that I have sent this money I can sleep. P.S. If I still can't sleep, I'll send the rest."

Defining "Love Covers," "Love Conceals" and "Overlooking a Transgression."

In order for a husband to take sin seriously, he must understand some easily misunderstood phrases in the Bible. One such phrase is "love covers." One way that the word *cover* is used in the Bible is in reference to God covering our sins. We need to ask ourselves, however, *how* and *when* does God cover our sins?

> **How blessed is he whose transgression is forgiven,**
> **whose sin is covered!**
> **Psalm 32:1**

God covers our sins by choosing to remember them no more. He chooses to hide them from His sight in that He chooses not to hold our sin against us (Jeremiah 31:34). But *when* does God cover our sins? He covers them *after* He convicts, and addresses our sin, and we confess and repent. The covering of our sin clearly comes *after* repentance and not before. This gives us an idea as to when we should cover our wife's sin.

The main verse that is cited in the New Testament for the popular "love covers sin without addressing it" idea is 1 Peter 4:8:

> **Above all keep fervent in your love for one another**
> **because love covers a multitude of sins.**
> **1 Peter 4:8**

The phrase "love covers a multitude of sins" here is probably referring to some Old Testament proverbs, which use the same phrase. For this reason we will briefly look at these Proverbs passages.

> **Hatred stirs up strife, but love *covers* all transgressions.**
> **Proverbs 10:12 [emphasis mine]**

The word *sins* in this verse is referring to personal offenses or sins committed specifically against us. It is essential to note that Proverbs 10:12 says that love covers <u>all</u> *transgressions* (personal offenses). The fact that the verse says "all" should help us to know that this word "covers" could not mean to *ignore* or *to forget about* clear sin *without dealing with it first*. We are clearly commanded by God to go to the person who sins against us in an effort to restore them (see again Matthew 18:15; Galatians 6:1). If covering means to forget about sin, then how can we obey the command to cover as well as the command to confront at the same time? We can't. These proverbs cannot be in opposition to the other passages that clearly teach us sin must be dealt with completely. So it must be that we are to first go to our wife when she sins against us, help her deal with her sin, and *then* cover it

A similar passage, Proverbs 17:9 shows us further what it means to *cover* a transgression. In this verse, the word "conceal" is used instead of "cover." We can understand more about the meaning of both words because of the second half of this verse.

He who *conceals* **a transgression seeks love, but he who** *repeats a matter,* **separates intimate friends.**
Proverbs 17:9 [emphasis mine]

Someone who does not lovingly conceal a sin repeats it to other people. This, in turn, destroys friendships. This verse and Proverbs 10:12, therefore are warning us against the hateful or bitter behavior of bringing up (probably to others) issues from the past. These proverbs are in no way telling us to ignore the sin in the present. They are telling us not to gossip about sin that has already been addressed.

Another related verse speaks about *overlooking* a transgression. The word "overlook" in Proverbs 19:11 means to "pass over."

A man's discretion makes him slow to anger. And it is his glory to *overlook* **a transgression.**
Proverbs 19:11 [emphasis mine]

In a typical Hebrew style, the phrase to "overlook a transgression" is explaining the first phrases of the verse—"slow to anger." Thus we can understand that overlooking a transgression is dependent upon the phrase "slow to anger." George Santa, in his commentary on Proverbs says, "A man's wise judgement delays his anger . . . {means} he will guard against offensive outbursts of temper, taking the time, instead, to carefully weigh the offense . . ."[1] A man's discretion makes him slow to anger . . . is clearly emphasizing our need for patience and self-control instead of having an impatient and uncontrolled reaction to an offense.

What does all this mean?

As best I understand it, **"love covers (or conceals) a multitude of sins" means, love does not take into consideration, bring up, or share sins that have** *already been dealt with.* So the answer to the question, "Do we cover sin?" is a definite, "Yes." We deal with it, and then we must cover it. If we do not hide (from others and ourselves) our wife's sin after it has been dealt with, we have not truly forgiven her.

Since *overlooking* or *passing over* a transgression cannot mean to live in some sort of non-reality as if nothing happened and it cannot mean to let our wife believe that her sin is not a problem, it must mean something else. To overlook means while you have indeed been personally offended, you chose not to react on the basis of that fact, but deal with the offense with patience and graciousness, because you are looking more to the glory of God and the good of the other person. Our need to initially"overlook" our own injury does not release us from our own duty to hold our wives accountable for sin.

We cannot gather from any of these verses that God wants us to do nothing about sin. Instead, He wants us to react in a godly way, deal with sin His way and then truly forgive by covering it.

---

1. George Santa, *A Modern Study in the Book of Proverbs* (Milford, MI: Mott Media, 1978), p. 373

- Those were the days.
- ~~Happy together~~
- San Fransic., Be sure
- I'm a Rock
-